Economomorphics

Economorphics

The Trends Turning Today into Tomorrow

LINDA NAZARETH

ISBN 978-0-9936510-0-7

Editor: Linda Pruessen
Proofreader: Michelle MacAleese
Page Design & Layout: Kim Monteforte, WeMakeBooks.ca
Cover Design: John Lee
Cover Author Photo: Tara Leigh, Tara Leigh Photography

www.economorphics.com

For corporate orders or special copies,
please contact sales@economorphics.com.

Printed in Canada

For Maddie

Contents

Introduction

Losing control—what could be worse? It's like that dream in which you wake up late for work, then scramble around in a panic as everything goes wrong, making you later still. There is no winning move in such a scenario; the only question is how late you are going to be. Of course, you don't have to wait until you are asleep to have that feeling of things swirling into chaos around you. The world we live in today is one where many people feel that they lack control—many organizations too. And with good reason: change is happening so quickly, and on such a widespread level, that it is difficult to feel that you are ahead of the curve, or even that you have a good sense of what is happening.

Economorphics: The Trends Turning Today into Tomorrow will help you regain control of your future—both personal and professional. To grasp what is going on in your own backyard, you need to understand the wider world and all that is happening in it. Failure to do so means the risk of making the wrong decisions, whether you are running a government, a corporation, or your own career and finances.

What do we mean when we say "economorphics"? The word encompasses the themes of economics, demographics, and change. Thanks to the first two factors, our world is morphing into another one, an unfamiliar one to many of us. This change is being powered by a series of "economorphic trends" that will transform our economy, sometimes for good and sometimes in ways we might not have bargained for. Understand each trend—its causes and effects—and you can strategize how to make them work to your advantage.

To be successful over the next few decades, you will need to make decisions ahead of the coming changes. You need to assess your human capital needs, your financing needs, and your production schedules, but you also need much more than that. You need information, and you need answers to some key questions. In 10 or 20 years—which will be here in the blink of an eye—what markets will you be serving? Will it pay to be in the business that you are in? What kind of an economy will you live in—and what does that mean for where you take your organization? And if you are planning your own financial future, is there a big-picture view that you need to have? One thing is clear: if you wait for tomorrow to happen, you will be nicely behind the curve.

For North America, the next two decades will be a time of significant challenges, and will perhaps feature a fight to hold on to a quality of life that we have been taking for granted. All things being equal, growth is going to slow, a victim of economic malaise and negative demographics. But this scenario is not carved in stone: the coming decades could be a time of renaissance, of people doing new things with new processes. These decades could feature a population that makes the best choices in terms of work and lifestyles. We have amazing technology already, and more is coming to the fore: the challenge will be to channel it in the right directions.

THE HUMPTY DUMPTY RECESSION

As much as the starting point for the future should not include a lot of backward glances, we cannot avoid acknowledging that the world economy has come through a time of severe economic upheaval. Following the longest post-war period of economic expansion since the end of World War II, the world was plunged into a U.S.-led recession that started in 2008. The causes of the Great Recession—as it's come to be known—will be debated for a very long time, but we do know that its aftermath has been trying. It is reminiscent of the story of Humpty Dumpty: something got smashed, and despite the best efforts of all the king's horses and all the king's men, it could not be put together again. In this case, the broken economy could not be repaired—at least not to a state of "good as new." Yes, it is once again on track, but it is a glued-together version of what came before, and it is taking us in a somewhat different direction than the one we'd expected.

Another thing about the king's horses and men? They don't come cheap. In this case, the "royal" efforts were made by policymakers and central bankers, and their solutions to the crisis have left us with debts to pay. In the past, some of the issues outlined in the pages to follow might have been tackled with comprehensive public sector spending programs—with both good and bad results—but those days are done. Around the world, governments in developed countries such as the United States, Canada, France, and Japan (to name just a few) have big debts to pay and big pressures on the horizon. We are going to be paying off what is owed for a long time, and at a time when the pressures on social and health spending are only going to increase. That means that, in many ways, government is going to be out of the picture as an economic force, and we are effectively going to have to find our own solutions.

How do we do that? First, we need to understand the forces shaping the future. And then we need to know how to make them work for us.

THE THREE FORCES

In this post-recession world—a world on the brink of enormous change—there are three major forces at work. Combined, they will cause today's economy to morph into a different one.

Force #1: Transformed Demographics

We have known for a long time that the economy of the developed world is aging, but there has been little discussion about how closely that trend is tied to economic growth. But economists know that there is something called the "demographic window," a period of time in which the stars line up, in terms of population distribution, and an economy can manage some fairly easy expansion. Given what we know about the populations of various countries, it is not difficult to calculate when the demographic windows will be open and shut—and the calculations are an eye-opener.

But the demographic trends are not just limited to population aging. Two of the most important economorphic forces of our time are the increasing mobility of the world's population, and increasing urbanization. We are a world on the move, both internationally and within individual countries. In North America, very definite patterns of movement are changing the map. Indeed, the movement of people across borders and within countries today is not unlike what we saw a century or two ago, when settlers decamped from Europe and moved to the "New World" in earnest. The trend toward urbanization also has gigantic consequences. When people live in cities, they tend to share ideas and create new businesses and institutions; they also use copious amounts of resources and cause environmental damage.

It all adds up to a world in which people are congregating in a different way, and, in the process, realigning everything in their path.

Force #2: An Economic Power Shift

Power is changing hands. We have come through 50 years in which the United States was top of the heap in terms of economic leaders, and in which Canada did pretty well too. When the European Union took on a single currency in 1999, there was talk that it was the new global powerhouse, and that we would all do well to tap into it as a market. That was then. Now, Europe is in shambles, and North America is still picking up after a devastating recession that left its fingerprints on all kinds of economic decision-making. On the bright side, a bevy of previously ignored countries are steaming ahead. They include giants like China and India and Brazil, as well as an assortment of smaller nations that were once considered less developed. If you're eager to pick tomorrow's growth stars, this may be the place to look.

Not that we should or could write off North America, but unfortunately, some of the changes afoot in the continent spell trouble. Globally, we are seeing the rise of a new "middle class," a swathe of people who will be able to pay for their basic necessities and still have something left over for luxuries. In North America, however, what was once the middle class is looking different than it did. Income inequality is a huge issue, one that is only going to get more serious. We are looking at a split market—some refer to it as an "hourglass," or even a "Victorian gown economy," with some on top and some on the bottom, but few in the middle. That means big paydays ahead for some and a shrinking share for others—a situation that might lead not just to social unrest, but to an economic morass.

Force #3: New Realities, New Attitudes

So you have economics, and you have demographics: What happens when those larger trends come together? Well, you get a bunch of new realities, and those will lead, in turn, to new attitudes. The end point may be social change, but the adjustment process will come first, particularly in North America.

At the crux of it will be a push to deal with the fallout from a (new) world where wealth is being created outside of North America. For one thing, that will mean higher commodity prices, which will be a shocker for a continent that has functioned nicely on cheap oil and even cheaper food. Will budgets have to be realigned to deal with the new realities (undoubtedly, yes)—and what will that mean for industry?

The world of the next two decades will also be one in which some people are trying to reconcile their economic needs with their need to have a balanced and meaningful life. For many others, this desire for balance and meaning is just mumbo-jumbo for rich people: these folks will be fighting to survive, and their numbers will include a large share of the baby boomers. The boomers are retiring, and many are doing so with a whole lot less economic security than they would have liked. What will their second act look like—in income terms, and in terms of what they do for the rest of their lives? Will they be pushed out of large corporations, and forced to accept retail jobs as a way to keep going? And what about the economic choices of women? Globally, there has been an inching up in the power of women, and in North America we may be headed to a much more powerful economic shift.

In a broad sense, one particular challenge will be to get all economic players to work together. Companies want profits, and they will increasingly need to be competitive on a world stage. Will the decisions that they make be the best ones for the economy as a whole, or for their own particular circumstances? Are the two things in conflict? "What's good for General Motors is good for the country," said former GM chairman Charles Erwin Wilson at his U.S. Secretary of Defense confirmation hearing in 1953.[1] More recently, the attitude has been somewhat different. "We sell iPhones in over a hundred countries," an executive from Apple told a reporter from the *New York Times*, when asked why Apple does not employ more people in the United States. "We don't have an obligation to solve America's problems. Our only obligation is making the best product possible."[2]

Is there a conflict between what employees want and what employers want to give them? In a perfect world, employees would be in heavy demand; companies would be so profitable that there would be plenty of nice-sized pieces of pie to go around. But as we have seen in recent years, that pie is getting served in pretty unequal slices, and it seems that situation is not about to change. Then again, those who are better compensated seem to be paying in other ways, such as working ever-longer and ever-more-stressful hours.

Technology should be able to make some things easier—but is it? In 2013, Virgin Group Ltd. boss Sir Richard Branson confidently declared that "in 30 years, as technology moves forward, people are going to wonder why offices ever existed."[3] But Sir Richard can't even get buy-in for this idea from his own peers in the executive suite. The same year he tweeted out his opinion, tech company Yahoo ordered all telecommuters back to the office, declaring, "We need to be one Yahoo!",[4] while New York City mayor Michael Bloomberg (the founder of one of the most successful financial services companies of all time) called telecommuting "one of the dumber ideas I've ever heard."[5] Companies save money by not having workers on-site—but do they pay in other ways? How they answer that question will shape more than just the workplace.

And yes, financial markets will continue to be challenging, and perhaps challenging in ways that are different from those to which we've become accustomed. That, too, will mean different planning (and lots more planning) for those looking for returns on their money.

TECHNOLOGY AND INNOVATION: UNDERLYING THEMES

There's a fourth force as well, but it's perhaps an invisible one—or maybe too highly visible to call it a force of its own. Over the next few decades, we're going to see previously unimagined technology imagined—on the scene, affecting our day-to-day lives, both personal and professional. So why not a section of its own? The reality is that technological change is playing a hand in *every bit* of economic change coming down the pipe, and it's a good thing that it is. To be sure, there are dislocations that go along with it, just as there were when buggy-whip makers had to come to terms with that newfangled automobile. The divergence in incomes in North America owes something to technological changes that give big rewards to people with certain skills, and relatively small ones to others. But the fact that it might actually be possible to feed and house and provide for a planet of nine billion or so people within a couple of decades has a lot to do with technology. And so, technological change is a big theme behind all of the economorphic changes ahead.

The other, related big theme is that of innovation. Finding new processes, new ideas, and new ways of doing things has been the driving force behind much economic progress in the last decades— and it must continue to be the driver of progress in the future. Many of the economorphic trends that we'll explore could suggest a future with slower economic growth and perhaps a weakening standard of living for much of North America. But it does not have to be that way. By encouraging an economy that thrives on new innovations and ideas, we can move things forward in ways that we never imagined. Forget the idea that the pie is being broken up into uneven pieces: with a little knowledge and foresight, we can create a much bigger pie, with generous slices for everyone.

So what's the upshot of all of this? Yes, change is coming, and yes, you need to be prepared. But more importantly, you need to be willing to change too. Understanding the economorphic forces means shrugging off the conventional wisdoms. What do you think of when someone talks about the Chinese economy? If your first thought was "economic powerhouse," you are only partly correct. China is indeed an economic powerhouse, but thanks to its aging population, it is well on its way to being just another developed economy. Do you wonder where your children are going to work—and are you prepared for the notion that it may not be in an office or for a company at all? When they tell you what they are going to be "when they grow up," do you tell them that whatever their choice—teacher, doctor, computer tech—they will likely have to be an entrepreneur as well? Have you prepared them for the fact that work may not be a place—and are you yourself ready to deal with that reality? And did you know—or care—that the new middle class we mentioned earlier has both increasing discretionary income and increasing economic clout? Their new taste for the good things—like meat on their plates, and air conditioning in the summer—may soon jack up the prices *you* pay for those things, which means you *will* care, sooner rather than later.

Change, transformation, a world economy that is morphing into a different one—these are the hallmarks of the next two decades. It will be a time of challenges, to be sure, but it could also be a time of great excitement and growth. Are you ready?

(ENDNOTES)

1 Actually, what Mr. Wilson said was: "For years I thought what was good for our country was good for General Motors, and vice versa." But he was misquoted in the popular press, and the inaccuracy became the motto for a generation of U.S. business practices. Over the years, Mr. Wilson apparently became resigned to the misquote; in 1957, he told *Time* magazine that "I have never been too embarrassed over the thing, stated either way." Source: Justin Hyde, "GM's 'Engine Charlie' Wilson learned to live with a misquote," *Detroit Free Press*, September 14, 2008. Retrieved from http://www.freep.com/article/20080914/BUSINESS01/809140308/GM-s-Engine-Charlie-Wilson-learned-live-misquote.

2 Quoted in Charles Duhigg and Keith Bradsher, "How the U.S. Lost Out on iPhone Work," *New York Times*, January 21, 2012. Retrieved from http://www.nytimes.com/2012/01/22/business/apple-america-and-a-squeezed-middle-class.html?pagewanted=all&_r=0.

[3] Tweeted by @RichardBranson, March 4, 2013. Retrieved from https://twitter.com/richardbranson/status/308577084593274880.

[4] Omar El Akkad and Suzanne Bowness, "Telework or Teamwork? Yahoo and the Evolution of the Office," *Globe and Mail*, February 26, 2013. Retrieved from http://www.theglobeandmail.com/report-on-business/careers/the-future-of-work/telework-or-teamwork-yahoo-and-the-evolution-of-the-office/article9099573/.

[5] "Mayor Bloomberg Agrees with Marissa Mayer, Says Telecommuting is Dumb," nbcnewyork.com, March 1, 2013. Retrieved from http://www.nbcnewyork.com/news/local/Bloomberg-Telecommuting-Dumb-Marissa-Mayer-Yahoo-Working-from-Home-194318371.html.

PART

1

Transformed Demographics

The Demographic Window Is Slamming Shut

Through the last 50 years or so, much of the developed world has benefited from a wide-open demographic window—a time when the age of the population creates the ideal climate for growth. That window is now slamming shut in the developed world, and increasingly in newly developed countries as well.

A closed demographic window will create worldwide challenges in terms of governance and economic growth. Still, the aging world should not be thought of as sounding a death knell for the global economy. Well-designed policies could go a long way toward reversing the "demographics as destiny" mantra that is sometimes taken as absolute.

I t has been a remarkable century: over the past hundred years or so the world has gotten bigger, and richer too. In North America, we have built cities and bought cars and created a society that is far from perfect but is nonetheless much wealthier and more inclusive than the one that existed a century ago. Technology played a part in all that; so did some great ideas and inventions, and maybe some social progress as well. But it may have been demographics that really drove the economic progress of the last century.

The age structure of the population in the developed world had a lot to do with the economic progress we've experienced. But that age structure is changing, and, all things being equal, that change is going to halt a lot of economic progress. The fact is that we cannot allow "all things to be equal" anymore; the world is going to have to change if we want to accommodate the new population structure and still move forward. The term *demographic* refers to a time when the age of the population creates the ideal conditions for economic growth. Economists generally agree that the window is open when the percentage of the population under 15 is below 30 percent, and the percentage over 65 is below 15 percent. For much of the world, that window is slamming shut. The key to economic growth will be to work with the new structure, and to work around it too.

BIG, GETTING BIGGER—AND GETTING OLDER

It's a big world we live in, and it's getting bigger. As of 2013, the United Nations (UN) estimates that there are approximately 7.2 billion people on planet Earth, up from a paltry three billion in 1960. We have seen exponential growth over the last century. The world hit the one billion mark sometime around the early 1800s, then did not reach two billion until 1927. There were three billion people on Earth 33 years later, four billion by 1974, five billion in 1987, and six billion in 1999. The last billion got added in 13 years, in 2012. UN projections suggest that it will take only a couple of decades—until 2025—for the planet's population to reach eight billion, and that there will be 9.6 billion of us by 2050.[1]

Of course, the growth is not expected to be exactly even across countries. Since the early 1960s, the rate of growth has been slowing, and in some areas—notably in Central and Eastern Europe—has actually turned negative. In others, including North America, population would also be on the decline if not for immigration.

So, is the world growing too quickly—or too slowly? A planet careening toward eight billion people can hardly be thought to be experiencing slow growth. The too-quickly fear has been around for a long time. In 1798, economist Thomas Malthus warned about the limits of growth and the potential for a catastrophe if the population did not stop increasing. That the worldwide famines he foresaw have not come to pass is mostly due to the fact that technological progress has increased at a quicker rate than population growth, and the world has effectively been able to accommodate more people. Still, as more of the world industrializes we do have to worry about the scarcity of some resources in the years ahead.

> The world is getting older. In 1950, approximately one in 12 people were over 65; by 2050, this ratio will be one in six.

But never mind the actual number of people crowding the planet: a bigger issue—especially for North America, and especially for a 20-year planning horizon—is that the world is getting older. In 1950, approximately one in 12 people were over 65; by 2050, this ratio will be one in six.[2] According to UN projections, in the more developed parts of the world the population over the age of 60 will increase about 1 percent per year between now and 2050, meaning that the total number of people in this group will rise from 287 million in 2013 to 417 million in 2050. That's slow growth, however, compared to the expected increase in the 60-plus age group in the less-developed countries, where the annual increase will be a stunning 3.7 percent over the 2010 to 2015 period, and about 2.9 percent per year through 2050.[3]

Aging is also prevalent in those countries that were supposed to provide a chunk of economic growth over the next decade. In, 2001 Goldman Sachs first identified the "BRIC" countries—Brazil, Russia, India, and China—as nations that were at a similar stage of economic development, and that were going to be economic out-performers over the coming decades. Over the first decade of the 21st century, those nations contributed almost half of global growth—but that may not last. Late in 2011, Goldman Sachs asserted that, "In terms of the role of the BRICs in driving global growth, the most dramatic change is behind us." The letter cited aging populations as the culprit.[4]

It is this aging of the population that is going to affect ... well ... everything. Be it government finances or labor markets or interest rates, the fact that the world is getting long in the tooth is arguably the biggest economorphic trend shaping the economy of the next 20 years.

DEMOGRAPHICS AND THE SWEET SPOT FOR ECONOMIC GROWTH

The Demographic Transition Model

The demographic window is effectively the sweet spot for economic growth—the years in which all conditions are "go" for economic progress. You can get an idea of how this works by looking a the *demographic transition model*, developed in 1929 by an American demographer named Warren Thompson to categorize the pattern of births and deaths that happen as a society industrializes. This theory says that a country moving from low industrialization to high industrialization goes through four stages, each with distinct patterns of births and deaths.[5]

Before going through the stages, a couple of ratios are instructive when you look at the demographic situation in any country. The first is the *youth-dependency ratio*, or the percentage proportion of persons aged under 15 as a percentage of those aged 15 to 64 (the age at which people are typically in the labor force, and which is called the *working-age population*). The other is the *elderly-dependency ratio*, or the proportion of the population aged over 65 as a percentage of the working-age population. In an ideal situation, each of these ratios is higher rather than lower, meaning that there are a fair number of people working and paying taxes compared to those receiving social benefits such as education or pensions.

With those notes in mind, let's look more closely at the four stages of demographic transition.

Stage 1

Stage 1 is associated with pre-modern or primarily agrarian times. Birth rates are high and so are death rates, meaning that population stays pretty stable or grows slowly. It is a time when disease is rampant, infant mortality is high, and sanitation standards are low.

Although most of the world has moved past these conditions, there are a few pockets in places such as Sub-Saharan Africa that are likely still in Stage 1.

Stage 2

In Stage 2, the country gets more industrialized; health improves and death rates decline, and there is an increase in life expectancy. Birth rates are generally unaffected at this stage and stay high. With lower death rates (including lower infant and child mortality), the population increases and there is also a subtle shift in the population's age structure, which becomes increasingly youthful.

The years associated with the Agricultural Revolution of the 18th century are thought to be a good illustration of this stage of development, but these conditions can also be found today in newly industrialized countries. You can certainly see the rise in life expectancy the world over: on a global basis, life expectancy in 1950 was 48; as of 2005–10, it was about 76 years.[6]

Stage 3

The third stage of economic transition is characterized by a decline in birth rates, much as we have seen in the developed countries of the world since the end of the 19th century. Actually, the measure to track is the *fertility rate*, which is roughly defined as the number of children a woman has over her lifetime.

Fertility rates fall with industrialization. As societies become more urban, there is less need for lots of kids to work the farm, and with lower child mortality there is less need to have multiple children to ensure some survive. As well, as a country industrializes, women become more educated and tend to enter the workforce, and have fewer children.

These factors, combined with continued health improvements, lead to population growth during this stage, but at a slower rate than in Stage 2.

Stage 4

Stage 4 is associated with an old and older population. Birth rates are low and so are death rates, and in some cases the former cannot keep up with the latter. You can possibly extend the model even further. In a possible fifth stage, fertility rates drop below the replacement level, and population declines.[7]

The key figure to keep in mind for fertility rates is 2.1: that's the number of children a woman has to have over her lifetime to replace herself and her assumed partner. At this point, about 48 percent of the world's population—including in North America, Europe, China, Brazil, the Russian Federation, Japan, and Vietnam—are in "low fertility" countries where this ratio is not met.[8]

The Demographic Window

The sweet spot for economic growth is when countries are moving from Stage 2 (high birth rates, declining death rates) into Stage 3 (declining birth rates, declining death rates). That's the point at which the working-age population is on the rise; it is also when a country experiences its first *demographic dividend*. When the labor force is expanding more quickly than the youth-dependency rate, more money is being paid in taxes and less is going into education, relatively speaking, and strong conditions are created for economic expansion. Arguably, much of Ireland's economic success in the 1990s, during the heady days when it was called the "Celtic Tiger," came about because of a sharp increase in the working-age population relative to the birth rate.[9]

A second demographic dividend for industrializing countries comes about when newly expanded workforces age—although not too much. Workers in their middle years are cognizant of the fact that they will live longer, so they start to put money away for retirement. That increases the supply of capital available, which facilitates lending and business expansion. It also juices the financial markets: more money going after the same stocks is going to send equity prices higher. Given that fact, you can argue that the intermittent bull market in North American stocks in the 1990s and early part of this century had a lot to do with aging baby boomers looking for returns on their retirement savings.

Overall, a country gets the most bang for its buck when the so-called demographic window is open—and that is a problem if you look at where things are in the world today. In North America, the demographic window is still open, but only just: it opened in 1970 and will shut by 2015. In Western Europe, the window was open between 1950 and 1995; it's been shut for years. Arguably, this is one of the reasons that the European economy is currently under such stress. China's economic window opened in 1990 and still has a few good years left, but it will slam shut by 2030.

India has the best potential profile, with the window open between 2015 and 2060.[10]

OPEN AND SHUT: THE DEMOGRAPHIC WINDOW

	Beginning	End
World	2005	2045
Africa	2045	2080
Asia	2005	2040
India	2010	2050
China	1990	2025
Latin America	2005	2040
Australia/New Zealand	1970	2010
North America	1970	2015
Eastern Europe	Pre-1950	2015
Western Europe	Pre-1950	1990

Source: United Nations Database/author calculations.

All of this is not to say that demographics are the only driver to growth. If productivity—the ability to squeeze more out of less—goes up, then an economy can grow without having lots of people to do the work. As well, what matters is not just the size of the working-age population, but the labor force participation rate (the percentage of people in the working-age population who choose to look for a job). A country with a high labor force participation rate (say because more women are in the labor force) will have less of an issue with aging than one with a lower participation rate.

Of course, not every part of the world is aging. In fact, the world as a whole is actually experiencing a population surge, although the quickest growth is taking place in very concentrated areas, including Sub-Saharan Africa, the Middle East, and parts of Asia.

The demographic window is wide open in these countries, and there should be an expansion in growth as well as population in these areas of the world.

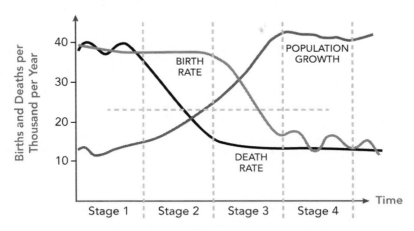

DEMOGRAPHIC TRANSITION MODEL

Based on the model specified by demographer Warren Thompson in 1929.

THE ECONOMORPHIC IMPLICATIONS

So what exactly does it mean that the demographic window is closing in the developed and even the developing world? Simply put, it means that the demographic circumstances that created many of our positive economic outcomes are disappearing. The new demographics will create an economic situation that is very different—unless policies are put in place to offset the adjustments.

A Global Economy with a Big Strike Against It

Growth in working-age population and growth in an economy as a whole go hand in hand. An older society means a growing proportion of people not paying taxes. As an official from the Bank of Canada put it in a 2012 speech, it is like a "pie growing more slowly than the number of eaters—less for everyone."[11]

The demographic structure of the population has arguably given economic growth a huge boost in the past decades—until the point when it did not. After all, when the baby boomers reached critical mass in the population, there were a lot of people smack in the middle of their prime consumer-spending years. They wanted cars and houses and washing machines and toys for their children, and their spending fueled the production and sale of those things, and created lots of multiplier effects through the broader economy. One study by the McKinsey Global Institute found that the presence of boomers in their prime buying years helped to fuel U.S. economic growth at an average rate of 3.2 percent per year between 1965 and the 2008—a level that they see dropping to 2.4 percent for the next few decades.[12]

> An older society means a growing proportion of people not paying taxes. As an official from the Bank of Canada put it in a 2012 speech, it is like a "pie growing more slowly than the number of eaters—less for everyone."

The Organisation for Economic Co-operation and Development (OECD), in a 2012 report[13], was a bit more upbeat, saying that better education in many countries would offset the impact of aging in others. In their view, global growth, which averaged 3.5 percent a year from 1995 through 2011, is set to actually rise, going to 3.7 percent per year through 2030 before falling to 2.3 percent for the three following decades. However, even in their view, that growth is going to be heavily skewed toward developing countries, while the more developed parts of the world will inevitably see a decline. In Canada, for example, projections by the Bank of Canada show that in the absence of any adjustments, the average incomes of Canadians could be as much as 20 percent lower by 2032 than they would have been without population aging.[14]

The Labor Market

The labor market is going to feel the pressure of an aging population. This may be hard to imagine in these days of high unemployment rates, but we are closing in on a time when there will be relatively high retirements relative to a low number of labor force entrants. As a result, there will be upward pressure on wages, and a potential boost to overall inflation.

Of course, there are ways to offset the demographically driven labor market issues. One is to encourage more people to enter the labor market, and to stay there for a longer period of time. Another is to discourage retirements, and encourage workers to stay in their jobs for longer periods (Canada, for example, recently scrapped its mandatory retirement laws). Arguably, the weak performance of the equity and stock markets—which has left many facing retirement feeling as if they have insufficient assets—might be the most persuasive factor of all.

Government Preparedness (or Lack Thereof)

So how much have governments prepared for this hurtling train called population aging? Not enough. To put it mildly, government purse strings will be affected by aging. More people will be looking for pensions, and fewer people (again, relatively speaking) will be paying taxes. As well, there will be higher demand for health services, which typically must be paid at least in part by the public sector. According to research done by the International Monetary Fund Group of 20, countries will have to spend four times the current output to pay for health care, pensions, and long-term residential care associated with aging over the period from 2009 to 2040.[15]

Canada and the United States are actually in the enviable position of being able to watch a giant learn-by-doing experiment in population aging currently taking place in Japan and Europe—countries which are much further ahead on the aging scale. In truth, however, not much is being learned, given that Europe's situation is being skewed by its economic crisis, and that Japan is moving very cautiously toward making any changes at all. As well, whatever knowledge is gleaned from watching other countries go through their adjustments, the menu of choices is going to be the same for all governments. The first choice is to offer less in terms of publicly funded programs, something that is already being tried in various places in limited ways. For example, new employees in the public sector might be offered much more limited pensions than were available to existing employees. In more extreme cases, governments might also have to claw back or not make good on previously negotiated pensions. The second (and perhaps the inevitable) choice when it comes to keeping existing systems going is to simply tax workers and businesses more as the bills mount. But that is a tricky proposition: high taxes in some jurisdictions will drive companies to others where the tax bills may be lower. All in all, the next decade is going to feature an ugly tug-of-war between regions as they struggle to adjust their tax structures, and between those with competing priorities as they struggle for what little government spending exists.

The Financial Markets

Another issue that will come with population aging is that the stock of capital—basically, savings—will be impacted. As the boomers earned money, they saved some of it too, not just in North America but in other countries as well. There was lots of liquidity available, and, as a result, interest rates could be relatively low, as indeed they were during the period from the 1990s on.

An older population saves less than a younger one, meaning that countries with older populations will see available capital decline, forcing up interest rates or forcing borrowers to access capital from outside the country. Of course, there are ways to encourage savings—providing tax breaks for money put into specific savings vehicles, for example—but any such program is fighting a generational trend.

A world with an older population is, therefore, likely to be a world with a tendency for higher, not lower, interest rates. If that happened, it would be a sea change from the very low interest rates experienced globally for the past decade or so, and it would have severe consequence for a younger cohort. While the older population would be thrilled to have higher rates—it would give them a decent return on their savings without having to take substantial risks—the younger population would be forced to borrow at high rates to finance mortgages or loans. The conflict between generations, already stoked by the taxes the working-age population has to assume to pay boomer health care, would only ignite further.

> An older population saves less than a younger one, meaning that countries with older populations will see available capital decline, forcing up interest rates or forcing borrowers to access capital from outside the country.

The stock market could also conceivably be a victim of an old and older world. After all, older people draw down on their holdings, meaning that they are more likely to sell their stocks than to buy new ones.

THE COUNTRY STORIES[16]

The details vary, but the big picture is the same: the world is getting older and that is posing a series of challenges, or at least adjustments. Some parts of the world have a little more time to figure out how to cope with the new realities, but for many, something close to a demographic crisis is already in full force.

European Union

Like other parts of the world, Europe experienced a baby boom in the post-World War II years, which resulted in a flood of labor force entrants by the early 1970s. The demographic window was open during the years from about 1950 through 1990. Now, the population is aging rapidly. The median age in the 27 nations that make up the European Union is now 41.5, up from 35.7 in 1992. In Germany, the largest nation in the Eurozone, it is 45.[17]

Even without the economic morass now engulfing the continent, the aging of the population would have been a nightmare in terms of finding a way to support a generous social and benefit system. According to data from Eurostat, by 2030 every 100 workers in Europe will have to support 40 people aged 65 and over, compared to the current ratio of 100 to 25.[18] With the added burden of an economy effectively in slow growth—or even in recessionary mode—for the next decade or so, the adjustments will be momentous.

While there is reason to believe that the current economic situation in Europe actually did have its roots in population aging, the country with the worst demographics (Germany) is ironically the one with the strongest economy. The reason? Very strong economic productivity, a situation that is not mirrored in many other European countries. Spain, for example, has a horrendous problem with unemployment (and particularly with youth unemployment), despite the fact that the population is aging sharply and the native-born population is actually on the decline.

Unfortunately, the signs suggest that the overall picture will only get bleaker in Spain, and elsewhere, as public finances become strained with ever-increasing numbers of elderly and a relatively smaller working-age population. Still, the German case gives a glimmer of hope, illustrating the possibility of triumphing over demographic change provided that there is an offset from productivity.

North America

The baby boom happened in full force in North America, and its aftermath is being felt six decades later. In the United States, births peaked in the years from 1946 to 1966, while in Canada (which actually experienced a larger baby boom, in percentage terms) the boom ended a year or two later. Despite a bit of skewing because of a later boom in the 1980s and a bit of distortion because of immigration, it is the baby boom that is still dominating the North American population pyramid, and it is the baby boom that will create a host of economic and social issues in the coming years.

As of 2013, the median age of the population was just over 37 in the United States and 40 in Canada. Both countries are hurtling toward having an "old" population. How this plays out in the labor market remains to be seen, particularly since so many boomers are ill-prepared for retirement, at least in a financial sense. Still, however long they put it off, the next few years will see an exodus of boomers away from the office and toward whatever comes next.

It is worth mentioning that there are actually some pronounced differences between the Canadian and U.S. population outlooks. Canada is following a European-style aging pattern, and births are falling precipitously. The United Nations estimates that the Canadian fertility rate will be approximately 1.66 in the years between 2010 and 2015. In the United States, there has actually been a rise in the fertility rate, thanks solely to higher-than-average births among some ethnic groups (notably the Hispanic population), and the fertility rate is expected to average 1.97—just a bit short of replacement level—for the 2010 to 2015 period.

In the U.S., the demographic window opened in about 1970 and will close around 2015. Those who wonder whether the current mini–baby boom will cause the window to open again in the foreseeable future are engaging in a bit of wishful thinking, given the huge elderly population. In Canada, the demographic window was open during the years from 1975 onward, and is set to close around 2015. The prospects of it opening again anytime soon are weak.[19]

Russia

As one of the BRIC nations, Russia was supposed to have a lot of economic promise. But in fact, its demographics are dreadful, and, in many ways, the country is self-destructing. As of 2012, life expectancy in Russia is 69.7, which is about a dozen years lower than in the European Union. A 20-year-old man in Russia has just a 63 percent chance of reaching the age of 60, compared to a 90 percent chance in the EU.[20]

There is a smattering of reasons for Russia's demographic problems, ranging from cardiovascular disease (caused by very high levels of alcohol and tobacco consumption), high infant-mortality rates, and infectious diseases through to relatively low-quality and inadequately financed public health care systems. The net result, however, is a stagnant population (an improvement over a decline during the last decade) and a rising elderly-dependency ratio. From 20 percent in 2000, the Russian elderly-dependency ratio is expected to rise to 45 percent by 2050. While this is not unlike other parts of the developed world, the rise here is for all the wrong reasons: birth rates are low, but life expectancy is also on the decline. To fulfill its economic promise, Russia will need a sharp reversal of health practices and economic policies. Even if these things do happen, they will take years to succeed.

China

Here is a scary statistic: in the year 2050, there will be more people over the ago of 60 in China alone than there were in the entire world in 2010. That's according to statistics from the World Economic Forum, and they illustrate a starkly different reality for China than the one that exists today. China has built an economic miracle by having a strong working-age population and by putting that population to work in the ever-growing factory sector. Now, the cohort that staffed the factories—those aged 15 to 24—is set to decline by 62 million between now and 2025. At the same time, the population above the age of 60 is set to double by 2030, rising by about 180 million. If not a recipe for disaster, it is a recipe for a completely different country, demographically speaking.

There is no mystery as to why China's demographic structure is changing so dramatically. The one-child policy has been in place in China since 1979. And while it was once a short-term solution to over-population, it is now a long-term economic disaster. The fertility rate in China is now around 1.4, well below what is now average in the developed world. Accordingly, between 2000 and 2010, China's population grew by just 0.6 percent annually, about half the growth of the previous decade, and about one-fifth of its growth rate in 1970. Clearly, the cheap labor that powered the country's boom is diminishing, and, at the same time, the pressure to finance an aging population is on the rise. Over the next 20 years, the ratio of working-age population to retirees will decline from five to one today to two to one by the early 2030s. With smaller families the norm, support for this aging population will have to come from the state.[21]

Were it not for China, the world economic crisis of 2008 would have been scarily worse: the country has been an economic power-house for the last decade or more, and that fact has papered over the cracks of weakness in the balance of the world economy. Now China is facing its own problems, which will put pressure on everyone else to solve their own problems too.

India

India is thought to have the best chance of a big demographic dividend over the next decade or so. And it's true that many things are lined up in the right direction. About half of India's population is under the age of 25, and 65 percent is under 35. Between 2010 and 2040, a quarter of the total increase in the global working-age population will stem from India, during which time the population in this age group will comprise 69 percent of the country's total population. As mentioned earlier, the demographic window in India will be fully open in 2015 (the first year that the population aged under 15 drops to less than 30 percent of the total) and will not close until 2050.

Still, there are some cautionary notes when considering whether India is going to be able to realize its full demographic dividend. For one thing, there is a huge split between demographics and conditions in the north of the country and in the south. In the north, where education levels and incomes are relatively low, the fertility rate is high and the population structure is that of a country in the early stages of demographic transition. In the south, the part of the country where the IT sector thrives and the economy is in a latter stage of industrialization, the demographics reflect a much later stage of demographic transition.[22] The country cannot just take workers from the north and plug them into the south, anymore than a shortage of workers in the U.S.'s Silicon Valley can be addressed by plugging in workers from a mining community in Appalachia. There is a skills mismatch at play, and it might stem some of the gains anticipated for the country.

Japan

Japan is the textbook case of an aging population. The country has the longest life expectancy in the world (81.25 years as of 2006) and a fertility rate of 1.35. And, unlike North America, the country has very low levels of net immigration. Accordingly, the population (which was at about 128 million as of the 2010 Census of Population) is declining by about one million per year. The population aged above 60 is already close to 25 percent of the total, and if present trends continue will be close to 40 percent by 2060.[23]

Japan is so far ahead of other developed countries on the aging curve that it is experiencing issues that are not even dreamt of elsewhere. For example, the aging population combined with a movement toward the city from the country means that many rural areas are experiencing big declines in population, to the extent that wildlife that had been driven out by development years ago is now moving back in.[24]

Japan is taking steps to boost the working-age population, partly by making it easier for young women to be in the workforce. As well, there are moves to delay retirement, and to boost immigration. It is the canary in the coal mine, though: what happens to Japan may well happen to other countries in the not-too-distant future.

CHANGING THE FUTURE

In spite of the oft-repeated phrase, demographics is actually *not* destiny and does not have to mean the end of a prosperous society. If the demographic train is going to be stopped, however, it will have to be through well-designed policies and safety nets, not through luck or blind hoping for the best.

At the heart of this entire issue is labor productivity: if you cannot get a larger mass of working-age persons to pay the bills, you need to get people working at more effective jobs, making more money and paying more taxes because they themselves are well-compensated. That takes good macroeconomic and tax policies, and the right kind of investments in technology, but if you push all the right buttons, you can solve the problem of demographics.

(ENDNOTES)

[1] United Nations, "World Population Prospects: The 2012 Revision," June 13, 2013 press release (New York: United Nations Department of

Economic and Social Affairs, 2013), p. 2. Retrieved from http://esa.un. org/wpp/Documentation/pdf/WPP2012_Press_Release.pdf.

[2] United Nations, "World Population Aging, 1950–2050," United Nations, October 2006. Retrieved from http://www.un.org/esa/population/ publications/worldageing19502050/pdf/80chapterii.pdf.

[3] United Nations, World Population Prospects, p. 3.

[4] Bloomberg News, "Global Growth Slows to 3.9% as O'Neill Sees BRICS Diminished by Population," January 2, 2012. Retrieved from http://www. bloomberg.com/news/2012-01-02/global-growth-slows-to-3-9-as-o-neill-sees-brics-diminished-by-population.html.

[5] For more on the demographic transition theory see Keith Montgomery, "The Demographic Transition." (Madison, WI: Department of Geography and Geology, University Wisconsin, 2009). Retrieved from http://www. uwmc.uwc.edu/geography/demotrans/demtran.htm.

[6] United Nations, "World Population Prospects," p. 3.

[7] There is also a possible sixth stage, at which point the high level of industrialization causes an increase in fertility.

[8] United Nations, "World Population Prospects," p. 3.

[9] For more on the Irish boom and demographics, see David Bloom and David Canning, "Contraception and the Celtic Tiger," *Economic and Social Review, 2003*, 34: 3, p. 229–34.

[10] The author calculated the demographic windows by the using data from the United Nations' "World Population Prospects, 2012 revision." The window is cited being open in the first five-year period in which the conditions are met, and closed in the first five-year period in which it is not.

[11] Jean Boivin, "Aging Gracefully: Canada's Inevitable Demographic Shift." Remarks from the Deputy Governor of the Bank of Canada to the Economic Club of Canada, Toronto, Ontario, April 2012.

[12] Diana Farrell et al., "Talking 'Bout My Generation: The Economic Impact of Aging U.S. Baby Boomers," McKinsey&Company, Insights & Publications, June 2008. Retrieved from http://www.mckinsey.com/insights/ economic_studies/talkin_bout_my_generation.

[13] A. Johansson, et al., "Looking to 2060: Long-Term Global Growth Prospects," OECD Policy Paper No. 3 (Paris: OECD, 2012).

[14] Quoted in Boivin.

[15] Lee Ronald and Andrew Mason. "The Price of Maturity." *Finance and Development*, International Monetary Fund, June 2011. Retrieved from "http://www.imf.org/external/pubs/ft/fandd/2011/06/pdf/fd0611.pdf

[16] Unless otherwise specified, data in this section is derived from the United Nations' "World Population Prospects, 2012 revision." Retrieved from http://esa.un.org/wpp/.

[17] Figures are from Eurostat, quoted in Norma Cohen, "Immigration: Demographic Crisis Pushes Outsiders to Fill Jobs," *Financial Times*, May 8, 2013.

[18] Eurostat, "Active Ageing," *European Barometer* 378, January 2012, p. 3. Retrieved from http://ec.europa.eu/public_opinion/archives/ebs/ebs_378_en.pdf.

[19] Data is based on the United Nations' "World Population Prospects, 2012 revision." Retrieved from http://esa.un.org/wpp/. The demographic window is said to open in the first five-year period that the conditions are seen to have been met, and to be closed in the first five-year period in which they are not.

[20] E. Tomluc, "Low Life Expectancy Continues to Plague Former Soviet Countries," Radio Free Europe, April 2, 2013. Retrieved from http://www.rferl.org/content/life-expectancy-cis-report/24946030.html.

[21] Feng Wang, "Racing Towards the Precipice," *China Economic Quarterly*, June 2012. Retrieved from http://www.brookings.edu/research/articles/2012/06/china-demographics-wang.

[22] For more on India's demographic divide, see James Tulloch, "India's Demographic Divide: Poles Apart," *Allianz Knowledge*, October 20, 2011. Retrieved from http://knowledge.allianz.com/demography/population/?1651/poles-apart-indias-demographic-divide.

[23] See "Japan's Population Decline: Estimate Shows One-Third Shrink by 2060," *Huffington Post*, January 30, 2012. Retrieved from http://www.huffingtonpost.com/2012/01/30/japan-population-decline_n_1240950.html.

[24] John W. Traphagan, "How Demography is Changing Japan," *The Diplomat*, February 26, 2013. Retrieved from http://thediplomat.com/2013/02/how-demography-is-changing-japan/.

A World on the Move

It is sometimes called the "third wave of globalization." After goods and after capital comes migration—the movement of people from place to place, country to country. And, as with goods and capital, the goal is to get the best returns, to put the people in the places where they can do best and where they, in turn, will ensure the best economic outcome.

The next decade will be a time of unprecedented economic mobility as people find their way to the parts of the world where growth is happening and where they can make more growth happen. It will not be a smooth process, however, either for the migrants or for the countries they enter. There will be debates over whether migration is the "best" thing in an economic sense, and very few solid conclusions will be reached. Over time, though, if things are allowed to work without too many interruptions, the results should speak for themselves.

First comes the flow of goods: bananas come from South America and silk comes from China. Next is the flow of capital: investment dollars go from banks in the United States to infrastructure projects in Malaysia, while British pounds go to the Shanghai stock market, hoping for good returns. The third wave of globalization is not, however, about things or money: it's about human beings—human beings looking for better prospects, or just hoping to get away from the dismal conditions in which they live. The force of a person picking up stakes and moving is every bit as powerful as that of a crate of bananas being flown from one destination to the next, and the force of *thousands* of people rethinking their economic positions and changing where they live is much more powerful still.

At the moment, much of the world is on the move, and that mobility is going to intensify. From south to north, from village to city, and from developed countries to developing ones—there are some new trends at work, and the direction they take will shape the world over the next two decades.

PEOPLE ON THE MOVE

When we talk about *migration* we generally mean the movement of people. However, a better word for the phenomenon we are seeing right now might be *mobility*: people are not necessarily moving from one place to another and staying put; instead, they are leaving some places and heading to others, and they may pull up stakes again. *Immigration* refers to people coming into a host country; *emigration* is the act of leaving one's country of origin. And although we talk the most about international migration trends, another important trend is that of *internal migration*, or migration within particular countries. This is the force that is powering people to leave small towns and villages and head for cities, and it is a pretty potent trend as well.

Whether we are talking about internal or international migration, the movement of people should improve economic efficiency—if done right. People generally pull up stakes and move to places where prospects are brighter and their skills can be better utilized than at their starting points. And indeed, statistics bear this out. According to research by the World Bank, migration causes aggregate incomes and output to rise, and a 3 percent increase in immigration by 2025 to OECD countries would result in gains of over $150 billion a year to world economic output.[1]

> People generally pull up stakes and move to places where prospects are brighter and their skills can be better utilized than at their starting points.

There are various reasons why people pull up stakes and leave their homes for a new region or a new country. Sometimes, as discussed, those reasons are purely economic—a new job and better prospects. Sometimes they are purely social, as when someone follows a new husband or wife to his or her homeland. They can also be political, as when people are forced to leave war-torn or unstable homelands. There are a handful of other factors too—things like famines, or natural disasters that literally force people from their homes. Whatever the motivating reasons, however, migration ultimately has a massive economic impact, moving resources, as it were, from one location to another.

You can see the economic impact of migration—as well as the economics that propelled that migration—if you look at the pattern established over the past hundred years or so. In the 19th and early 20th centuries, there was a wave of migration from Europe to the "New World" of the United States and Canada, as well as to Australia and parts of South America, propelled by the promise of better economic prospects. Similar reasons prompted the movement of Britons to Australia, South Africa, and New Zealand in the first couple of decades of the 20th century. Political strife was responsible for the next waves of migration—Russians to Siberia, European Jews to the United States, those from India and Pakistan to Sri Lanka and the United Kingdom in the post-war years. More recently, we have seen a distinct wave of migration from Asia toward North America and Europe.

Migration is now taking place at the most intense pace in human history. The United Nations tallies the number of migrants across the globe, and, as of 2013, about 232 million people, or 3.2 percent of the world's population, was "living abroad." Europe and Asia are the homes of two-thirds of the migrants, with 72 million and 71 million migrants residing in each as of 2013. North America hosts the third-largest number (53 million), followed by Africa, Latin America, and the Caribbean. In absolute terms, however, North America has attracted the largest number of migrants since 1990, with 25 million people, which translates to a growth rate of 2.8 percent per year, heading to the continent.[2]

The recent economic crisis has had a huge impact on migration. To some extent, it has forced more people to move, but it has also made them very cautious regarding the areas that they choose to move to. On balance across the developed countries, net migration over the 2008–10 period was positive, although more muted than the period between 2006–07. Countries that got hit hard (such as Spain and Ireland) saw less net movement, while those who experienced less of a downturn (Denmark and Switzerland) saw higher net migration than during the pre-recession years. Since the "end" of the recession, the levels of migration have ratcheted up sharply once more. For example, immigration into Ireland rose a stunning 41 percent in 2011.[3]

Looking forward, those countries with the highest rates of industrialization and the quickest-growing economies will increasingly look attractive to migrants, perhaps even more so than will richer but slower-growing developed countries. For example, oil-producing countries are a hot destination for those on the move, with places such as Malaysia increasingly bringing in labor.

These trends raise questions for those economies that are look-ing to migration to fuel their labor forces and economic growth. That is true for Europe, and for North America as well. Already we are seeing that educated residents of countries with strong inter-nal economic growth (such as India) are considering staying put as a viable alternative to moving abroad. The next step will be for countries like this to perhaps attract immigrants from other places.

China may get increasingly aggressive about bringing in work-ers. It is a country that is still industrializing, but also one in which the so-called demographic window is closing (for a full discussion of the demographic window, see chapter 1).[4] For China to con-tinue its industrialization process, it will not only have to get more aggressive about losing population to other parts of the globe, but perhaps also become equally aggressive about attracting the right kind of immigrants themselves.

There is no better example of how this trend might pan out than Mexico. For years we have heard of the flow of migrants between Mexico and the U.S., as people travel north looking for better opportunities. That flow is still happening, but with a new twist: these days, many workers are leaving the United States and entering Mexico.

The U.S. recession and so-called recovery, long and arduous as they have been, have been well publicized around the world. All of this coverage has amounted to a giant advertising campaign against migration to the U.S. In contrast, Mexico has been going from strength to strength. China, which has been a manufacturing powerhouse, has been getting relatively expensive. As companies look around for a place to be, they have increasingly cast their eyes on Mexico, and opened factories there instead.

Mexico now has a bit of cachet, and a lot of economic potential. As a result, it has become a destination for international immigra-tion. True, plenty of Mexicans still want in to the U.S., but it is no longer one-way traffic. In fact, according to data from the two countries, over the past few years more Americans have been added to the population of Mexico than the other way around. People are also teeming into Mexico from many other locales, including Central America, Japan, and Europe.[5]

Whether Mexico stays a hot destination is yet to be seen. The country has a lot of issues, including crime, and its economic expansion has slowed over the past couple of years. The more important point, however, is that the tried-and-true destinations for immigrants may be looking a lot less appealing than they once did. If you are looking for tomorrow's economic star as a place to move your family, it might make more sense to consider up-and-comers like Mexico rather than the more developed countries. As countries such as India and China strengthen economically, we could also see former emigrants—or their children—heading back to their homelands in search of what might be better opportunities than exist in their developed-world homes.

STARTING SMALL: IMMIGRATION AND THE PRIVATE SECTOR

When speaking about immigration and whether or not it is "good," debates often focus on the macroeconomic picture. What does bringing people in mean for unemployment, for wages, for growth? All of those things matters, of course, but maybe we need to start our analysis by thinking smaller, and, in fact, concentrating on individual companies. If migration and immigration is good for companies, then presumably it is good for the broader economy as well.

One clear example of this can be found in the technology sector, where companies have lately been arguing that competitiveness is clearly tied to free migration. In the U.S., a very contentious issue over the last few years has been the issuance of H-1B visas for skilled foreign workers. These visas are issued to U.S. companies, including such giants as Microsoft and Facebook, so that they can temporarily fill positions with foreign workers. The regulations behind the visas require that the workers must be in a field requiring a specialized knowledge, must possess at least a bachelor's degree, and must work for the employer that sponsored them. At least in economic terms, it is all fairly straightforward: the program is meant to plug gaps in employer demand by increasing worker supply. In an economic sense, there is some evidence that the H-1B program has been a winner for tech companies. According to an analysis by Carl Lin of Rutgers University, when the H-1B regulations were passed in 1998, there was a quick 15 percent gain in the stock prices of the high-tech companies that primarily took advantage of them.[6]

In many ways, the H-1B program is a microcosm of all that is debated about mobility policies. Tech companies want to be able to use it, and to use programs like it, arguing that they are in dire need of workers with specific skills, and that those workers are simply not available in the United States. Critics say that those skills are certainly available, but not at a price that the companies are willing to pay. As a result, there are unemployed new graduates and veteran technical workers at the same time that the industry is pleading a shortage.

There is a little bit of truth in both arguments. The companies are anxious to fill their positions quickly, with employees who can hit the ground running. They can do that by bringing in workers who have specific experience, rather than training other workers. As such, it might be legitimate to suggest that the companies should participate in continuous retraining, rather than using only workers who meet their immediate needs. But the arguments regarding training are old ones, and complicated as well. Should companies be forced to train workers at all, given that those workers can leave and take their skills elsewhere? Should governments encourage training (and cover some of the costs), given that it is a necessity to the economy to have skilled workers? Or should it be completely up to the individual to get industry training, given that they will reap most of the benefits?

What is certain is that when companies do choose the right things for themselves, there are spillover effects (economists call them "externalities") through the rest of the economy. You can see this pretty clearly through a case study like the massive oil sands project underway in western Canada. To make that project viable, the companies involved have been bringing in people from all over, some from other Canadian provinces, and others from far-flung reaches of the globe. As they do so, they not only create wealth for themselves and for the province in which they are operating (Alberta), but also for other provinces. According to a study by the Conference Board of Canada, given that the actual drilling has to be supported by a host of other goods and services (ranging from custom manufacturing through to financial consulting), one-third of the benefits from the oil sands will accrue to other provinces.[7]

Keep in mind, though, that we are not talking about a "if it's good for General Motors it must be good for America" type of argument here, but rather something more nuanced. The situation regarding companies setting the tone for immigration is more in line with that 2012 remark from an un-named Apple employee, who, when asked why they did not make iPhones in the U.S., said: "We sell iPhones in over a hundred countries . . . we don't have an obligation to solve America's problems. Our only obligation is to make the best product possible."[8] But, of course, by making the best product possible, Apple does create employment and incomes within the U.S. And by being profitable, the company raises the value of stocks held by Americans. So, there is a "win" whether the company cares about U.S. welfare or not. A similar situation arises when it comes to choosing workers from elsewhere to fill positions: wherever they are from, those workers allow a company to be productive, and that ultimately benefits the country that the company is in.

THE BIG ECONOMIC QUESTIONS

So, is mobility "good," "bad," or somewhere in between? This question—and others like it—will be asked often over the next decade.

Is Immigration Good for Economic Growth?

This is hands down the biggest economic question associated with the issue of migration, and it is easy to see why. We know that people move to ensure their best outcomes, but in a broader sense, we need to measure the spillover effect. When people immigrate, do their host countries get an economic return, or do those returns accrue only to the migrants themselves? Given that we are seeing such a massive movement of people across the globe, we want to know that it is going to result in higher economic efficiency and growth than if the movers had just stayed put.

The short answer is that, yes, the so-called immigration effect is a positive one, but indeed it is possible to find studies and analyses on all sides. One recent analysis of the U.S. economy, however, is worth noting. In a 2012 study, researchers looked at the impact of immigration over a cross-section of U.S. communities. What they found was that in the regions where immigrants settled, there was less crime, more growth, and, in general, positive benefits to the regions, whether they were urban or rural. Initially, there might have been some adjustment costs (relating to language and religion, in some cases), but the overall net benefit was seen to be unambiguously positive.[9]

If you are talking about ensuring global growth, however, there should also be some thought to keeping high-skill labor in developing economies and avoiding a so-called brain drain effect through emigration. And that is a paradox that has been felt for years: the fastest-growing countries do not necessarily attract immigrants; they send workers away instead. Here's how it works: When a country gets more industrialized, it gets richer, and some of that wealth eventually gets spent on education. As young people finish high school and consider a third level of education, they may look abroad. Some may never return. Or, as they are able to earn a better living where they are, they save until they have enough to emigrate. Their education and skills make them attractive to developed countries. It may be a win for them, and it may be a win for their new countries—but it's definitely a loss for the regions that educated them.

The fastest-growing countries do not necessarily attract immigrants; they send workers away instead.

For some of the newly industrializing parts of the globe, the brain drain could be a major issue for the next decade. Nigeria, for example, is frequently pointed to as a country with substantial economic potential and a growing middle class. However, the brain drain is an ongoing problem, as professionals leave the country for various reasons.

Another way to evaluate the "immigration effect" is to ask whether immigrants do better or worse after they move. The answer to this one is usually "better," although here again the economic crisis has taken its toll. As a rule, it seems to be taking longer than it once did for immigrants to "catch up" to native-born workers. According to data from Statistics Canada, immigrants at one point earned 85 to 90 percent of the wages of the native-born; now it is closer to 70 percent.[10] However, the real answer may require analyzing multiple generations, rather than looking at the outcomes for just one generation of immigrants.

Does Immigration Push Wages Down for the Native Population?

At a very basic level, there is concern as to whether immigration pushes down wages for the native-born. That's a relevant question in the developed world these days, given that wages for many are stagnating or even falling.

It's a complicated issue. If immigrants come in to take jobs that natives are unlikely to fill—say to work on farms in agricultural jobs—than clearly everyone wins. The workers win, since they want the jobs. The farmers win, since they get to increase production. And, assuming that the new workers spend their money and eventually purchase homes and services, the economy as a whole wins.

Fear and distrust often result when the native-born suspect that they will be competing with new immigrants for the same set of jobs. That tends to be more of an issue, particularly these days, in the case of workers with lower skill levels. If, say, there are lots of people competing for low-paying factory work, then there will definitely be downward pressure on wages.

A study by economists George J. Borjas and Lawrence F. Katz looked at the wages of high-school dropouts and the ways they had been affected by the wave of Mexican immigration into California that occurred between 1980 and 2000. They did find some evidence of a negative impact—specifically, a decline of 8.2 percent in the wages that they attributed to the increase in labor supply stemming from immigration.[11] However, the authors did not take into account the positives that occurred as a result of immigration over the same period, such as the fact that many businesses would not have even existed without immigration. Other studies, including a comprehensive one for the Brookings Institution, have found that the opposite is true, and that immigrants (in this specific case, immigrants into the United States) raise average wages slightly for a country as a whole.[12]

Do Immigrants Use More in Government Services Than They Contribute in Taxes?

This is at the crux of things for many people: Do immigrants pay their way in terms of tax contributions, or do they consume more than they bring in? It is a particularly important question for developed countries, which are facing years of aging populations. Given that the retired typically pay less in taxes than those of working age, the argument is frequently made that bringing in relatively young immigrants is good for government revenues.

From time to time, there are studies that suggest that immigrants cost more in taxes than they bring in. A 2013 study by Canada's Fraser Institute, for example, suggested that the average immigrant into Canada led to an overall bill of $450 an immigrant, or $2 billion a year.[13] As pointed out in critiques of the report,[14] however, it is very difficult to make direct comparisons between the tax rates and earnings of natives and the foreign-born, since the latter tend to be younger at the time of immigration and hence will have lower wages (and thus pay lower taxes). As well, evidence from the U.S. suggests that immigrants are less likely than the native-born to access social services such as social assistance and subsidized housing.[15]

Another flawed argument about immigration is that it causes governments to spend on services. To an extent, that is true, of course: more people mean more schools and more hospitals and more of just about everything. However, as economist Bryan Caplan points out, many government services are what economists call "non-rival," meaning that once you provide them, more people can use them without significantly increasing the cost. For example, military spending does not have much to do with the size of the population.[16] If you want to run a program to spray for mosquitos in the summer or a public service campaign to educate the population about nutrition, you can provide those things without regard to how many people are in a country. So, it is not a one-to-one progression between population growth and services.

The most comprehensive analyses on the fiscal impact of immigrants are those done by the Organisation for Economic Co-operation and Development (OECD), which actually show that the whole thing is a bit of a wash: immigrants cost something in services, but they also bring in revenues and pay taxes.[17] With the right policies—particularly those that favor younger immigrants who will have years to pay taxes before collecting a pension—it should be possible to nudge the fiscal impact into the positive. Indeed, that is the goal for many developed countries.

Does Immigration Push Up Unemployment Rates in Host Countries?

Instinctively, this one seems as if it must be true: surely bringing in more workers to a country with a finite number of jobs is going to leave more people out in the cold and push up the unemployment rate. But bringing in more people to any country has ripple effects. The people coming in need to buy things, and educate their children, and find housing. They increase the size of the economic pie in that way, and in other ways too. Without a certain amount of labor, some projects—such as oil drilling in various parts of the world—could not take place. And so, bringing in more people would have a very positive effect on employment, and a negative effect on the unemployment rate. It is not a zero-sum game.

As well, in many cases the skills of the native-born and immigrants do not overlap. Frequently, when we are talking about developed countries, immigrants are willing to take jobs in which natives are not particularly interested—things like agricultural and domestic work. In that sense, there can be an additional positive impact on employment. If, for example, there is a shortage of child-care workers that is preventing parents from accepting employment, bringing in foreign-born nannies makes it easier for the native-born to enter the labor market.

Immigrants do tend to have high employment rates. An OECD study of immigrants into Canada finds that employment rates for foreign-born Canadian citizens has risen since 2008, while it has plateaued for the native-born.[18] As well, at least in North America, immigration policy is structured such that immigrants are more likely than the native-born to be entrepreneurs (and hence create jobs).[19]

CLOSE TO HOME: IMMIGRATION AND NORTH AMERICA

So, there are major trends afoot in terms of global migration patterns. Looking at things through a North American lens, the question is whether those trends will be a source of economic strength for the Canadian and U.S. economies, or whether they will be another potential negative in terms of economic development.

In North America, there are two patterns of migration to watch. The first is the pattern of international migration that delivers people to North American shores. This may or may not address labor force imbalances and budget shortfalls—for good or bad. The second migration trend to watch is internal migration, the reshuffling of the deck within Canada and the U.S. that is sending people to different cities and redrawing the map in terms of human capital. That can also have some major economic ramifications.

Let's start by looking at the pace of international immigration into Canada and the United States. The U.S. accepts around one million immigrants a year, or about 0.4 percent of its population, while Canada brings in a little more than 250,000 a year, or about 0.8 of its population.[20] In each country, there are ongoing debates as to whether the pace of immigration is too high, and whether the "right" people are being brought in. New immigrants are often viewed with suspicion and mistrust, particularly in economies that are still traumatized from the effect of the last recession.

At the moment, with the effects of the recession still being felt, it can be difficult to argue that immigration is happening to deal with immediate labor force needs, at least on the face of it. In mid-2013, the unemployment rates in the United States and Canada were each around 7 percent, which, although not as high as they were in the depths of the recession (when the U.S. rate touched 10 percent), still do not represent anything close to what could be called "full employment."[21]

But looking at things in such a simplistic framework may not be the best approach. We do know that even amidst the "surplus" of workers, there are still occupations (such as high tech) and locations (such as the regions of western Canada where the oil sands are being developed) where there are dire shortages of appropriate workers, and where immediate immigration makes sense to fill labor market needs. Still, when talking about immigration to Canada and the U.S., most analysis centers on filling needs in the future, when an aging population will take its toll.

In Canada and the U.S., as in many developed countries, a tidal wave of baby boomer retirements (put off a bit by the recession, maybe, but unlikely to be put off forever) looms. There will be labor force needs or, quite simply, jobs to fill—although it is very difficult to know exactly how many. Demand changes, technologies change, and methods of work also change over time. A job that was filled by one baby boomer may eventually be filled by a part-timer, a freelancer, and/or some new technology. The departure of so many boomers from the labor market will mean some reshuffling, and that will create a need for workers, even if they do not take the form of nine-to-five, 40-year employees.

Even with immigration, labor force growth is going to be fairly weak for the next decade or so, at least compared to the norms of the last few decades. Without immigration, particularly immigration in the younger age groups, there would be an actual decline in population. At best, that would cause a spike in wage rates and an inflationary spiral. At worst, it would cripple the productive capacities of North America.

But economic output is not just boosted by people at work. Look at the other side of the equation: productivity. What the slower-growth parts of the world (that is, the developed parts) need in order to kick up their economic growth rates is a boost in productivity. Productivity is typically encouraged by new inventions and processes that are then brought forward—through some form of entrepreneurship—to a wider audience. It is the process of innovation—and, yes, immigration plays a role.

> Without immigration, particularly immigration in the younger age groups, there would be an actual decline in population. At best, that would cause a spike in wage rates and an inflationary spiral. At worst, it would cripple the productive capacities of North America.

When we talk about innovation, we are typically talking about shiny new ideas that will move the world forward. There are many theories as to what you need to breed innovation: people cite everything from the correct government policies through to the correct education system through to a removal of government red tape for patent applications. All are important, as are scores of other factors. Innovation happens when you put the right people in the right places, and, frequently, that means bringing in the best and the brightest from wherever they may be. The right places for innovation may well be universities and workplaces in the U.S. or Canada or Europe, and the right people may well be in Asia or Africa or South America, as well as in the same countries as the universities. Universities award a disproportionate number of PhDs to foreign students, and, after graduation, U.S.-educated foreign workers frequently take out patents in electronics, machinery, pharmaceuticals, and tech products.[22] So, at least in the case of the highest education and skill levels, there is an argument for open mobility.

But it is not just the highest-skill migrants who contribute to productivity: lower-skill workers do as well, particularly because they are willing to move as many times as possible. Native-born workers are more likely to own homes and have ties in their communities. As a group, they tend to be somewhat resistant to picking up their families and moving when economic fortunes change. Not so for more recent immigrants.

Actually, the need for immigration is much easier to see if you look at the housing markets of North American countries. The U.S. (and much of Europe) has already gone through a housing market meltdown, while many are watching Canada's booming market with a wary eye, wondering if it will be next. If Canada is to avoid a collapse—and if the U.S. is to avoid another one in the foreseeable future—population in the age groups that feed housing demand will have to grow. That is not a guarantee of housing market strength, of course—the U.S. meltdown was not primarily driven by demographics—but without a growing market of buyers, the housing situation will be doomed. Luckily, there is some growth in the 20- to 44-year-old age group projected for the next two decades. But in the absence of immigration, there would not be.[23]

As much as international immigration and the policies that govern it are important to North America, it is also important to ensure the correct outcomes from internal migration, or people moving *within* Canada and the United States. Actually, as with all policies regarding migration, you would think that leaving things alone would ensure the best outcomes, simply because when people are looking out for their own economic welfare, you can generally count on them finding their way to where the opportunities are best. Unfortunately, however, there may be policies afoot that are making this outcome less likely.

Overall, people are moving from state to state and province to province. In the U.S., the recession did put a damper on things for awhile as people stayed in one place and waited for the value of their homes to improve before they thought about selling. By 2012, however, people were pulling up stakes again, with 16.9 million people—the highest in five years—on the move.[24] In Canada, migration has also been gaining steadily over the years. According to a report by TD Economics (using data from Statistics Canada), as of 2012, about 320,000 people, or 1 percent of the population, moved between provinces during the year, a figure that was greater than the net increase in immigration in Canada that year.[25]

In the Canadian case, particularly, it is easy to see that population shifts are all about people moving to where their prospects are better. Canada's western provinces have been booming, economically speaking, and there has been a corresponding boom in east-west migration. That is one trend that will likely continue, but there will be others as well. For example, as baby boomers retire, they are going to look for cities—or, more likely, towns—where their money will go as far as it can. That should cause another spur in migration over the next decade.

Still, despite the recent spike in migration, mobility in the U.S. is being hurt by the housing market crisis that engulfed the economy over the 2008–09 period, and whose aftereffects still linger. People who lost a chunk of the value of their home (and, in many cases, who now have homes worth less than the value of their mortgages) are understandably hesitant about selling their house and moving, even if there is work available elsewhere in the country. What can make that situation worse are policies that effectively encourage people to stay where they are. Employment insurance is arguably one such program, given that it gives would-be workers a cash subsidy to stay put and wait for things to pick up rather than forcing them to go where economic activity might be stronger.

You can also see the negative impact that employment insurance has on mobility in Atlantic Canada, which is an area that is disproportionately rural. Prince Edward Island (the smallest province in Canada) has a population that is 54 percent rural, while New Brunswick's population is 48 percent rural.[26] The rural parts of both provinces tend to be older, and to have more economic issues, than the rest of the province. Ideally, there would be a shift from those rural areas, where unemployment is high, to larger urban areas, or to other parts of the country completely. Arguably, this is not happening more quickly because there is employment insurance and social support for holding on to the "rural way of life."

But if those who are stuck in "old" industries are less likely to be mobile, there is evidence that those with the highest education and skills are more mobile. According to research by economist Enrico Moretti, the more education a person has, the more mobile he or she is, which is a contrast to earlier periods of migration, when it was the least educated who hit the road. Still, Moretti also notes that when the educated head for cities to take new jobs, they also have a multiplier effect, and create positions in the service industry, meaning that migration effectively creates jobs for people with a wide variety of backgrounds and education levels.[27]

And there is one more trend to keep an eye on as regards North American migration: a small but growing migration of U.S. citizens to Canada. According to data from Citizenship and Immigration Canada, the number of Americans becoming permanent residents in Canada rose from 2,792 in 2003 to 4,753 in 2012. The numbers are certainly still tiny, but the trend is unmistakable: over a nine-year period, immigration from the U.S. into Canada rose by 70 percent. Over the same time period, the U.S. went through a much more severe recession than did Canada, and the unemployment rates in the two countries diverged. That clearly encouraged some households to look north, particularly given the resource boom in Canada's western provinces. It is a trend to watch, particularly given recent changes to Canada's immigration rules that some believe will favor Americans.[28]

FITTING THE JIGSAW TOGETHER

And so we have a world on the move. Economic adjustments are happening very quickly, and that will see people scrambling to fit themselves into the right places. It is as if they are all a part of a large jigsaw puzzle, and need to find their spot. All of that considered, the focus should be on guiding people to the places where their skills can best be used and, in turn, using that labor effectively when it is in place. Each is easier said than done.

Are there things we should do to prepare for the next decade? Certainly, although when working against a tide of people who want to be where they want to be, policy measures will only go so far. For one thing, social change will be the order of the day, and institutions need to prepare for it now. This has happened already: in North America alone, we have seen progressive influxes of immigrants speaking different languages and bringing different traditions, and this has caused various adjustments to take place. But, given that the next wave is happening even faster, we will need more and better measures to facilitate the adjustment of newcomers, whether that means language training from governments or sensitivity training from companies. And, by the way, "newcomers" does not necessarily mean people from faraway lands. We are already seeing Americans coming to Canada, and rural dwellers heading for cities in the same states or provinces in which they live; these people, too, face adjustments.

Another challenge will be to use labor effectively. In fact, in developed countries, "credentialism" is one of the things that make it most difficult for those who come in from elsewhere to effectively use their abilities. Under Canada's "points" system, for example, immigrants are awarded points coincident with their level of education. Once they are in the country, however, the education that got them accepted in the first place may not be recognized by employers. That is a problem that is especially prevalent in any industry where a licensing exam must be taken. Difficulties in having foreign degrees either formally or informally recognized not only lead to a loss of talent, they lead to the loss of potential tax revenue that would have been paid had the individual in question been able to be employed in a higher-paying position.

Yet another challenge? Getting the right people into the right places will be increasingly difficult as a global war for "talent" heats up. Yes, Europe and North America are hitting the latter years of their demographic cycles, but so are many other places. China, for example, will see its own demographic window close by the mid 2020s, and Brazil by 2040. These countries—fast-growing economic powerhouses that are rapidly increasing the size of their respective middle classes—will also want to bring in the most qualified migrants, or at least keep the ones they already have. Indeed, many of the countries that we think of as sources of immigrants may become immigrant-receiving countries themselves. Also, keep in mind that we are seeing huge amounts of urbanization around the world, and that cities are becoming magnets for those with talent and ambition. In many countries, that will mean that there is an alternative to actually leaving national borders in order to better economic prospects. None of this means that Canada or the United States will find themselves with a shortage of potential immigrants, but it does mean that the pool of applicants with strong economic attributes may contract a little. After all, knowledge is power. Knowing that people want to move, we should be able to help them find the best places to be, both for them and for our economic future.

(ENDNOTES)

[1] National Intelligence Council, *Global Trends 2030: Alternate Worlds*, Military Bookshop, December 1, 2012. Location 1052 in the Kindle edition.

[2] United Nations, Department of Economic and Social Affairs, Population Division, "232 million international migrants living abroad worldwide–

new UN global migration statistics reveal." Retrieved from http://esa.un.org/unmigration/wallchart2013.htm.

3 OECD, "International Migration Policies and Data: International Migration Outlook 2013." (Paris: OECD, 2013). p. 19. Retrieved from http://www.oecd.org/els/mig/imo2013.htm.

4 The demographic window is the time period over which there is a sweet spot for economic growth. This corresponds with a relatively large number of people entering the labor force, compared to those who are out of it. Roughly speaking, it happens when the percentage of the population under the age of 15 is less than 30 percent, and the percentage over the age of 65 is less than 15 percent. In China, that window is still open, but given the trend to low birth rates, it will close by 2030.

5 Darien Cave,, "For Migrants, New Land of Opportunity is Mexico," *New York Times Magazine*, September 21, 2013. Retrieved from http://www.nytimes.com/2013/09/22/world/americas/for-migrants-new-land-of-opportunity-is-mexico.html?_r=0.

6 Carl Lin, "Give Me Your Wired and Your Highly Skilled: Measuring the Impact of Immigration Policy on Employees and Shareholders," Institute for the Study of Labor Discussion Paper No. 5754, May 2011, p. 3. Retrieved from http://ftp.iza.org/dp5754.pdf.

7 Conference Board of Canada, "U.S. Workers May Hold the Key to Canada's Skills Shortage," *Briefing*, October 2013, p. 10.

8 Quoted in Charles Duhigg and Keith Bradsher, "How the U.S. Lost Out on iPhone Work," *New York Times*, January 21, 2012. Retrieved from http://www.nytimes.com/2012/01/22/business/apple-america-and-a-squeezed-middle-class.html?pagewanted=all&_r=0.

9 John M. MacDonald and Robert J. Sampson, "Don't Shut the Golden Door," *New York Times*, June 19, 2012. Retrieved from http://www.nytimes.com/2012/06/20/opinion/the-beneficial-impact-of-immigrants.html.

10 Tamsin McMahon, "Why the World's Best and Brightest Struggle to Find Jobs," *Macleans*, April 24, 2013. Retrieved from http://www2.macleans.ca/2013/04/24/land-of-misfortune/.

11 Eduardo Porter, "Cost of Illegal Immigration May Be Less than Meets the Eye," *New York Times*, April 16, 2006. Retrieved from http://www.nytimes.com/2006/04/16/business/yourmoney/16view.html.

12 Michael Greenston and Adam Looney, "Ten Economic Facts About Immigration." The Hamilton Project, Policy Memo, The Brookings Institution, September 2010. Retrieved from http://www.brookings.edu/~/media/

research/files/reports/2010/9/immigration%20greenstone%20looney/09_immigration.pdf.

[13] Herbert Grubel, "Canada's Immigrant Selection Policies: Recent Record, Marginal Changes and Needed Reforms." Fraser Institute, August 29, 2013. Retrieved from http://www.fraserinstitute.org/uploadedFiles/fraser-ca/Content/research-news/research/publications/canadas-immigrant-selection-policies.pdf.

[14] Patti Tamara Lenard, "Indecent Proposals: Why the Fraser Institute Is Wrong on Immigration." Broadbent Institute blog, September 13, 2013. Retrieved from http://www.broadbentinstitute.ca/en/blog/indecent-proposals-why-fraser-institute-wrong-immigration.

[15] Sara Pekkala Kerr and William Kerr, "Economic Impacts of Immigration: A Survey," National Bureau of Economic Research Working Paper #16737, January 2011. Retrieved from http://dl.kli.re.kr/dl_image/IMG/03/000000011124/SERVICE/000000011124_01.PDF.

[16] Christopher Matthews, "The Economics of Immigration: Who Wins, Who Loses," *Time*, January 30, 2013. Retrieved from http://business.time.com/2013/01/30/the-economics-of-immigration-who-wins-who-loses-and-why/.

[17] For more, see http://www.oecd.org/els/mig/.

[18] Clement Gignac, "For Canada, Immigration is a Key to Prosperity," *Globe and Mail*, October 7, 2013. Retrieved from: http://www.theglobeandmail.com/report-on-business/economy/economy-lab/for-canada-immigration-is-a-key-to-prosperity/article14711281/.

[19] Associated Press, "Luring New Entrepreneurs from Silicon Valley to Canada," June 6, 2013. Retrieved from http://www.obj.ca/Technology/2013-06-06/article-3270692/Luring-new-entrepreneurs-from-Silicon-Valley-to-Canada/1.

[20] Andy Radia, "Canada's immigration numbers peaking for seventh consecutive year: 2012 statistics," Yahoo!News, February 27, 2013. Retrieved from http://ca.news.yahoo.com/blogs/canada-politics/2012-immigration-statistics-released-canada-remains-one-most-235820655.html.

[21] Sources: U.S. unemployment rates are as per the U.S. Bureau of Labor Statistics, http://www.bls.gov/home.htm. Canadian unemployment rates are as per Statistics Canada, www.statcan.gc.ca.

[22] Jennifer Hunt and Marjolaien Gauther-Loiselle, "How Much Does Immigration Boost Innovation," National Bureau of Economic Research Working Paper #14312, September 2008. Retrieved from http://www.nber.org/papers/w14312.

[23] Gignac.

[24] Greg Toppo and Paul Overberg, "Census: Americans Are Moving Again," *USAToday*, October 26, 2013. Retrieved from http://www.usatoday.com/story/news/nation/2013/10/26/americans-moving-again-census/2986963/.

[25] "Interprovincial Migration Shifts in Canada," TD Economics, June 17, 2013. Retrieved from http://www.td.com/document/PDF/economics/special/jb0613_interprovincial_migration.pdf.

[26] Statistics Canada, "Section 5: Rural and urban populations by sex and age for total population and farm population," Table 5:1, Canada, 95-633-X. Retrieved from http://www.statcan.gc.ca/pub/95-633-x/2007000/t/6500022-eng.htm.

[27] Jim Russell, "The Great Creative Class Migration," *Pacific Standard*, August 22, 2013. Retrieved from http://www.psmag.com/business-economics/burgh-disapora/the-great-creative-class-migration-64912/.

[28] Trevor Melanson, "Why Canada Could See a Boom in Immigration—from the U.S.," *Canadian Business*, February 6, 2013. Retrieved from http://www.canadianbusiness.comToppo, Greg and Pau /economy/canada-us-uk-immigration-rules/.

More Urbanization (However You Define It)

The world is becoming an increasingly urban place, and cities are becoming more important as economic entities. Over the next 20 years, this will become a planet on which the majority of people live in cities of one size or another. What urban living means will vary: sometimes it will mean living in the center of a large city, while other times it will mean living in a far-flung exurb. And that is an important point: although we hear a lot these days about how cool it is to live in or near downtowns, in truth what suits many people is to live in the suburbs—with no apology.

Regardless of the specifics, there will be new opportunities to build productive communities and enhance economic growth, as well as challenges to provide enough resources—and appropriate policy—for the new urban dwellers.

Pick a city, any city, and take a close look. Look at its sidewalks and suburbs and the people you see and the buildings that surround them. You'll find a story not just about that particular urban area, but about the global economy as a whole.

Urbanization is happening at a rapid clip these days, and for positive reasons: expanding economies create opportunities, and they tend to create them in urban areas. If we are looking forward to 20 years of economic development in North America and around the globe, we are also looking forward to a world in which more people live in cities, and sometimes in increasingly large cities. Once upon a time, the best bet for people was to stay on the family farm and tend the land. Now, the best bet is not the farm, or even the village in which one is born. Instead, the best chance many have to achieve success is to head for an urban area. *Urban*, however, can mean many things, particularly in North America, and some of the fastest growth in the years ahead may be in what used to be called *suburbs* and in fact these days are actually little cities on the periphery of bigger ones.

And so we are fast becoming a world of urban dwellers, with all of the opportunities and challenges that presents. Cities are places where incomes are higher and ideas flow freely; they are also places in which development can be too rapid and the strains on resources can cause social and economic problems. Increasingly, they are places that need strong leadership and thoughtful strategic plans. How each of these challenges are met will go a long way to deciding whether we end up with livable cities and a vibrant economy, or a host of economic problems.

THE NEW URBAN WORLD

Let's start with the big picture: cities are indeed becoming more important, but there is no one-size-fits-all answer to which kind of city is going to lead the pack in terms of economic force and opportunity. From megacities like Mexico City or Manila through to up-and-comers like Chongqing (in China's interior), there are different models of urbanization, and each presents its own unique strengths.

Before looking at what is happening and where it is happening, a few definitions are needed. We are talking about a trend toward *urbanization*, although the meaning of that word differs depending on where you live. According to the United Nations Demographic Yearbook,[1] Norway defines an urban area as one in which there are 200 or more inhabitants, while Switzerland puts the cutoff at 10,000, and the Netherlands is somewhere in between, at 2,000. In North America, Canada defines a place as urban if it has 1,000 or more inhabitants and a population density of 400 or more per square kilometer, while the United States puts the cutoff at 25,000 or more. So although we will refer to overall urbanization, bear in mind that this might encompass different things in different countries.

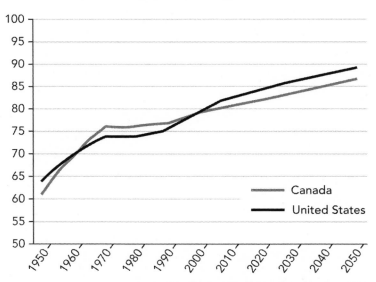

CITY DWELLERS

Proportion of population living in urban areas

Source: United Nations, World Urbanization Prospects, 2011.

Whatever your country's definition, urbanization is on the rise. According to the World Health Organization, a century ago about two out of every 10 people on the planet lived in an urban area. That had grown to five out of 10 by 2010, and is expected to hit six out of 10 by 2030, and seven out of 10 by 2050.[2]

The reasons for this recent wave of urbanization are not too different than the reasons for previous waves. Historically speaking, the first country in the world to really urbanize was arguably the United Kingdom, which did so during the Industrial Revolution in the 18th and 19th centuries. Technology created opportunities for people to better their earnings, but to take advantage of those opportunities they had to abandon rural life and head for the cities, where the metal working industry had started to flourish. The circumstances were a little different but the motives were pretty much the same when the U.S. and Canada urbanized at around the same time as the U.K., as did European countries such as Germany. More recently, we have seen waves of urbanization in Japan, South Korea, China, and India. As geographic areas from Asia to Latin America grow in economic terms, they create factories and job opportunities, typically in non-rural areas. As industrialization blazes around the globe, clusters of factories are created, and these draw ever-larger clusters of people to work in them.

Over the next two decades, the globe is likely to see all regions become more urban, albeit at different rates. The U.S. and Canada, already urban with 82 percent and 81 percent of their total populations living in urban areas, respectively, will get a little more so, increasing their shares to 85.2 percent and 82.5 percent. Europe (including all countries) will go from 72.7 percent to 76.1 percent. Although not insignificant, these increases pale in comparison to the expected growth in urban dwellers in Asian and South American cities. China's urban population is expected to increase from 49.2 percent in 2010 to 65.4 percent in 2025, a figure that is even more stunning when you consider that only 31 percent of the population lived in urban areas as of 1995. India's urban population will rise from a very modest 30.9 percent as of 2010 to 37.2 percent by 2025—which is still significant considering that in 1995 the urban population was just 27 percent.[3]

Much of the global urban growth of the next decades will be in megacities, areas that house populations of 10 million plus.[4] Megacity growth has already been astronomical, with the number of people residing in them increasing tenfold to 359.4 million between 1970 and 2011. This figure is expected to double, to about 630 million, by 2025. Today, one in 20 of the world's population lives in a megacity, a figure expected to reach one in 13 by 2025.[5] The growth of megacities by geographic region will mimic the pace of population and economic growth by region, with the lowest growth rates expected to be in the developed countries, and the highest in Asia, as well as in parts of Africa (specifically Nigeria's Lagos). In the more developed regions of the world, megacities are expected to expand by 21 percent by 2025, which although robust is much less than the 43 percent growth expected in the developing world.[6]

Perhaps an even more interesting story than the growth of the megacities is the expected expansion in what the McKinsey Global Institute has termed the "middleweights." These are cities with populations between a (very modest) 200,000 up to 10 million, and which the Institute sees growing at about 8 percent a year, in gross domestic product (GDP) terms, between now and 2025. Many of us in the developed world have never heard of these places, yet they will be setting the pace for global growth in future. McKinsey also believes that of the six hundred cities they now see as middleweights, 13 will join the megacity ranks by 2025—and, with the exception of Chicago, all of these will be in emerging markets, with seven in China alone.[7]

In North America, growth patterns suggest that *somewhat* smaller cities will see the greatest expansions. In the United States, the megacities (New York and Los Angeles at present, with Chicago expected to join soon) are expected to grow by 30 percent by 2025, while cities with five to 10 million inhabitants will grow by 59 percent. Smaller cities (those with populations of one to five million, which would include such cities as Austin, Texas, and Raleigh, North Carolina) are expected to decline in aggregate by 8.7 percent. In Canada, the sharpest growth will be in cities with populations between 500,000 and one million (a group that includes cities such as Winnipeg, Manitoba, and Ottawa, Ontario), which are expected to grow by 78 percent. The larger urban areas, with one to five million inhabitants and five to 10 million, are expected to grow by 6.8 percent and 4.9 percent, respectively, between 2010 and 2025.[8]

DOWNTOWNS AND EXURBS

As we've established, the term *urbanization* can cover a lot of ground. Does it mean living in a city's core, or in a suburb that may be a long way from the city's center but still technically considered part of the city? For many of the world's largest cities, urban growth will not mean growth in the downtown cores, but rather over an increasingly large metro region.

The growth of "downtowns" is an interesting topic, especially as it relates to North America. Over the past few years, there has been a blitz of condo building in North American cities of all sizes, and with that a sharp increase in the number of people who live in the core areas. According to the U.S. Census Bureau, between 2000 and 2010, the population living in American downtowns (defined as being within two miles of City Hall) in cities with five million or more rose by 13.3 percent, compared to a 9.7 percent increase for the population as a whole. Downtown Chicago, with an increase of 36.2 percent, saw the heftiest growth, but Washington (14.2 percent), Philadelphia (9.7 percent), New York (9.3 percent), and San Francisco (5.9 percent) also experienced healthy growth.[9]

Why the increase? The revitalization of cities and, in some cases, specific campaigns to get people downtown are key reasons. As well, there is a general weariness with the time and cost of commuting. Interestingly, the demographics do not really argue for growth at this pace. The group that has traditionally lived in urban downtowns is twenty-something college graduates starting their exciting new jobs, or early thirty-somethings who have not yet had kids. That demographic group, however, did not grow particularly quickly between 2000 and 2010. According to the Census Bureau, it was up just 2.9 percent in the U.S. over the ten-year period. In addition, we know that younger workers, indebted and underemployed as they are, have become more likely to live with their parents for a period past college. So it really is not this group that is likely driving the downtown boom.

There is an argument to be made that some of the downtown growth comes from baby boomers seeking downtown pieds-à-terre. Between 2000 and 2010, the U.S. population aged between 55 and 64 grew by an incredible 50.3 percent—12.2 million in absolute numbers.[10] There is a great fit between this group and downtown living. They do not need as much space as they might have in the past, when they were more likely to have had kids at home; they are more likely to have the time to enjoy the things a downtown has to offer; and they are at a point in their lives when they want to shake things up, so selling the suburban home and moving downtown makes sense. If this group is interested in downtown living—or could be sold on it—then there is indeed a real likelihood of a boom in city centers.

The retirement decisions of baby boomers could make a difference to the growth of cites in North America (and abroad) over the next few years in another way as well. Many boomers have equity built up in their homes in larger centers, and, faced with not having saved enough for retirement, might want to liquidate those holdings and choose retirement homes in smaller centers.

The first wave of boomers to have tried that found mixed results: small towns that looked bucolic from a distance ended up feeling more like Twin Peaks than Mayberry. And for the next wave of U.S. boomers in particular, selling homes in larger centers has been postponed because of the recent housing crash. Most likely, boomers will choose to stay in their own markets, although perhaps in smaller housing units. If they make a different decision, the face of cities in North America might change dramatically.

> Many boomers might want to liquidate holdings and choose retirement homes in smaller centers. The first wave of boomers to have tried that found mixed results: small towns that looked bucolic from a distance ended up feeling more like Twin Peaks than Mayberry.

If downtown living is at one end of the urbanization scale, then exurbs are at the other. Typically, the term is used to define cities someplace outside a city's official suburbs. In a recent analysis, the Brookings Institution exurb status is contingent on having 20 percent of the population commuting to the core city. Other terms for exurbs include *rurban areas* (a European term), *peri-urban areas*, or, less flatteringly, *urban sprawl*.

Although the last of these might be said with a sneer by those who live in downtown cores, scores of people apparently are uninterested in their opinion. According to the U.S. Census Bureau, the total U.S. population grew by about 10 percent between 2000 and 2010, while the exurb population grew by a stunning 60 percent.[11] The trend seems to be the same in Canada. According to the Canadian Census of Population for 2011, the fastest growing community in the country was Milton, Ontario, a town of 84,362 that is 55 kilometers from Toronto.[12]

Whether this trend toward exurbanization continues will depend on several factors, most importantly the cost of fuel: every time that it costs more to fill up the tank, people rethink the cost of commuting and wonder about moving closer to the city. Also important, however, will be the decisions that are ultimately made by companies as to how much telecommuting is okay. After rising in popularity in the 1980s and 90s, the work-from-home trend took a hit in the recent recession.[13] Since then, several large companies (most notably Yahoo) have tightened the rules on telecommuting and ordered everyone back to the office. The ultimate resolution of this conflict over where people work will be a key factor in how population is divided up between downtowns, suburbs, exurbs, and those retirement towns that are far from existing large metropolises.

AN URBAN BOOM, A SPENDING BOOM

Urbanization has always been and will continue to be a positive economic force. People seek out bigger markets because they see the benefit of them, but as they create those bigger markets the economic benefits for others also snowball.

In fact, the biggest bonanza from the growth of cities could conceivably be a boom in innovation and economic productivity. Historically, city populations have brought together thinkers and artists and those with a vision of the future, and that has benefited the larger world. These days, you could argue that big ideas can get exchanged over the Internet, and in fact, in the 1990s there was some conjecture that technology might sound the death knell for cities. During the dot.com era in the late 1990s, Harvard economist Edward Glaeser posed the question, "Are cities dying?"— pondering whether a mix of technological improvements could offset the gains of being in a city.[14] But in the same way that telecommuting has a cost in terms of the productivity gains from impromptu interactions in the hall, doing everything virtually also has a cost in terms of the way that face-to-face interactions can spur activity. As urbanization spirals, we can only hope that it also brings with it a new wave of innovation and productivity.

But even without any productivity gains, the fact that cities are growing will have a huge economic impact. According to the McKinsey Global Institute, between 2010 and 2025 the gross domestic product of cities[15] will rise by over $30 trillion—or, to put it another way, by about 65 percent of global growth. Given that growth, there will be over $10 trillion in additional annual investments needed in cities by 2025. And, of course, the new urbanites will consume more, to the tune of $10 trillion more in consumption by 2025. Again, McKinsey is upbeat about the prospects for the middleweight cities with populations between 200,000 and 10 million, which they see growing at about 8 percent a year, in GDP terms, between now and 2025.[16]

Much of the growth will come simply from consumer spending. The move to cities typically comes because of the motivation of a higher income, and some of that income is inevitably going to get spent. Of course, some of the city dwellers' spending has nothing to do with income increases. City dwellers are simply exposed to more, and many take advantage of that fact. For example, the average resident of Manhattan spends 59 percent of their food budget on dining out, compared to 42 percent in the average U.S. household.[17] You can see the potential repercussions if you look at the case of China. According to calculations by China's government, data for 2010 showed that urban residents spent 3.6 times more per capita than did their counterparts in rural areas. Carrying that through suggests that every rural resident who moves to a city increases consumption by the equivalent of U.S.$1,631. If you figure on 10 million rural residents moving into China's cities every year, it translates to $16.3 *billion* dollars a year of spending. That is certainly a business opportunity for someone, but more than that, it is money that will ricochet through the system, creating multiplier effects.[18]

Even more than the consumer products industry, the infrastructure sector will see a demand surge because of urbanization. From roads to ports to airports to railways to telecommunications equipment, there will simply be a need for more—more of everything—in both developed and developing countries. Some estimates suggest that over $40 trillion will be invested in urban infrastructure over the next couple of decades.[19] Some of that will be remedial repairs on old infrastructure that is being tested by new demands. In other cases, though, it will be new construction. And consider this statistic: midsize cities in emerging markets are posed to generate nearly 40 percent of global growth over the next 15 years. That's more growth than the combined total of all developed economies *plus* the emerging markets' megacities.[20]

So who will finance the new projects? Governments maybe, but even in the fastest-growing countries the demands on funds are growing at least as quickly as the urban populations. Traditional financial institutions maybe, except that many of those are in cash-strapped Europe, and all of them, wherever they are located, are primly risk-averse as a result of the global crisis. So it will be a mix: floating bonds, public-private partnerships, and traditional and non-traditional lenders. Given the volume of the demand, there will be some need for oversight and caution: building booms—indeed booms of any kind—have a history of causing questionable decision-making, and this particular expansion will likely be no exception to the rule. As well, no matter who handles the lending, the sheer explosion in demand for capital, unless it is matched by a corresponding increase in global savings, could inevitably push up interest rates worldwide.

THE CHALLENGES OF AN URBAN WORLD

If all of this sounds very upbeat, spare a moment think about Detroit, Michigan—a poster child for all that is wrong with cities.

In the summer of 2013, the city declared bankruptcy, effectively declaring that its economic prospects were so poor that it would not realistically be able to pay its creditors. The city had been ravaged by decades of industrial restructuring, and the hollowing out of its once-mighty auto sector. By the time of the bankruptcy, what in 1950 had been a prosperous blue-collar city of 1.8 million people was an urban jungle of just over 701,000,[21] where hungry dogs roamed the streets and houses could frequently be purchased for less than what people paid for cars in other cities.

Detroit was initially lifted up by migration and growth and industrialization; it now offers us a look at how bad a situation can get when a few things go wrong and then spiral out of control. If the world is to become increasingly urban, it is important to ensure that those newly prosperous cities do not follow in Detroit's path. It is a good time to take stock of some of the problems that might ensue, and whether (and how) they can be prevented.

We also have to be mindful of the fact that the path taken by cities will affect everyone, not just those who live in them. Perhaps the best example of this comes from commodity prices. More city dwellers and bigger cities will inevitably mean a pull on the world's resources. If cities make bad decisions, resource use can spiral out of control, causing spikes in demand that can raise the prices across the board. You can see how that might happen in the case of oil, in particular, which is an input to all kinds of urban activity. Higher urban demands for energy will result in higher energy prices, which will raise the production cost and inevitably hit consumers as higher final prices. Those higher prices will slow global growth. However, if cities implement plans to keep energy consumption in

> Higher urban demands for energy will result in higher energy prices, which will raise the production cost and inevitably hit consumers as higher final prices. Those higher prices will slow global growth.

check, the price increases could be controlled to some extent.

As well as changing our mindset to deal with this new urban world, we are also going to have to make some practical adjustments. At the moment, most economic data that is available is on countries, not cities. Although from time to time special tabulations of the gross domestic product of various cities are done, for the most part large purveyors of data do not bother with this layer of coverage. That has to change. To quote Michael Bloomberg, the mayor of New York City from 2001 to 2013, "If you can't measure it, you can't manage it."[22]

And so, with all of that in mind, let's explore some of the issues that will come to the fore in an increasingly urban world.

Poverty and Crime

If you look at the urbanization of cities such as New York or Chicago or London, you can see that there were "negative externalities" that went hand in hand with growth. As people flooded into these urban areas, public health issues grew more quickly than any corresponding plans to deal with them. Sanitation was an issue, as was housing. Crime and poverty were endemic. Some of those concerns are going to surface again as cities around the world expand, and progress will be in fits and starts.

It is worth noting that urbanization actually helps people out of extreme poverty. According to a joint report from the World Bank and the International Monetary Fund, 11.6 percent of those who live in urban centers around the world are considered to live in "extreme poverty" (defined globally as living on less than $1.25 a day), compared to 29.4 percent of those who live in rural areas. That's easy to understand as a phenomenon: in rural areas, the primary way to earn a living is through agriculture, which in many parts of the world does not offer much in the way of income. Cities provide many more opportunities to earn, whether in factories or on construction sites or in service businesses. True, some of those earnings are eaten up by the higher cost of living that comes with urbanization, but moving to a city and clawing your way up the economic ladder is a tried-and-true path out of poverty.[23]

An inevitable byproduct of increased urbanization is the development of slums, or at least "less prosperous" areas. Urbanizing without the development of impoverished areas or slums may be impossible, but in the successful models of urbanization, these areas are "transitional" rather than permanent.[24] That's easier said than done, of course, but if the next wave of cities is going to avoid the mistakes of the past, the idea of urbanization without creating slums has to be a policy priority.

Dealing with Environmental Issues and Natural Disasters

If the majority of future growth is going to be urban, then the factors that most effect the environment are going to be urban as well. Any discussions on the environment over the next two decades must involve cities and municipal governments. That is already starting to happen: for example, the Mexico City Pact of 2010 brought cities together to develop guidelines on climate change. Also on the bright side, according to a study by the Carbon Disclosure Project (CDP), based on a survey of 140 cities worldwide, the threat of climate change is already causing cities to take steps to reduce their carbon footprint, with some success.[25] Still, rapid construction and rapid flows of people to new urban areas will inevitably create strains, and so continued dialogue on the subject will be needed.

In a similar vein, it is notable that as cities get larger, countries get more vulnerable to natural disasters. High population concentrations mean there is a lot at stake if an earthquake or hurricane hits. It is therefore crucial to make good design and infrastructure decisions as urbanization grows. That is doubly important given that eight out of the 10 most populous cities in the world are at risk of being severely affected by an earthquake, and six of 10 could be affected by a tsuanami or storm.[26] In recent years, we have seen examples such as the impact of Hurricane Katrina in New Orleans in 2005—proof positive of how bad urban planning can cause huge losses of lives and livelihoods. As the stakes get higher, more and more efforts must be made to ensure that there are plans in place to deal quickly with these types of situations.

Who Sets Policy?

Some of the challenges from the next decades of urbanization will relate to power, and specifically to who needs to set policy for those living in cities. As cities get larger, in both the developed and developing world, policies in general will increasingly be set by cities, and there will be a push for more resources (specifically financial resources) to be transferred from other levels of government toward metros—and with good reason. At the Federation of Canadian Municipalities conference in May 2013, Canadian cities made the case that the current division of powers forces cities and towns to choose short-term solutions to their problems rather than having the funds to choose longer-term ones. Translation: we are dealing with large issues and we need larger amounts of money than we currently have in order to do so.[27]

With so many more pulls on their resources and so many demographic changes underway, cities must know their strengths and weaknesses. That can start with a fact-based assessment of the population and demographics, but it needs to be extended to projections as to where things are likely to go in future, both in terms of population changes and economic strengths. Most larger regions already have strategic plans in place, although frequently these are done at a fairly high level and are more concerned with mission statements than practical assessments. As well, few city strategic plans look at alternate economic scenarios or the various possibilities in terms of population growth. Finally, many smaller metros do not have such plans in place, and lack the resources to put them together. That could be a large missed opportunity, both in terms of their own outlook as well as in the management of environmental resources.

Make no mistake: cities do need to be managed, and managed properly. There has to be an acknowledgment that they will need more resources and more capital and more care than ever before. If all those things are in place, then cities will be the leading edge of good decision-making on everything from how to deal with a rising middle class through to how to manage natural disasters. They already have economic might behind them, and that is growing. Next, they need the financial and political power that goes along with it, and which will inevitably be a hallmark of the next decades.

A WORLD OF CITIES

And so we are headed into a different world—one where countries will matter, but cities may matter more in economic terms. We will still be talking about the United States versus China, but increasingly we may also be talking about New York versus Beijing, or Seattle versus Ningbo (a port city in East China). When we talk about policy decisions in future, we will increasingly be talking about those that come from municipal, not federal, governments. Those decisions will have been made with different priorities in mind, and if a lot of things fall into place, they may be better decisions for the kind of global economy that is evolving.

(ENDNOTES)

1 United Nations, Demographic Yearbook 2005, Table 6 (United Nations: Geneva, 2013). Retrieved from http://unstats.un.org/unsd/demographic/sconcerns/densurb/Defintionof%20Urban.pdf.

2 World Health Organization, Global Health Observatory, "Urban Population Growth" (WHO: Geneva, 2013). Retrieved from http://www.who.int/gho/urban_health/situation_trends/urban_population_growth_text/en/.

3 United Nations, Department of Economic and Social Affairs, "World Urbanization Prospects, 2011 revision" (United Nations: Geneva, 2011). Excel spreadsheets available at http://esa.un.org/unup/CD-ROM/Urban-Rural-Population.htm.

4 Often a megacity is the result of several cities clustered together that end up with a single municipal government. For example, Tokyo, which with a population of 37.2 million is the largest city in the world, is actually an agglomeration of the city itself plus 87 surrounding cities and towns.

5 UN, World Urbanization Prospects, 2011 revision, p. 6.

6 Ibid.

7 Richard Dobbs, Sven Smit, Jaana Remes, James Manyika, Charles Roxburgh, Alejandro Restrepo, "Urban World: Mapping the Economic Power of Cities," McKinsey Global Institute, March 2011. Retrieved from http://www.mckinsey.com/insights/urbanization/urban_world.

8 United Nations, World Urbanization Prospects, 2011 Revisions. Retrieved from http://esa.un.org/unup/CD-ROM/Urban-Rural-Population.htm.

9 Steven G. Wilson, David A. Plane, Paul J. Mackun, Thomas R. Fischetti, and Justyna Goworowska, "Patterns of Metropolitan and Micropolitan Population Change 2000 to 2010," U.S. Census Bureau Special Report, September 2012. Retrieved from http://www.census.gov/prod/cen2010/reports/c2010sr-01.pdf.

10 William H. Frey, "The Uneven Aging and 'Younging' of America: State and Metropolitan Trends in the 2010 Census," June 28, 2011. Brookings Instituttion, June 28, 2011. Retrieved from http://www.brookings.edu/~/media/research/files/papers/2011/6/28%20census%20age%20frey/0628_census_aging_frey.

11 Nat Berg, "Exurbs, The Fastest Growing Areas in the U.S.," The Atlantic Cities, July 19, 2012. Retrieved from http://www.theatlanticcities.com/neighborhoods/2012/07/exurbs-fastest-growing-areas-us/2636/.

12 Joe Friesen, "Fast-Rising Milton's Battle of the Bulge," *The Globe and Mail*, December 26, 2012. Retrieved from: http://www.globalworkplaceanalytics.com/wp-content/uploads/2009/02/Table6.jpg.

13 According to data from www.globalanalytics.org, there was a 26 percent increase in the number of U.S. teleworkers between 2007 and 2008, which was the year the recession took hold. Since that time, the average increase has been 3.7 percent. See http://www.globalworkplaceanalytics.com/wp-content/uploads/2009/02/Table6.jpg.

14 Edward L. Glaesar, "Are Cities Dying?" *The Journal of Economic Perspectives* 12:2, Spring 1998. Retrieved from http://www.csus.edu/indiv/c/chalmersk/ECON180FA08/GlaeserDyingCities.pdf.

[15] The McKinsey Global Institute figures pertain to what they call the "City 600," or the top six hundred cities in the world in terms of their contribution to global GDP growth from 2010 to 2025.

[16] Richard Dobbs, et al., "Urban World: Cities and the Rise of the Consuming Class," McKinsey and Company, June 2012. Retrieved from http://www.mckinsey.com/insights/urbanization/urban_world_cities_and_the_rise_of_the_consuming_class.

[17] Bonnie Azab Powell, "What U.S. Citydwellers Really Spend on Food and Drink", www.grist.org, August 19, 2010. Retrieved from http://grist.org/article/food-what-us-citydwellers-really-spend-on-food-and-drink.

[18] T.P., "City Chickens and Country Eggs," *The Economist*, August 4, 2013. Retrieved from http://www.economist.com/blogs/analects/2013/08/urbanisation-and-growth.

[19] David Aldred, "Urbanization: A Major Driver of Infrastructure Spending," Citi Perspectives, Citibank, Volume 6, Q1/Q2 2012.

[20] Ricard Dobbs, Jaana Remes, and Sven Smit, "The World's New Growth Frontier: Midsize Cities in Emerging Markets," *McKinsey Quarterly*, March 2011. Retrieved from http://www.mckinsey.com/insights/economic_studies/the_worlds_new_growth_frontier_midsize_cities_in_emerging_markets.

[21] Kofi Myler, "Detroit's population from 1840 to 2012 shows high points, decades of decline," *Detroit Free Press*, July 23, 2013. Retrieved from http://www.freep.com/interactive/article/20130723/NEWS01/130721003/detroit-city-population.

[22] Michael Bloomberg, "Why Sandy Forced Cities to Take Lead on Climate Change," CNN.com, August 26, 2013. Retrieved from http://www.cnn.com/2013/08/21/world/europe/bloomberg-why-sandy-force-cities.

[23] World Bank, "Urbanization is Helping Power People Out of Extreme Poverty and Assist Delivering on the MDGs, Says Report," April 17, 2013. Retrieved from http://www.worldbank.org/en/news/feature/2013/04/16/urbanization-is-helping-power-people-out-of-extreme-poverty-and-assist-delivering-on-the-MDGs-says-report.

[24] Judy Baker, "Urban Poverty: A Global View," World Bank Group Urban Papers, UP-5, January 2008. Retrieved from http://www-wds.worldbank.org/external/default/WDSContentServer/WDSP/IB/2008/03/24/0003330 37_20080324021722/Rendered/PDF/430280NWP0Glob10Box327344 B01PUBLIC1.pdf.

[25] AECOM/Carbon Disclosure Project, "Wealthier, Healthier Cities: How Climate Change Action is Giving Us Wealthier, Healthier Cities." July

2013. Retrieved from https://www.cdproject.net/CDPResults/CDP-Cities-2013-Global-Report.pdf.

[26] Mark Tran, "Vulnerability to Natural Disasters is 'Soaring', Scientists Warn," *The Guardian*, November 27, 2012. Retrieved from http://www.theguardian.com/global-development/2012/nov/27/vulnerability-natural-disasters-scientists.

[27] Andy Radia, "City Governments Call for a 'Re-Inventon' of the Federal-Municipal Relationship," Canada Politics on www.yahoo.com, May 31, 2013. Retrieved from http://ca.news.yahoo.com/blogs/canada-politics/city-governments-call-invention-federal-municipal-relationship-002058237.html.

PART

2

An Economic
Power Shift

TREND # 4

A Re-Shuffling of the Economic Deck

What may be the most important economorphic trend of them all is already taking place: the economic deck is getting shuffled and new countries are headed to the top—and to the bottom.

The next 20 years are going to see the world moving away from what has become a familiar economic hierarchy to something else altogether. Europe and North America will have less power, Asia, much more, and unfamiliar countries will crop up on the list of the world's 10 largest economies. New attitudes, new sources of economic power, new economic realities—all are in the cards, so to speak, as countries change economic positions.

The good news? The world economy is growing, and actually growing at a nice pace. The bad news, depending on where you live, is that some regions are growing at a much nicer pace than others. Over the next few decades, this seemingly simple fact is going to shake up the world economy. Lots of things go into calculating which are the most "powerful" countries in the world, and things like military might and population size certainly matter. Ultimately, however, true power tends to come down to economics—and when considering measures such as gross domestic product (GDP), wealth, and financial market capitalization, we can see that a definite shift is taking place.

Contrary to some popular opinions, the next 20 years are, in fact, unlikely to bury the U.S. economy; they are also unlikely to see Europe disappear from the map. However, the developed parts of the world *will* see their power erode a little, just as Britain's did when the United States ascended into power following World War II. At the same time, the developing world, with its young population, expanding consumer markets, and new reserves of capital, will move steadily up the rankings, and some countries whose names have never been associated with economic might will look like increasingly interesting places for investors.

THE MOST POWERFUL: NOW AND IN THE FUTURE

Before looking at any kind of top 10 list of powerful countries, it is helpful to put things into a broader context: How does a country ascend or descend in the rankings? One interesting way to look at it is to use the approach of Douglas McWilliams, chief executive of the Centre for Economics and Business Research. McWilliams postulates that there are "sunrise" and "sunset" countries in the world. The sunrise countries are gaining strength, while the sunset countries' strength is waning. What's more, each trajectory follows a predictable cycle.

The sunrise cycle creates economic winners. These countries typically start with well-educated but cheap labor forces that allow the relatively inexpensive and efficient production of manufactured goods. As these countries produce, their profits rise and are funneled into new investments, which, in turn, typically causes productivity to rise. (This last step is a key factor in the equation, and one that is absent from many developed countries these days). As a sunrise country progresses along its economic path, wages do tend to rise. But that increase in costs is often nicely offset by the new productivity gains, which effectively mean that more is being produced for each hour of human capital used. And so it goes: people are earning more money, so they pay more taxes; those taxes pay for better services and infrastructure, and, presumably, for a workforce that continues to become healthier and more educated. McWilliams calls this "economic nirvana."[1]

The sunset cycle is the reverse, the story of a country with high costs and falling competitiveness. As a result, it faces declining exports and declining growth, and, inevitably, declining profits. Investment suffers, and productivity gets hit. Tax revenues are affected, so governments run deficits and are forced to raise taxes to deal with them. Growth stagnates.

While both of these scenarios could be criticized as economic generalizations, they neatly describe the phenomenon behind economic ascension and descension. Our recent economic history has seen many developing countries hitting their stride, and many developed ones hitting roadblocks. The changes started decades ago, but have intensified over the past 20 years. According to research from the Peterson Institute for International Economics,[2] between 1960 and 1990, only 30 percent of developing countries grew at a quicker pace than the United States, meaning it was just a matter of time before their GDP share increased and they became the dominant economic power in the world. From 1990 onward, however, 70 percent did so. In fact, as of 2013, emerging markets account for more than half of world GDP.[3]

The starting point behind which countries have been classified as "sunrise" and which as "sunset" since 1990—cheap and efficient labor—is influenced by a many factors, most notably demographics. Policies and social tastes play an interconnected role as well. The countries who were primed to rise a couple of decades ago were China and India; the fact that they have indeed done so has had a lot to do with trade. The big sources of efficient and relatively cheap labor were in China and India; the big pools of consumers were in North America and Europe. Technology made communication and coordination of trade easy, and energy prices cooperated by remaining at a tolerable level. It all made for a cozy east–west trade pattern. As their manufacturing sectors expanded, China and India prospered, and as they did, the prosperity spread, albeit very slowly, to more and more people.

China and India are two of what are called the BRIC countries (the others are Brazil and Russia), a moniker coined by Goldman Sachs economist Jim O'Neill in 2001.[4] At the time, those countries looked to be the growth superstars of the coming decades, a prediction that has indeed come to pass. All four economies now rank squarely on any list of the top 10 economic winners in the world. Much of their success is linked to a rise in the value of the commodities they produced, a value that was, in turn, influenced by the rising prosperity of the developing countries.

At the same time that the developing countries were ascending in economic influence, other economic stories were playing out as well. When ranking the biggest economies in the world over the past 50 years or so, the United States has inevitably topped every list. In 1970, the world's second-largest country was the Soviet Union. By 1980—following the breakup of the Soviet Union into Russia and more than a dozen smaller countries—Japan was the second largest. It held this position until (arguably) 2010, when it was overtaken by China. If you look at current World Bank rankings, the top 10 are as follows: the U.S., China, Japan, Germany, France, Brazil, the United Kingdom, Russia, India, and Italy. No need to memorize it; it will switch up again—many times, no doubt—over the next couple of decades.[5]

So how do businesses, investors, and other curious human beings figure out which economies will be the biggest in 10 years or so? Whichever source you use, you have to take any predictions—actually, *projections* is a better word—with a degree of caution. All projections will have been generated by some kind of economic model that makes assumptions about growth. Depending on what those assumptions are, the rankings could change sharply. For example, if you assume that China will grow at 12 percent a year (as it did for some time) and that the U.S. will grow by 2 percent (a fairly downbeat but not impossible pace), then it would not take long before China was the largest economy in the world. But if you assume that China will grow at only 7 percent for awhile (certainly a possibility) and that the U.S. will grow by a slightly improved 3 percent, the shift in rankings would clearly take longer.

> If you look at current World Bank rankings, the top 10 are as follows: the U.S., China, Japan, Germany, France, Brazil, the United Kingdom, Russia, India, and Italy. No need to memorize it; it will switch up again—many times, no doubt—over the next couple of decades.

Not surprisingly, then, different forecasters are bound to come up with different scenarios. From investment banks (Citi, Goldman Sachs) and consulting groups (PricewaterhouseCoopers, McKinsey) to government organizations (United States Security Council) and international organizations (the International Monetary Fund, the Organisation for Economic Co-operation and Development), projections as to the most powerful countries for the next 10, 20, 30, and even 50 years are regularly made. It's worth remembering that these are projections—no more, no less—and are certainly not cast in stone. Things can, and do, change. In 2006 the Economist Intelligence Unit projected that the long-term GDP growth potential of the United States would be close to 3 percent a year.[6] That still might be the case, but in 2008 the United States was rocked by a major recession and has had a hard time finding its footing since. That scenario was not assumed in the 2006 projections.

With all that said, let's use the estimates from Pricewaterhouse-Coopers (PWC)—which were published in December 2012 and which use fairly conventional assumptions about demographic and economic growth—and flash forward to 2030.[7] By that time, Asia will, in terms of gross domestic product, have grown to a size that is larger than North America and Europe combined, and China will easily have the largest economy in the world.[8] Meanwhile, other countries will be on the decline. Japan, which by 2030 will be decades into fighting the demographic burden of an aging population, will be much smaller in relative size, to the point where China's GDP will be about 140 percent larger than Japan's.

If all of this unfolds the way PWC expects it to, China will be the economy on top, followed by the United States and then India, Japan, Russia, and Brazil. Germany will have dropped down two places from its 2011 position, going from number five on the list to number seven, while France will have dropped from eighth to 10th. In contrast, Indonesia is expected to have ascended to 11th place, up five spots from its 2011 ranking, and Mexico will have climbed from position 11 to position eight. Canada will be in 16th place in 2030, down a couple of spots from 2011.[9]

How about if we go further ahead, to 2050? That's a long way from now—and a lot of things in terms of economic cycles and shocks could take place between now and then. Then again, we do know a fair bit about demographics and the way that it is powering various economies, as well as the likely impact of those changes. If you look at PWC's expectations, the top three countries—China, the U.S., and India—are likely to stay just where they are. Brazil, however, is expected to be number four in the world, followed by Japan (who was number two as recently as 2012). Mexico will have moved up to number seven, and the U.K. down to number 11. A couple of new names will be on the list by then too: Nigeria (number 13) and Vietnam (number 19).[10]

Or not. No one who compiles these lists would suggest that they know for sure exactly how things will stack up five decades from now. What is clear, however, is that the list of top economies is a game with moving pieces, and one in which complacency does not rule.

PROSPECTS FOR INDIVIDUAL COUNTRIES

Although we've clearly established that long-term projections require a certain amount of guesswork, that guesswork can be educated. Based on the best information we have available, here's a closer look at where some key players in the world economy may end up over the next few decades.

United States

One key takeaway from all projections is that the United States is headed to a point where it will no longer be the biggest economy in the world. Whether China takes the lead in 2018, 2020, or 2022 doesn't really matter. What matters is that the United States, in the aftermath of the Great Recession, has slipped into a lower growth trajectory, and that fact will have serious social and economic repercussions.

On the plus side, the demographics of the U.S. economy are actually relatively positive compared to many developed countries. As well, the U.S. has a relatively high income base, and is an acknowledged leader in technology development and adaptation. Those are all key advantages, but unfortunately they are being set against a host of challenges. In the aftermath of the recession, the U.S. has a heap of public and private debts, and a growing problem with income inequality. Education is not what it could be, and the health care system needs far more attention than the recent "Obamacare" initiatives can possibly provide. The housing market has crashed, taking the assets of many with it, and the unemployment rate five years after the recession's end is still not at what many would consider an acceptable level. The aggressive efforts by monetary and fiscal authorities to kick-start things have arguably made a difference, but they will also need to be paid for down the road.

So what does this mean for economic growth? There are a lot of variables, but it is difficult to create a scenario in which the U.S. vaults back into the kind of growth it's enjoyed for most of the past several decades. In a piece for the Carnegie Endowment for International Peace, economist Uri Dadush sketches out two separate scenarios for the U.S. In the first, "good" scenario, none of the worst-cases happen, and the U.S. grows at about 2.7 percent a year through 2030. This is actually better than the 2.5 percent it averaged between 1990 and 2010, although that timespan included several periods of recession. In the "bad" scenario, a lot of things go wrong (for example, the Eurozone

> In the aftermath of the recession, the U.S. has a heap of public and private debts, and a growing problem with income inequality. Education is not what it could be, and the health care system needs far more attention than the recent "Obamacare" initiatives can possibly provide. The housing market has crashed, taking the assets of many with it, and the unemployment rate five years after the recession's end is still not at what many would consider an acceptable level.

is assumed to break up). The U.S. heads to a 1.5 percent rate of growth through 2030 and becomes firmly entrenched as a country on the downslide.[11]

Will either of these cases—or a different one altogether—take place? Whatever happens, the U.S. is extremely unlike to grow at a 3 or 4 percent pace for any length of time, which means the gap between its size and economic might and that of the developing countries (which, over time, will become developed) seems sure to grow.

The European Union

Europe is the site of some of the world's "oldest" economies (in 2011, the median age in Germany was 44, compared to 37 in the United States) and, at present, the center of some of the world's most dire economic issues. Given all of that, can anyone be bullish on the long-term prospects for the European Union (EU)?[12]

Let's set aside the fiscal crises that have snared individual countries (Greece, most notably, but also Italy, Spain, and Ireland, to name a few others) and look at the larger picture. It was only a few decades ago—in 1982—that the total economic output of the EU15 countries (the EU members pre-2004) was actually higher, by 15 percent, than that of the United States. If nothing changes, however, consulting firm Bruegel estimates that output in the same countries will be 17 percent lower than it is in the U.S. by 2017.[13] Even assuming no further crises, something will have to change to keep Europe at even close to a modest level of growth.

The list of things that do need to change is long, and it includes fiscal reforms (in virtually every country) and banking reforms. Most importantly, however, there is a need to increase the productivity in Europe, which by most measures has been disappointing over the past several years. What cannot be changed, however, is the rapidly aging population and the pressure that it is going to put on the cost of social services. Whether that issue is solved (by either productivity or immigration) will be one key determinant of Europe's future.

Canada

After managing to escape the Great Recession relatively unscathed, Canada has become something of an economic poster child over the past few years. Canadian banks are relatively cautious compared to their U.S. counterparts, and the country did not suffer a housing market collapse (although doomsayers say it could still happen). As well, Canada went into the recession with a fair degree of fiscal flexibility, meaning that government stimulus was and continues to be a remedy for economic weakness.

Over the short term, the economy faces several potential problems. The low interest rates the country has enjoyed for several years will at some point have to be brought back to "normal," which will be a slap in the face to Canadians who have taken advantage of them and piled on the debt. As well, despite steadily building trade relations with European and Asian nations, Canada's largest trade partner is still resolutely the United States, and the fate of the country is in many ways tied to that of the United States, which means that things are not assured.

Over the long term, Canada will face the problem of retiring baby boomers and a resulting slowing in labor force growth, and, hence, tax revenues and overall growth. Like virtually all developed nations, it will also have to figure out a way to pay for the demographic transition.

On the plus side, Canada is well positioned to benefit from the sustained high commodity prices that will go along with growth in the developing world.

China

When we talk about countries that are moving up that Top 10 list of economic powers, the most obvious is China, which will certainly have the largest economy in the world within a few years. Growth cannot, however, continue at the blistering pace that has come to be taken as the norm over the past few years. Over most of the next 20 years, China will be dealing with increasingly unfavorable demographics. What powered the Chinese economy through the '90s and '00s was a sharp rise in working-age population that translated into lots of people who could come to the cities and work in the factories. That supply mechanism is headed lower: the 15 to 24 age group is now waning, or will be within a very few years. In addition, the overall working-age population will start to decline by about 2015, and by 2030 will be lower than it was in 2010.[14] China is arguably already a developed country, but that fact will be undeniable in coming years when, just like other developed countries, it faces massive bills in terms of paying for its older population.

Over the next two decades, China's economy will shift from being all about exports to also being about domestic consumption, fueled by a growing middle class. The expansion will not be without its problems. In particular, in order to avert social unrest China will have to meet the needs of those who feel that the spoils of the country's economic progress are not being adequately shared. Another concern is that in the absence of a committed public and private sector effort to turn things around, the environmental problems that have plagued China to date will only worsen. As well, imbalances in the Chinese economy—including property market and financial market shocks—could skew the growth profile in the years ahead, with repercussions felt outside the country as well.

India

In the wake of the 2008 economic crisis, the Indian economy has had a hard time to returning to its potential growth rate, and has been plagued by a series of economic problems, including high inflation and high fiscal and current account deficits. Still, the country has positive demographics and is slowly opening up to foreign investment. Many analysts (including Goldman Sachs, which first suggested that India be included in the BRICS)[15] still believe the country can manage 10-percent-plus growth over the next two decades, although few believe it can be done without serious, further reforms.

The reforms needed for India to reach its full potential range from changing the way the central bank sets interest rates (perhaps keeping a closer eye on inflation through formal targets) through to ensuring more children attend school (and attend it from an earlier age).

Brazil

With its strong commodity base and solid demographics, Brazil was a growth success story for many years. The economy started to flag around 2010–11 and has been growing at a sub-par pace ever since, but the potential is still there for a very strong decade or two. Unfortunately, that growth will also feature some bumps along the way.

One of the mixed blessings that have beset Brazil is the creation of a still-new but very large middle class. Many Brazilians are now in a place where they can cover their bills and have a bit left over— a change from the situation Brazilians faced in previous decades. As the pressure to eke out a living has eroded, however, there has been some social unrest. Many Brazilians are looking around and wondering why, if the country is getting richer, the social services on offer are only getting poorer. By bidding for—and winning—the 2014 World Cup (and the 2016 Olympics), Brazilian authorities no doubt expected to create a nation of deliriously happy people. Instead, they got a nation in full-out protest, unhappy that a stadium was being built while health care stagnated.

Over the medium term, Brazil needs to deal with a series of growing pains as its middle class expands, making sure that it solidifies rather than loses its footing. Although it is unlikely to match its growth trajectory of recent years, the country is expected to expand in economic size and global importance through the next several decades.

Russia

Russia's economy is closely tied to the energy sector, which has been to the country's benefit in a big way over the past decade. Along with the economic reforms of the 1990s and 2000s, high oil prices in the early years of this century boosted income, albeit income that was not particularly well distributed. Like most of the world, the country was hard hit by the recession of 2008–09, but arguably bounced back as well as the rest of the developed world.

The outlook for the next two decades will mainly depend on two factors: oil prices and demographics. In the case of the first, Russia faces the same risks as any commodity-driven economy, in the sense that booms and busts may be in its future. As well, reforms are needed with respect to the management of the energy sector.

In the case of demographics, Russia faces a much more dire future, with population aging (similar to what exists in Europe, except with higher mortality rates thrown in) as a major concern. Altogether, the issues facing the economy make it difficult to picture Russia continuing to be a BRICS superstar to the same degree that it has been in the recent past.

The Next 11

In 2007, Goldman Sachs came up with the designation of the "Next 11" to describe those countries that they saw as the potential growth leaders of the 21st century.[16] They can be thought of as the "replacement" BRICS—the countries that are going to zoom ahead when others move further along the sunrise cycle toward sunset. The list is an interesting smorgasbord— including some countries with fairly developed economies (Iran, Mexico, the Philippines,

Turkey, and Indonesia), some that are definitely developing (Egypt, Nigeria, Pakistan, and Vietnam) and at least one (Bangladesh) that ranks among the world's least developed.

The economies of each of these countries are quite different from each other but all have notable strengths—and notable challenges. Bangladesh, for example, is close to India and has the kind of large, relatively young population that has made other sunrise economies successful. The Philippines has similar advantages, and an extra one in that much of its population speaks English. South Korea is actually a fairly developed economy already, with the potential to get much more economically powerful still.

One interesting inclusion on the Next 11 list is Nigeria, a country of 162.5 million people, and one that the United Nations predicts will be more populous than the United States by 2050.[17] Nigeria is blessed with reserves of oil and a demographic window that is still wide open, which is to say it has a high proportion of working-age population. The problem with citing Nigeria as a Next 11 winner, however, is that—like so many countries on the list—there are still wildcards in its future. The country is already experiencing a bit of a brain drain as educated young Nigerians seek their fortunes elsewhere. As well, it has its share of internal violence—enough so that foreign companies will continue to be somewhat wary about investing. So the potential is there, but as with so many Next 11 countries, the risks are high.

THE ECONOMORPHIC IMPLICATIONS

So the deck is being shuffled, but in an economic sense does it matter where the growth originates, or does it simply matter that there is growth? The answer is that it sort of matters, at least in terms of a few major areas.

The Implications for World Growth

All things being equal, the new economic structure will send the world into a somewhat slower growth trajectory than has been the case over the past couple of decades.

Think about it: since roughly 2000, the biggest growth players in the world have been the BRICS countries, the superstars with economies that were rapidly industrializing. Their speed of development made up nicely for the fact that the United States and Europe were expanding at a somewhat slower rate. The BRICS will still grow over the next few decades, but at a somewhat more muted pace. China, for example, is rapidly moving to a point where its demographic window is closed. Its economy will still grow, but not likely at a double-digit pace. Similar fates will hit countries like Brazil and India, albeit somewhat later.

For sure, there will be new growth superstars—maybe Indonesia or Nigeria or Vietnam—but these countries are relatively small compared to the BRICS. And there will also be steady growth from the "old" industrial powers, but it will likely be a notch below the levels we have gotten used to. End result? Well, if we are not talking about a world recession (and we really very likely are not), we are certainly talking about a world where growth will be at a somewhat slower pace. That will take some of the sting off of hikes to commodity prices (which will still likely be on the rise). It will also, however, create a new series of economic challenges for developed and developing countries alike.

Opportunities for Business and Investors

So how does one decide where the best business and investment opportunities will be in this new world order? The "old" economies are not necessarily without opportunities, and the risks are certainly well-known. But choosing some of the better-known players in the developing world doesn't guarantee much either. As growth leaders like China continue to expand, they will change from scrappy upstarts to the blue-chip countries of the world—and the blue chips are generally not where you get your biggest paybacks. That's why some analysts suggest that if what you are looking for is quick growth, you need to look further afield, at least for investment purposes.

The first place to look is probably at countries that are steadily building their middle classes. Whether the objective is to find financial markets with good returns or to find a source for direct investment, those places where people are acquiring more disposable income are going to offer interesting opportunities. There is a massive change going on in many economies of the world, taking them from being producers to being consumers (China is a prime example). That means that they will be looking for things to consume—which will benefit someone.

The most obvious opportunities are for retailers and companies with global brands, so investors would be well served to look at those—but make it a good look. North American companies will be competing against local brands that have already developed a foothold, meaning that many larger players may be forced to find local partners.

Companies that deal in services have as many opportunities as those that deal in goods. As people acquire more income they certainly acquire more things, but they also make the jump to spending more on leisure pursuits. In a way, leisure pursuits are the ultimate luxury—money spent on experiences rather than goods. Golf in China is the prime example. Less than three decades ago, there was not a single golf course in the country. By 2004, there were about 170, a figure that has grown to 600 in 2013, with some predicting an eventual increase to 1,000 by 2020. The courses host about 400,000 golfers, a figure that could double over the same period, in tandem with growth in the middle class.[18] As more people play, more people will watch golf and more people will buy golf merchandise. Now multiply that phenomenon across all the countries that could embrace golf, and add in all the other leisure activities they could also try out (figure skating is increasingly popular in Asia). Looking for trends and opportunities like this could become a formula for growth for CEOs who are attuned to the changing global environment.

The One Who Has the Gold

There's no doubt that calculating the GDPs of various countries tells you something, but if you really want to get a sense of who has power, the best place to look might be the financial markets. Right now, a cursory glance shows that the United States and the developed world hold the assets and hence set the tone for trading and economic policy. Not long from now, however, that will not be the case.

According to an analysis from the McKinsey Global Institute, as of 2010 investors in developed economies held nearly 80 percent of the world's financial assets (about $157 trillion at the time), with developing countries holding the remaining 20 percent. By their calculations, the financial assets of investors in emerging economies was poised to hit 36 percent by 2020—and presumably to grow further as those parts of the world continue to gain economic strength. That mass of assets also means a (potential) mass of power than can be exercised however the holders of the capital see fit.[19]

Not only do emerging markets investors increasingly hold assets, the countries they reside in are also increasingly the recipients of investment, presumably investment that could have been placed in more traditional venues. In a report on foreign direct investment (FDI) released in July 2013, the United Nations found that for the first time ever the share of FDI going to developing countries was higher than that going to developed ones.[20]

As the power shifts among countries, financial assets will also shift, and not always in an orderly way. Already we are seeing a massive flight of capital from the developed world toward Asia as investors seek what they assume will be high returns from a part of the world that is growing more quickly than their home economies. In April 2013, the International Monetary Fund (IMF) announced that it was "carefully" monitoring what they saw as massive capital inflows into Asia, and also urged the region's policymakers to guard against the "risks of overheating."[21] Put another way, the IMF, like many others, is observing that the pace at which money is entering Asia is sending up the prices of both financial and non-financial assets (such as property) at what might be considered an unhealthy pace. And, based on historical lessons, we know that too much money chasing too few assets often ends in burst bubbles. Financial bubbles may crop up in the fastest-growing parts of the world over the next decade or two as investors seek to rejig their portfolios to take advantage of the growth superstars.

Another potential issue is the possibility of an "equity gap" as expanding wealth in Asia leads to that part of the world controlling an increasing share of global assets. In most developed countries, investors typically put 30 to 40 percent of their assets into the equity markets. In the emerging world, however, that ratio is typically more like 15 percent. Based on their reading of the trends, McKinsey sees a drop in the share of publicly traded equities from 28 percent now to 22 percent by 2020. In practice, this means that there would be relatively less capital available to companies. Less capital, in turn, presumably means less growth for the economies affected. As a consequence, there could be a shift from equity to debt finance.[22]

A SHINY NEW WORLD

Good, bad, indifferent—or just different? How does one characterize the economy that will unfold over the next couple of decades? The answer depends on who you are, but it also depends on how comfortable you are at dealing with change.

In many ways, the 21st century has, thus far, been a North American century; it has also been an investor's century, at least in the equity markets. There was always risk involved in investing, but there were fairly discernible rewards for those who were willing to look for them. That is not exactly changing, but finding the rewards in the coming decades will mean looking further afield. And that will also mean assuming more risk than perhaps the average investor has found palatable up until now.

An adjustment in attitudes will also have to take place as North America and Europe are overtaken by Asia as the growth leader of the world. From innovation technology to capital, many things will emanate from a part of the world, and from countries, which up until now have been unfamiliar. The end result, however, will be a world that keeps growing—and that will be a winning hand for all countries.

(ENDNOTES)

[1] Douglas McWilliams, "Winning and Losing Nations." Transcript of a lecture given March 12, 2012, Museum of London, London, UK. Retrieved from http://www.gresham.ac.uk/lectures-and-events/the-winning-and-losing-nations.

[2] Arvind Subramanian and Martin Kessler, "The Hyperglobalization of Trade and Its Future." Peterson Institute Working Paper 13-6, July 2013, p. 1.

[3] As measured by purchasing power. See "When Giants Slow Down," *The Economist*, July 27, 2013.

[4] See Jim O'Neill, "Building Better Global Economic BRICs." Goldman Sachs Working Paper No. 66, November 30, 2001.

[5] The World Bank, "GDP Ranking" (Washington, D.C.: The World Bank Group, 2013). Retrieved from http://data.worldbank.org/data-catalog/GDP-ranking-table.

[6] Economist Intelligence Unit, "Foresight 20/20: Economic, Industry and Corporate Trends," *The Economist*, 2006. Retrieved from http://bc.fdo.msu.ru/Nik_s/WorkFiles/DOC_files/World_shares_foresight_2020.pdf.

[7] PricewaterhouseCoopers, "The World in 2050: The BRICS and Beyond: Prospects, Challenges and Opportunities," January 2013. Retrieved from http://www.pwc.com/en_GX/gx/world-2050/assets/pwc-world-in-2050-report-january-2013.pdf.

[8] Matthew Burrows, "Global Trends 2030: Alternative Worlds," U.S. National Security Council, December 2012, location 779 on electronic version.

[9] PricewaterhouseCoopers.

[10] Ibid.

[11] Uri Dadush, "The Long-Term Outlook for the United States and Its International Implications," Carnegie Endowment for International Peace, December 2011. Retrieved from http://carnegieendowment.org/2011/12/08/long-term-economic-outlook-for-united-states-and-its-international-implications/84dj.

[12] The European Union refers to those 28 member countries that share a single currency and monetary policy and are subject to various political agreements.

[13] Zsolt Darvas, Jean Pisani-Ferry, Guntram B. Wolff, "Europe's Growth Problem and What to Do With It," Bruegel Policy Brief, April 12, 2013. Retrieved from http://www.bruegel.org/publications/publication-detail/publication/776-europes-growth-problem-and-what-to-do-about-it/.

[14] United Nations, "World Population Prospects: The 2012 Revision," June 13, 2013 press release (New York: United Nations Department of Economic and Social Affairs, 2013). Retrieved from http://esa.un.org/wpp/Documentation/pdf/WPP2012_Press_Release.pdf.

[15] In 2010, South Africa was formally invited to join the association of BRIC nations, at which point the name was changed to "BRICS." It now comprises Brazil, Russia, India, China. and South Africa.

[16] Jim O'Neill, Dominic Wilson, Roopa Purushothaman, and Anna Stupnytska, "How Solid are the BRICS?" Goldman Sachs, Global Economics Paper No. 34, December 2005.

[17] United Nations, World Population Prospects, 2012 Revision.

[18] Brook Larmer, "Golf in China Is Younger than Tiger Woods, But Growing Up Fast," *New York Times Magazine*, June 11, 2013. Retrieved from http://www.nytimes.com/2013/07/14/magazine/golf-in-china-is-younger-than-tiger-woods-but-growing-up-fast.html?pagewanted=all.

[19] Charles Roxburgh, Susan Lund, Richard Dibbs, James Manyika, and Haihao Wu, "The Emerging Equity Gap: Growth and Stability in the New

Investor Landscape," McKinsey Global Institute, December 2011, p. 1. Retrieved from http://www.mckinsey.com/insights/global_capital_markets/emerging_equity_gap.

[20] United Nations Conference on Trade and Development, "World Investment Report 2013" (New York and Geneva: United Nations, 2013), p. ix. Retrieved from http://unctad.org/en/PublicationsLibrary/wir2013_en.pdf.

[21] Staff, "Asian Officials Must Respond Early to Overheating Risk IMF Says," Bloomberg News, April 28, 2013. Retrieved from http://www.bloomberg.com/news/2013-04-29/asian-officials-must-respond-early-to-overheating-risk-imf-says.html.

[22] Roxburgh, et al., p. 1.

TREND # 5

An Expanding Global Middle Class

The next 10 years will see a narrowing of global inequities as a large part of the world's population becomes "middle class." In an economic sense, this will be a positive change, as the new spenders from places like Asia will offset economic weakness in Europe and elsewhere.

The geographic distribution of the new middle class is going to cause a sea change in terms of production and consumption. Currently, most companies produce with the large North American market in mind; in the years to come, however, producers will more likely look to newly industrialized parts of the world. This shift will create huge opportunities for business—although it will be quite a fight to see who gets a piece of the pie.

In North America, we have become accustomed to hearing about the shrinking middle class. It may come as a surprise, then, to learn that the rest of the world is having a contradictory experience. More people than ever before are heading to income territory that lets them buy more than what they need for basic human survival. That's a very big deal for the global economy.

The rise of this middle class will mean economic goodies the world over. For one thing, the fact that wealth is rising anywhere will be a nice offset to the fact that Europe and North America are set to be stuck on slow speed for the next decade. Companies frustrated at the stagnant markets in their traditional strongholds will be vying for a share of the pocketbooks of the newly rich—although they are going to have to do a lot more than just show up to get it. Firms from within the newly middle-class countries will be springing up, and everyone is going to want a piece of the expanding pie.

MEASURING THE MIDDLE CLASS

The idea of a "middle class" seems to touch a nerve: it is the "just right" space where many people are apparently happy to be. After all, no one wants to be poor, which suggests not having enough. Lots of people are okay with the idea of being rich, but many will tell you that they do not need to be. Middle class is good enough, suggesting the means to purchase the essentials plus some of the extras that make life worth living.

Politicians seemingly love the middle class, and are constantly speaking to them when promoting their views: according to search engine Google's count, the middle class has been called "the backbone of the country" at least 2.3 million times.[1] There is a general view that a middle class supports the political process and progressive economic policies, and that is probably true. A group not struggling for a bare-bones existence has some freedom to act in the political arena.

In an economic sense, however, the middle class has a slightly different definition, which at least in the beginning was not entirely tied to income. The term first surfaced in 1913, when, in a report for the U.K. Register General, statistician T.H.C. Stevenson identified the middle class as that falling between the "upper class" (roughly speaking, those "to the manor born" who possessed significant capital without having to work for it) and the "working class" (those who worked in trades or unskilled professions).[2] Later on, other yardsticks were used to measure membership in the middle class. If, for example, you had enough money to employ a servant, you were there. More recently, it has been suggested that you are "in" if you can afford a car.[3]

Still, the question of exactly what makes someone middle class can be hotly debated both in North America and around the world. When President Obama visited Mexico in May 2013, he made a point of saying that "because of the sacrifices of generations, a majority of Mexicans can now call themselves middle class." His words created a furor: at the time of his remarks, about 46 percent of the Mexican population was living in poverty.[4]

So what is the best way to define and quantify the middle class? Perhaps the place to start is with this issue of poverty.

The first gateway to the middle class is to escape extreme poverty, and that is happening globally. Data from the International Labour Organization (ILO) show that between 2001 and 2013, 400 million workers in developing countries have joined the middle class, with incomes sufficient to consume between $4 and $13 a day per person—a figure that doubled over the time period in question. A further 186 million now live on more than $13 a day. More importantly, the ILO estimates that there will be an additional 390 million middle-class workers in the developing world by 2017.[5] Although a chunk of the world's population is still living in what can be called extreme poverty (defined as living on less than $1.25 a day), and about 472 million are defined as moderately poor (living on $1.25 to $2 a day), these percentages are on the decline.

Once someone is out of poverty, the next step to the middle class is to keep climbing the income ladder so that you have a bit of discretionary income. A few years ago, *The Economist* defined "middle class" as the point at which people have roughly a third of their income left for discretionary spending after paying for basic food and shelter.[6] And that's maybe a good way to think of it: a person becomes middle class when he or she has the economic flexibility to make choices. It is these choices, after all, that shape economies and lives. Having money on hand that was not there before might buy education, or better health care, or a car, or something else. The bottom line is that this "new" money means new opportunities, for consumers and for the companies that serve them.

That's why the best way to define the middle class is probably in terms of purchasing power rather than income. Brookings Institution scholar Homi Kharas did just that in a 2010 paper for the Organisation for Economoic Co-operation and Development (OECD), defining the middle class as those households with daily expenditures between $10 and $100 per person in purchasing power parity terms.[7] Choosing these boundaries means excluding those who make less than the poverty level in Portugal and Italy (the two advanced European countries with the strictest definition of poverty), and those who make more than twice the advanced median income in Luxembourg, the richest advanced country. The idea is to exclude those who are considered either "rich" or "poor" in advanced countries. Following this through and looking at data for 145 countries, Kharas estimated that there were 1.8 billion people who could have be considered middle class in 2009, and that between 2009 and 2030 the size of the global middle class would more than double to about 4.9 billion.[8]

That's a huge adjustment: in less than two decades, apparently, there will be another 2 billion–plus people in the world with discretionary spending power. Or, to look at it a different way: in 2009, the world had a population of about 6.7 billion, about 27 percent of whom could be called middle class. By 2030, the world population will have risen to about 8.4 billion.[9] Assuming that Kharas's estimate of 4.9 billion middle class is correct, that means 58 percent of the world's population will be middle class—more than double the percentage in 2009. It will be a stunning change, and one that will mean stunning changes for the world economy.

> By 2030, 58 percent of the world's population will be middle class—more than double the percentage in 2009.

RESHAPING THE GLOBAL ECONOMY

You can say that the new middle class will change the world, but it might be more accurate to say that the geographic composition of the new middle class will change the economic power structure of the world. The people with the buying power will not be where they used to be, and that will have big consequences.

Let's start by looking at where the middle class was in 2009, and where it is likely to be in 2030. As of 2009, 36 percent of the world's middle class was in Europe, and a further 18 percent was in North America. Together, the two accounted for 52 percent of the total. Among the rest of the world, the Asia-Pacific region had a 28 percent share. Now let's flash forward. If projections are correct (and the ones here are based on Homi Kharas's OECD report, but all sources basically show the same pattern), then by 2030 only 21 percent of the world's middle class will be in Europe and North America. In contrast, 66 percent will be in the Asia-Pacific region. Share-wise, there will not be much difference to Sub-Saharan Africa, the Middle East and North Africa, or Central and South America, but all will see increases in their numbers (in Africa's case, a tripling in the absolute number is expected).[10]

There are several forecasts out there, but all show a similar pattern of growth by geographic region, and, in particular, of growth in Asia. Ernst & Young, for example, figures that by 2030 as many as 500 million Chinese will be part of the middle class. Taking into account the already existing middle class in that country, this means that a total of 1 billion people—or 70 percent of China's population—will be middle class. India, which is further behind in the growth trajectory than China, has not yet created an "almost middle class" that can become officially middle class over the next decade. The increase in the Indian middle class is expected to be even more dramatic. Ernst & Young expects the current 50 million people classified as middle class (as of 2010) to reach 200 million by 2020 and 475 million by 2030, which would mean that India would actually add more people to the global middle class than China over the same time period.[11]

In economic terms, the rise of a middle class can certainly allow a country to rejig its economic composition. Given the consumer spending power that goes along with middle-class growth, the point at which countries go from having mostly poor to mostly middle-class consumers is a fairly magical one in terms of economic growth: the rule of thumb is that every 10 percentage-point increase in a nation's middle class creates a 0.5 percentage-point rise in its growth rate.[12] At that point in the cycle, labor is still relatively cheap, making it a good time to build up trade. It also tends to be a time when people leave rural areas for the riches that city life is said to offer, and find themselves working in factories and boosting a country's output. China offers a textbook example of this theory in action. Over the past two decades, a flood of young people moved from the country to the city, filling the factories and turning the country into an economic powerhouse.

Countries in the midst of developing a middle class are effectively looking at a makeover of their economy. Small countries without a strong middle class, particularly those with a commodity base, are often very dependent on exports—and, hence, the fortunes of other countries—to drive economic activity. For countries with a middle class, growth is more driven by internal consumer spending. A good example of this can be seen by looking at the experiences of Brazil and Korea. In the 1960s, both countries had similar rates of a growth and the beginnings of a middle class. In Brazil, however, income inequality increased in the following years, and by the 1980s, the middle class represented only 20 percent of the population, as compared to 53 percent in Korea.[13] As a result, Brazil was much more export-dependent than Korea. (Since that time, Brazil has indeed developed a middle class, with some putting its size as high as 52 percent of the population). Looking at this in broader terms suggests that we are headed toward a world where fewer economies will be entirely trade-dependent, a fact that might cushion them from economic collapse when one of their trade partners hits a rough spot.

A BONANZA FOR BUSINESS—MAYBE

So what happens when people get money? They spend it, of course, and the spending choices they make have serious consequences. And let's be clear: we are talking about a lot of money—new money —to spend. According to an analysis by the McKinsey Global Institute, the new market of middle-class consumers will include almost 2 billion people, spending about $6.9 trillion annually, and perhaps going as high as $20 trillion in a decade.[14] Let's put that into perspective: U.S. consumer spending is now about $10 trillion a year[15], so we are talking about a substantial adjustment.

Again, it is worth noting where the growth is going to be. According to the OECD, the growth in middle-class consumer spending in North America will rise from $5.5 trillion in 2009 to $5.6 trillion in 2030—an increase of 1.8 percent. Europe is going to see a 37 percent increase. In contrast, the increase in middle-class spending in the Asia-Pacific region—which includes China, India, and Indonesia, will increase by 571 percent over the same time period. From accounting for over 25 percent of world consumer spending in 2009, North American spending will fall to just over 10 percent by 2030, while Asian-Pacific spending will go from 23 percent to 59 percent over the same time period.[16]

Still, whichever definition of "middle class" you choose to use, it is worth noting that a lot of the new middle class will still be considered "poor" by developed-country standards. The ILO data shows that the "working middle class" (defined as those living on at least $4 a day) now comprises more than 40 percent of the developing world's workforce.[17] That level is not likely to be enough to catch the eye of businesses looking for worthwhile markets to enter. A study by Ernst & Young suggests that for businesses, the more useful sweet spot is when a chunk of a country's population earns the equivalent of over $10 day.[18]

For businesses, pursuing the middle class may mean thinking in terms of class, rather than about any particular country. Apple, for example, sells mostly high-end products (the price point for an iPhone is high, relative to other competing products, even in North America). When thinking about the middle class in other countries, however, Apple—and other companies like it—will need to adjust to a "lower" middle class than is present elsewhere. This could mean the development of different products, ones that appeal to a more entry-level consumer.

A study on the buying habits of newly affluent Brazilian consumers suggests that it may not be that simple for established North American brands to simply pick up the new middle class as customers. Professors Alberto Salvo and Alon Eizenberg looked at the buying habits of consumers in Brazil, a country that has seen a surge in its middle class over the past 20 years. Splitting up their test group into the "poor," the "established affluent," and the "newly affluent," and examining brand choices for soda, they found that less-affluent consumers tended to buy generic brands. Interestingly, when that group became more affluent, they tended to stick with their budget-conscious choices rather than automatically gravitating to the Coca-Colas of the world. These findings suggest that companies may have more difficulty than they expect when it comes to attracting the new consumers. The situation becomes even more challenging when we consider the fact that many countries have significant barriers to entry for foreign firms. In some industries, this may make it almost impossible for new players to enter and compete in local markets.[19]

Then again, grabbing up market share early may be a key if you want to keep your customers over the long term. If you look at the market leaders in the U.S. in 1925—a time when a new middle class was emerging—you see names like Kraft Foods (who led in the scale of biscuits), Del Monte (canned foods), and Wrigley (chewing gum). Look at the market leaders for these same categories at the end of the 20th century and you will find the same names at the top of the leader board.[20] Lesson? If history repeats itself, the early leaders in attracting the new middle class could well be the leaders for a long time.

It's also worth noting that the newly middle class typically want more than just "things": they also want leisure, and ways to spend their leisure time. We saw a similar phenomenon in North America during the late 1800s (a period sometimes dubbed "the second industrial revolution"). During that period, productivity improved to the point where workers were paid more and typically put in shorter weeks than had been the norm up to that time. A new middle class emerged, and its members found new pastimes, like going to the theater or listening to the newly developed gramophone. Leisure, which has been the most luxurious of luxuries up to that time, was suddenly within reach, albeit in small ways, for a much larger swathe of people.[21] Things do not always proceed so smoothly, however. China, for example, has built a bunch of ski resorts over the past decade that have been slow to attract skiiers. But even if this "new consumption" comes in fits and starts, it will come. Slowly but surely, a new group of people will see their horizons expand along with their incomes.

> It's worth noting that the newly middle class typically want more than just "things": they also want leisure, and ways to spend their leisure time.

NEW CHALLENGES

For the most part, the externalities that generally accompany a rising middle class are positive ones. For example, the ILO points out that there is a "virtuous circle" that comes with a rise in the middle class. As people earn more, they spend more on health and education, which in turn boosts productivity and growth. Higher productivity and growth, in turn, lead to further increases in incomes.[22] There is also the prospect of a more peaceful globe: a rising middle class could mean a concurrent rise in liberal democracies.[23]

But along with the good comes the bad, which in this case means a skyrocketing demand for Earth's finite resources. People with higher incomes want to eat more, they want to heat their homes when it is cold and cool them when it is warm, and they want running water. As they open their wallets to pay for these things, the prices of the resources connected with these "wants" will rise. In certain cases, the price mechanism will not be enough to regulate supply, and some parts of the globe will experience scarcities and shortages. With good management, technological advances, and some luck, that scenario might be avoided—but it will require a juggling act to deliver enough resources to everyone, particularly if it is to be done in a way that avoids serious environmental damage.

Another note: the fact that more countries will be classified as middle class within a few years means there will be a bit less income divergence between countries—but it says nothing about the income distribution *within* countries. Ernst & Young points out that in China, urban dwellers now earn three times as much as those who live in rural areas, and that India, Russia, and others have similar splits.[24] This means that there is likely to be a growing number of people who feel they are being shut out while others are making big gains—a situation that is primed and ready to create social unrest (we have already seen signs of this in North American in recent years, with such things as the Occupy Movement grabbing headlines). It's also possible that the mere existence of a middle class in a country that has not traditionally had one could set the stage for conflict and disagreements with government. Consider the protests in Brazil in the summer of 2013, when thousands took to the streets to protest spending for the 2014 World Cup rather than for much-needed health and social services. No doubt there was some bewilderment from the soccer organizers over the whole thing: Brazilians love soccer, so what could be better than hosting the World Cup? That might have been true a decade or so previously, when the best that many Brazilians could hope for was a distraction from their hand-to-mouth existence. These days, the fairly new Brazilian middle class clearly has a much longer wish list.

> In China, urban dwellers now earn three times as much as those who live in rural areas, and India, Russia, and others have similar splits. This means that there is likely to be a growing number of people who feel they are being shut out while others are making big gains—a situation that is primed and ready to create social unrest.

A DONE DEAL?

Then again, we may be putting the cart before the horse. The rise of the middle class is not exactly a "done deal." To assume that China or India or Indonesia is going to see a huge surge in the middle class is to also implicitly believe that those countries are going to grow steadily—or more than steadily—over the next few decades. A lot of things (like, for example, another 2008-style economic crisis) could happen to throw those projections off—and force a lot of people off the middle-class bandwagon.

As well, if resource prices rise too quickly throughout the world, some of the "new" middle class might be only an inflationary surge away from a return to "have not" status, and the expected size of the middle class may turn out to have been somewhat exaggerated. Case in point: one estimate suggests that if food and energy prices were to rise more than 20 percent over the course of a year (something that is certainly possible), the size of the Asian middle class might fall by up to 100 million (85 million in China alone).[25]

But let's put the negatives aside, and let's especially refrain from any thoughts that the middle-class explosion will not take place. The developed world is facing a demographically driven economic slowing in the years ahead, and in many ways is still coping with the aftermath of the global downturn. If there is to be an offset, it must come from legions of newly flush consumers, primed to buy what's on offer. It is a future that needs to be well managed, but also one that needs to happen.

(ENDNOTES)

[1] Dan Horn, "Middle Class a Matter of Income, Attitude," *USA Today*, April 24, 2013. Retrieved from http://www.usatoday.com/story/money/business/2013/04/14/middle-class-hard-define/2080565/.

[2] Stevenson's 1913 classification conceived society as divided into three basic social classes (the upper, middle, and working classes), although he actually introduced intermediate classes between the upper and middle classes and between the middle and working classes, and added three industrial groups for those working in mining, textiles, and agriculture. See David Rose, "Official Social Classifications in the UK," *Social Research Update*, Issue 9 (Guildford, UK: Department of Sociology, University of Surrey, July 1995).

3 Uri Dadush and Shinelse Ali, "In Search of the Global Middle Class: A New Index," July 23, 2012. (Washington, DC: Carnegie Endowment for International Peace, 2012). Retrieved from http://carnegieendowment. org/2012/07/23/in-search-of-global-middle-class-new-index/cyo2.

4 Ioan Grillo, "Mexico is on the Rise but What About Its Middle Class?" *Time*, June 13, 2013. Retrieved from http://world.time.com/2013/06/13/ mexico-is-on-the-rise-but-what-about-its-middle-class/.

5 International Labour Organization, "Rise of middle-class jobs in the developing world could spur growth," Global Employment Trends 2013, January 23, 2013. (Geneva: ILO, 2013. Retrieved from http://www. ilo.org/global/about-the-ilo/newsroom/news/WCMS_202481/lang--en/ index.htm.

6 Staff, "Burgeoning bourgeoisie," *The Economist*, Special Report, February 12, 2009, Retrieved from http://www.economist.com/node/13063298.

7 Homi Kharas, "The Emerging Middle Class in Developing Countries," OECD Development Centre, Working Paper 285, January 2010, (Paris: OECD, 2010). "Purchasing-power parity terms" means that exchange rates have been adjusted to allow comparisons within countries.

8 Ibid.

9 Based on United Nations, "World Population Prospects: The 2012 Revision," June 13, 2013 press release (New York: United Nations Department of Economic and Social Affairs, 2013), p. 2. Retrieved from http://esa. un.org/wpp/Documentation/pdf/WPP2012_Press_Release.pdf. The data on middle-class population comes from an earlier version of population projections. Given that the 2012 revision to population shows an upward revision to world population, the estimate of percentage of world population that is middle class is likely slightly understated.

10 Kharas.

11 Ernst & Young, "Hitting the Sweet Spot: The Growth of the Middle Class in Emerging Markets," 2013. Retrieved from http://www.ey.com/Publication/vwLUAssets/Hitting_the_sweet_spot/$FILE/Hitting_the_sweet_ spot.pdf.

12 Calculation is by the economist Surjit Bhalla, as quoted in Ernst & Young.

13 Mario Pezzini, "An Emerging Middle Class," *OECD Observer*. Retrieved from http://www.oecdobserver.org/news/fullstory.php/aid/3681/.

14 David Court and Laxman Narashimhan, "Capturing the World's Emerging Middle Class," McKinsey Quarterly, July 2010. Retrieved from http:// www.mckinsey.com/insights/consumer_and_retail/capturing_the_worlds_ emerging_middle_class.

[15] St. Louis Federal Reserve, "National Economic Trends, updated through November 1, 2013." Retrieved from http://research.stlouisfed.org/publications/net/page24.pdf.

[16] OECD data, quoted in Kuo Lily, "The World's Middle Class Will Number 5 Million by 2030," *Quartz*, January 14, 2013. Retrieved from http://qz.com/43411/the-worlds-middle-class-will-number-5-billion-by-2030/.

[17] International Labour Organization.

[18] Ernst & Young.

[19] Alon Eizenberg and Alberto Salvo, "Buying Behaviors of Emerging Middle Classes," Kellogg Insight, July 2, 2012. Retrieved from http://insight.kellogg.northwestern.edu/article/buying_behaviors_of_emerging_middle_classes.

[20] Court and Narashimhan.

[21] For a further discussion, see Linda Nazareth, *The Leisure Economy* (Toronto: John Wiley and Sons, 2007), p. 29.

[22] International Labour Organization, "Global Employment Trends 2013" (Geneva: ILO, 2013).

[23] Dadush and Ali, p. 3.

[24] Ernst & Young.

[25] Estimate is by Silk Road Associates, as of 2010. See Ben Simpfendorfer, "Asia's Rising Middle Class—Not Always What It Seems," Fung Global Institute, April 2012.

TREND # 6

The Stuck
Teeter-Totter

As we learned in chapter 5, people the world over are ascending income categories and finding their way into the middle class. The possible exception? North America. Within North America, a series of economic changes are creating a society where the rich are getting richer, the middle is losing some ground, and the poor are falling off the wagon altogether. Those changes are going to create a restructured economy, and perhaps some social issues that will have economic implications.

Think of a teeter-totter, or a seesaw, depending on where you grew up. Unless you're dealing with some very diligent children who wish it to be so, getting a teeter-totter to balance is almost impossible. Instead, one person is usually in the air, and the other is on the ground. That's what it's supposed to look like, and that's fine: a teeter-totter is a piece of park equipment, and the thrill is in the divergence of places. Now think of the economy, and specifically of income distribution. Unlike on a teeter-totter, things do *not* work better if some are up in the air and some are stuck on the ground—and yet this is the economic situation we seem to be facing in North America.

In Canada and in the United States, we are increasingly seeing an economy where a relatively small number of super-earners are enjoying a very good life. On the other side of the equation, however, a lot of people seem to have been thrown off the path to prosperity. The reasons for the split are varied, but the end result is the same for all—and it's not positive. If people start believing that their prospects are diminishing, they are going to act differently than if they believe they have a strong chance to move forward. The Occupy protests that spread around the world in 2011 expressed that sentiment very clearly, and drew attention to a situation that is not "fair." But the protests may have missed a larger point: income inequalities do not hurt just those at the bottom of the ladder—they can actually hurt everyone else as well. Unless real steps are taken to acknowledge and deal with the stuck teeter-tooter, there is a very real possibility of more economic upheaval ahead.

IT'S NOT "FAIR": MEASURING INCOME INEQUALITY

How exactly do we measure income inequality? There are different yardsticks, and although they can tell slightly different stories, all more or less show that there are rising numbers of "rich" and "poor." Actually, the biggest disparities are fairly new. According to the Organisation for Economic Co-operation and Development (OECD), over the two decades before the advent of the global economic crisis, real disposable household incomes (after tax and accounting for inflation) grew by a respectable 1.7 percent a year in its member countries.[1] The catch, however, was that the incomes for the top 10 percent of households grew more quickly than the incomes of the bottom 10 percent, meaning that income inequality effectively widened. Given that the rising economic tide was raising all boats, the situation might have been tolerable had it continued—but, as the numbers show, it did not.

In the case of North America, there are a few different indicators you can use to measure income inequality.

The Decline of the Middle Class

There is general agreement that the North American middle class is shrinking. But why? One of the most common answers is that incomes are stagnating or falling. Is this true?

We can analyze the situation by taking all incomes in a country and dividing them into "quintiles" (five shares, from the top-earning fifth of earners through to the lowest-earning fifth). The first quintile is the top 20 percent; the last is the bottom 20 percent, and the remaining three quintiles represent the middle 60 percent of earners. If you look at how this middle group's earnings and share of earnings has moved over time, you get a good idea of how the middle class has done.

In the United States, data from the Census Bureau shows that between 1976 and 2011, the income of the top quintile of families rose 15.8 percent while the income of the workers in the bottom quintile (data is in 2011 constant dollars) was up by 12.2 percent in 1976. The lowest income earners saw their average incomes fall by 0.8 percent between 1976 and 2011, while those in the three middle quintiles saw their average rise by 14 percent (which translates into less than 1 percent a year). In contrast, earners in the top quintile saw their incomes rise by a stunning 51.8 percent.[2]

DIVIDED FORTUNES

Average incomes include Capital Gains, constant 2012 dollars

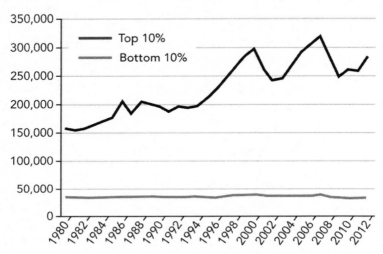

Source: The World Top Incomes Database http://topincomes.
g-mond.parisschoolofeconomics.eu/#Database.

Statistics Canada data shows that between 1976 and 2010, depending on the year, families in the top 20 percent of earners received between 7.2 and 9.5 times more than families in the bottom 20 percent of earners (data is in constant 2010 dollars and is net of taxes). That split got more pronounced from the 1990s onward; by 2010, the top 20 percent was earning 9.3 times more than the bottom 20. Between 1976 and 2010, the median incomes of those in the lowest quintile rose by 16 percent, while those in the highest were up by 27 percent. Middle-income earners saw the smallest gains, at 11 percent. What it comes down to is this: the norm for "rich" was superseded by something new—"richer." Earners in other income groups saw gains too, but in inflation-adjusted terms they were not as impressive.[3]

The Notorious 1 Percenters

As much as the modest gains of middle-income earners is an issue, another concern is that those at the very top of the income pile have made such amazing gains in recent years.

According to the OECD, the share of the richest 1 percent of earners rose between 1980 and 2010 in all countries monitored.[4] The richest of the rich also saw their shares of the pie grow very sharply: the 0.1 percent accounted for 8 percent of total pre-tax incomes in the U.S. in the years just prior to the recession, and about 4 to 5 percent in Canada.

The United States is a particularly dramatic story. In 1970, the richest 1 percent received 7.8 percent of total income; in the decade that followed, this increased to 8.2 percent. That inched up to 13 percent in 1990 and 16.5 percent in 2000. From then on, however, the split got more pronounced, and the top 1 percent reached a peak of 18.3 percent of total income in 2007, a figure that slipped a bit to 17.4 percent by 2011. The Canadian story is a bit more muted, with the top 1 percent of those filing taxes accounting for about 7 percent of the country's total income in the early 1980s, a figure that reached 8 percent in the early 1990s and then 10 percent by 1995. The peak for Canada was also in 2007, when the top 1 percent of earners hit 13.7 percent of total income earned; the percentage dropped to 12.2 in 2010.[5]

> These days, pictures of every party, every place, are beamed throughout the world pretty much in real time, so everyone knows exactly what they are missing. The OECD put a name to this phenomenon, calling it the *Hello!* magazine effect.

Of course, what you don't know cannot hurt you, right? So if the super-rich were quietly partying on yachts in St. Tropez, well, no harm done. Wrong. These days, pictures of every party, every place, are beamed throughout the world pretty much in real time, so everyone knows exactly what they are missing. The OECD put a name to this phenomenon, calling it the *Hello!* magazine effect; in essence, people were feeling poorer because the excesses of those at the top (that 1 percent) were being reported so copiously by the media.[6]

Gini Coefficients

The most standard way to measure income inequality is through the Gini Coefficient, which is calculated to show the disparities between low and high incomes. The Gini Coeficient is expressed as a value between 0 and 1; the lower the value, the more equality exists. So at 0, for example, there is no income inequality at all; at 1, there is total inequality (that is, income is not just going to the top 1 percent, but to just one person). This measure, too, shows increasing inequality across most developed countries over time. In the OECD as a whole (the top 20 countries), the Gini Coefficient stood at 0.316 in 2011, up from 0.29 in the 1980s.[7]

The U.S has always had more inequality than the OECD average, and that inequality has worsened over the past 20 years. From about 0.316 in the mid-1980s, the Gini Coefficient was up to 0.38 as of 2011.[8]

Interestingly, the Gini Coefficient shows a different story for Canada. For a time, until the mid-1990s, the Canadian Gini Coeficient was a little lower than the OECD average, although in the latter part of the 1990s that pattern changed. As of 2011, the Gini Coefficient for Canada was 0.32.[9]

"Shares" of the Economy

Another way to look at income equality is to calculate the share of the total income generated by an economy that accrues to labor. That share has been on the decline for a couple of decades now: the OECD calculates that within the countries it monitors, the median labor-share of income fell from 66.1 percent in the mid-1970s to 61.7 percent in the mid-2000s. What does this mean?

In essence, the economies were growing faster than labor's share. In other words, workers are getting less, on average, for the time they are putting in.[10]

In the United States, an analysis by the Federal Reserve Bank of Cleveland found that, for decades, labor's share of income sat at around two-thirds of all income. Recently, however, that share has declined, falling from 65 percent in 1980 to a current level of 57.6 percent.[11]

According to the OECD, labor's share has fallen by more in Canada than in the OECD area as a whole, from 65.3 percent in 1990 to 60.3 percent in 2006. And, as the OECD points out, if you were to exclude the earnings of the top 1 percent, labor's share would have declined by even more.[12]

THE TRENDS AFFECTING INCOME INEQUALITY

So, the evidence clearly points to both the existence of and increases in income disparity. The question is why. Most of the answer lies with earnings, and, more specifically, the returns on having a particular skill set. In the decades prior to the 1980s, the economy had a higher orientation toward "goods-producing" industries such as manufacturing, mining, and construction, and, at the time, this was fairly labor-intensive work. Accordingly, employees with minimal education could still receive relatively high compensation. The recession of the 1980s, however, caused a marked loss of jobs in these sectors, and, in many cases, this loss has been permanent. Over the past 20 years, the biggest economic gains have accrued to those with the highest skill levels and the best education, attributes that tend to skew toward those at the top of the income distribution.

In their analysis of the U.S. situation, the Federal Reserve identifies three factors that have caused labor's share of the economy to fall over time. (Since we know that not all earners saw their earnings decrease over time, their analysis is really an examination of why workers in lower- and middle-income brackets saw declining shares). Although the end result was negative for many workers and, by extension, may have done damage to the broader economy, each factor was, in and of itself, a rational response to a global economy that was becoming increasingly competitive.

The first factor flagged is a decline in the bargaining power of labor as a result of lower unionization. That's part and parcel of the shift in the broader economy: the sectors that were paring back were traditionally unionized. Next, globalization has made it easier (and more efficient, in many cases) to move labor-intensive sectors from advanced economies to less advanced ones. Finally, technological change has raised the returns to capital rather than labor.[13]

And then there was the Great Recession of 2008–09, an event that took workers who were on the edge and decisively shoved them off. One fascinating analysis of the unemployment situation in the United States shows that as the recession was ending, both the unemployment and underemployment[14] crises were situated squarely on the shoulders of the two lowest income quartiles. In a study prepared for the C.S. Mott Foundation, economists Andrew Sum and Ishwar Khatiwada used data from 2008 to establish 10 income deciles: the bottom decile included all households with annual incomes at or below $12,160, while the top decile was comprised of households with pre-tax annual incomes over $138,800. They then looked at data from the U.S. "household survey" of employment that is gathered each month and used to calculate statistics including the unemployment rate. Each employed person in the survey was assigned to one of the deciles.[15]

Their results were startling: the incidence of underemployment problems in the fourth quarter of 2009 was 13 times higher among those workers in the bottom household income decile as opposed to those in the top decile. For the bottom decile, the incidence of underemployment was 20.6 percent; for the top 10 percent, it was 1.6 percent. When they looked at unemployment for the same sample, they found that workers in the lowest income decile faced what they termed a Great Depression–type unemployment rate of 31 percent, while the second-lowest decile had a rate of 20 percent. Workers in the top two deciles had unemployment rates of only 4 percent and 3.2 percent, or what economists would term "full employment." The relative size of the gap in unemployment rates between workers in the bottom and top deciles was close to 10 to one.[16]

As much as it is easy to blame the global economic situation for the income disparities in North America, at least some of the causes are social. Family incomes are being skewed downward thanks to a sharp increase in the number of single-earner households, both for those who have children and those who do not. And that trend is true across the OECD: in the 1980s, about 15 percent of all households in the developed countries were "single-headed," a figure that rose to 20 percent by the mid-2000s.[17]

> The incidence of underemployment problems in the fourth quarter of 2009 was 13 times higher among those workers in the bottom household income decile as opposed to those in the top decile.

Another trend that has caused family incomes to become skewed is "assortative mating"; that is, people marrying those in similar careers (for example, doctors marrying other doctors as opposed to nurses). If you look at the employment rate of women over the past couple of decades, the group whose employment rate has increased the most is women married to high-income men. By the OECD's count, these days, 40 percent of couples where both spouses are in the labor force are in the same or neighboring income deciles, up from 33 percent a couple of decades ago.[18] Effectively, we have been creating high-income two-earner households at the same time that there has been an increase in single-earner households.

In some cases, efforts to redistribute income have mitigated some of the larger trends. For example, the Gini Coefficient for Canada tells a different story than the country's income figures. In the latter case, there was clearly a deterioration of incomes in the 1980s and the earlier part of the 1990s—the result of a couple of very brutal economic recessions. Prior to the 1990s, however, Canada had a different system in place to redistribute income, which by some measures did result in a lessening of inequality. In fact, the OECD report urges both Canada and other countries to make more efforts in those areas, perhaps through human capital investment starting with education and continuing through skills training. They also suggest that income redistribution be pursued through the tax system, perhaps by a tax on the rich. But the OECD acknowledges what is obvious in countries around the globe: this is a time of fiscal discipline, and a time when such reforms are somewhat unlikely to be given high priority.[19]

A PROBLEM FOR THE LARGER ECONOMY

There is something to be said for letting the economy function as it will, but presumably you have to draw the line when leaving things alone leads to an economic collapse. And so it is with income inequality: there is a plausible case to be made that the Great Recession of 2008–09—a worldwide event—was caused to some degree by income inequalities in the U.S.

> There is a plausible case to be made that the Great Recession of 2008–09—a worldwide event—was caused to some degree by income inequalities in the U.S.

The story is easy to understand. For years, the majority of U.S. households had to deal with stagnation in terms of their after-tax earnings. In the five years from 2002 to 2007 (the expansion years of the George W. Bush presidency), the real average income growth in the U.S. was 16.1 percent. However, there was a pretty big split between gains by income group. For the top 1 percent, the gain during these years was 61.8 percent, while for the other 99 percent it was a paltry 6.8 percent (barely enough to get them back to where they were before the recession of 2001–02).[20] At the same time that income growth was languishing, however, lax policies regarding the financial sector and the housing market were turning the homes of the 99 percent into what seemed like super-piggy banks. So the solution to the disparity became pretty clear, particularly given that interest rates were low: tap into what you have and get what you want.

Perhaps it did make some sense for people to use the value of their homes (through what used to be called a "second mortgage," but has been re-dubbed "refinancing") to fix up their kitchens and hence raise the value of their properties. It made a lot *less* sense to refinance for a trip to Disney, but households did that too. In fact, as they siphoned money out of their homes, the amount of home equity that Americans held was only prevented from getting perilously low through the fact that home prices were rising at such a nice clip. According to a study by the U.S. Federal Reserve, for each percent increase in home prices, homeowners increased their mortgage debt by 1 percent, on average, so that their equity remained about constant.[21]

To be sure, consumer credit and borrowing look attractive during times of stagnant earnings growth, and that can lead to dangerous situations. In the 1920s, income inequality was also at a peak. The earnings of the 1 percent were well into the double digits, and hit an all-time high of 18.7 percent in 1927 (a level that has not been approached since). At that time, Americans were also drawn to credit, which led to the creation of farm credit and installment loans.[22] The problem, of course, is that an economy that runs on credit is not on particularly strong footing, and it can fall apart like a house of cards when something goes wrong—as we saw both in the 1920s and in more recent experience.

Another theory is that too much money at the top leads to a lot of bad ideas, or at least encourages those at the top to take risks. If you think about it, most of the 2000s was characterized by extremely low interest rates. Following the terrorist attacks of September 11, 2001, there was a very real risk that the world would be plunged into a deep recession. As a preventative measure, central banks around the world, including the Federal Reserve in the United States, cut interest rates to extremely low levels. As a result, traditional financial instruments such as treasury bills yielded very little, and offered very little in terms of returns. Accordingly, Wall Street firms found it to their advantage to dream up new kinds of investment vehicles—things like mortgage-backed securities—that could offer their clients better returns. Theoretically, if less wealth and power had been concentrated on Wall Street, there would have been more regulation and more opposition to what turned out to be extremely high-risk vehicles.

The exact causality is a bit fuzzy, and it is not entirely clear that the rise of high-income earners in itself led to any kind of crisis. In fact, in an analysis of 14 advanced countries and their experience with credit and economic cycles over the period from 1920 to 2000, economists Michael D. Bordo and Christopher M. Meissner found no such relationship, instead concluding that it was the pattern of low interest rates and rising asset prices that caused booms and busts.[23] Still, you can argue that the desire to take full advantage of the low rates (and hence fuel the booms) had a lot to do with a society-wide dissatisfaction with the poor gains that Americans were seeing from their incomes, and a desire to make up the difference somewhere else.

And so here we are, post-recession, in a world of fairly unsatisfactory growth and a seriously skewed income structure. Unless the disparities are lessened to some degree, there are some serious economic consequences ahead.

A Restructured Economy

In the most basic sense, the eroding of the middle class means that companies need to let go of their middle-class marketing model, something that the larger players are already starting to do. In 2011, Procter and Gamble came out with a dish soap in the U.S. that it marketed at a "bargain" price—the first time in 36 years that it had done so.[24] Companies that have zeroed in on the economic crisis facing the majority of North Americans—even years after the official recessions have ended in Canada and the U.S.—have also found their strategies to be successful. Walmart struggled a bit, and since the recession has faced years of tough quarterly results. Still, the company has always been cognizant of the fact that its core customers live "paycheck to paycheck," and in 2011 stated that its customers were "running out of money faster" because energy bills were high.[25]

At the same time that the middle-market brands are trying to be price conscious, however, the most expensive brands of all are thriving. From Tiffany to Hermes to LVMH (the company that owns brands such as Moet et Chandon champagne and Louis Vuitton), you can see it in the annual results: as others make blustering apologies for why they did not sell more, the purveyors of luxury goods are happily totaling up how much they did sell. For awhile, those brands were mostly driven by Asian growth, which sparked a taste for luxury among the newly rich. More recently, however, the figures have shown solidly good results in the United States and even in Europe. Although to some extent those figures are skewed by Asian tourists, the fact that the 1 percent are an expanding market is enough to keep luxury brands like Prada and Chanel in prime market locations on New York's Fifth Avenue and anywhere else the rich cluster.

If the income split continues at the rate it is going, look for a more pronounced difference in product offerings, as well as in stores and experiences. And if you are an investor, look carefully at the companies you buy into: if they rely on a middle-income market, you may want to think twice.

Another Economic Crisis?

Given the income disparity in North America, could we soon find ourselves in another economic crisis? Although this is always possible, it seems somewhat unlikely. For one thing, if income inequality caused the last crisis, it was because cash-strapped households went overboard with their borrowing. Although world interest rates have been kept very low, for a very long time, more stringent lending rules have restrained borrowing in some countries, including, to a degree, the United States.

One side note, however: although U.S. borrowing has leveled off, post-crisis, Canadian borrowing certainly has not. As of early 2013 Canadians were the most leveraged to debt that they had ever been.[26] This means that Canadians would be extremely vulnerable to any new crisis, whatever its causes.

New Divisions, New Battles

As the battle of the haves and have-nots escalates over the coming decades, we may see the rise of other sharp divisions in North American society. There is, for example, the matter of young versus old. Younger workers now face very high unemployment rates, hefty student debts, and an uncertain economic future. To their eyes, baby boomers had it pretty good, and will have it very good indeed when they pick up indexed pensions paid for by the wages of the young. Will the young generation of workers protest, demanding tax breaks for themselves and higher taxes on senior wealth?

There is also the issue of inequality *within* the baby boomer community. This division isn't easy to discern while the boomers are still in the labor force. When they retire, however, it will be clear that some boomers are set for travel and adventure, while others are struggling to scrape together enough money to pay off the mortgage on the home they refinanced during the boom. What kind of societal split might that cause?

Inequality between men and women is another potential issue—one that could actually lead to a lessening of income inequality among households. As we've seen, the OECD has pointed out an increase in "assortative mating" over the past couple of decades. Going forward, a reversal may take place. We know that women have scooped up degrees and moved into professional jobs, meaning that it is now easier for high-earning men to find high-earning wives. Over the next decade, however, high-earning women may find it increasingly difficult to find high-earning spouses.

A Smaller Talent Pool

Economists sometimes speak of "virtuous circles," times when one thing goes right and, in turn, sets in motion a chain of other things that go right. With income inequality, however, we may experience the opposite: a cycle of things getting progressively worse. Consider the implications, for example, of a shrinking middle class. A smaller middle class would wield less political influence. In turn, policy will shift in a way that might be construed to be negative for mainstream interests.

As an example, let's look at the issue of government support of post-secondary institutions. With governments squeezed across the board, it is no surprise that funding for colleges and universities is under pressure across North America. In the United States, for example, in the three years following the start of the Great Recession there was a 28 percent reduction in state spending on education. But, as an analysis by the Center for American Progress points out,[27] states (like Canadian provinces) can choose how to prioritize their spending. Does the fact that education is not the biggest priority have something to do with the skewing of incomes? After all, the wealthy may support public spending on education, but they have less of a stake in it, given that they can afford tuition at public or private institutions. As a result, spending on post-secondary education is likely to skew lower on priority lists, replaced by issues that are more important to that wealthy class. As that happens, fewer in the middle class get a chance to pursue higher education, and the cycle gets worse.

The recent furor over unpaid internships is another example of a system that makes life easier for those at the top of the income pyramid. In many fields these days—particularly those with a per-ceived "glamor," such as media or arts—one way to get your foot in the door is to take an entry-level job as an unpaid intern. These positions have always existed, and typically paid very modest salaries. These days, though, employers have figured out that they needn't pay anything, and can still have their pick of candidates. Of course, the candidates from which they are choosing will be from a more stratified economic background than would have been the case if modest pay were involved. That money might be irrelevant to a younger man or woman whose parents are paying for tuition, rent, and so on, but absolutely necessary for someone who cannot survive without a paycheck—regardless of its size.

These types of situations are bad for the broader economy. If an ever-smaller group of people is being groomed to fully participate in the economy—either because of poorer educational opportunities or more difficult paths to employment—then the potential economic output of the economy is getting ever smaller too. In these days of flagging productivity and worries about economic growth, that is worrisome, to say the least.

WHAT TO FIX AND HOW TO FIX IT

Does income inequality needs to be fixed—and if so, how? Given past and recent experience, the answer to the first part of the question has to be *yes*. The world is heading into an era when demographics will work in opposition to economic growth, and problems like rising resource prices will further hamper things. Adding brewing social unrest to the mix will breed inefficiencies at best and a crisis at worst.

The standard solutions tend to come from the left side of the political spectrum. Some are fairly straightforward: for example, enforcing employment standards legislation and ending the exploitation of new immigrants and foreign workers is not only fair in itself, but also ensures that the wages of workers on the bottom of the pile are not pushed lower. Most other suggested measures to end inequality, however, involve government intervention that could compromise the larger productivity picture. Raising entitlement programs and changing the tax system may be short-term solutions, but they will not do much to change the characteristics of workers or of the economy in a way that will raise wages over the long term. Encouraging unionization also works against a larger need to raise productivity in a way that will boost growth.

What about raising the minimum wage? Unfortunately, this measure is only likely to hurt those in the lowest earnings brackets. In 2013, workers at McDonald's restaurants across the U.S. staged protests over their wages, which, at $7.50 per hour (or around $15,000 a year for an employee with full-time hours), put workers squarely below any poverty line estimate.[28] But would hiking pay to $15 an hour (the protesters' goal) solve the problems? Very likely not. For one thing, if workers became that much more expensive to hire, fast food chains would look closely at how many of them they really needed, perhaps replacing jobs with technology. There would also surely be a sharp hike in food prices, which would hurt low-income consumers who buy fast food.

So, time to face facts: we are now at a place where those with lower levels of education and skills are simply not going to see any meaningful gains in their economic situations. Among other things, that could lead to pronounced social unrest—although a way around that might be to increase income mobility. After all, if you think you (or your children) have a shot at being the next Bill Gates or Oprah Winfrey (both fixtures on any "top earners" list), then being wherever you are temporarily is not such a bad thing. The problem is that so many people these days *do not* believe that they can get to the next rung of the ladder, never mind all the way to the top.

There are two ways to think about income mobility. The first is as an inter-generational issue: If you come from a lower-income family, are your kids doomed to suffer the same fate? According to the Conference Board of Canada, the answer appears to be *maybe*. In a study of 13 countries, the Conference Board found that inter-generational mobility was highest in Denmark and lowest in the United Kingdom, with Canada ranked fourth and the U.S. 11th. Put another way, the study found that if you looked at how much less than the national average a Canadian family earned, and compared that with the same information in the next generation, 19 percent of the family's disadvantage was passed on to their children. In quantitative terms, if a family in one generation earned $10,000 less than average, its children would earn $1,900 less than the average. In the United States, the children would earn $4,700 less, meaning that 47 percent of the disadvantage is passed on.[29]

The other way to look at income mobility is as "intra-generational mobility," or mobility through one's own lifetime—the old "start at the bottom and move to the top" thing that the American dream is supposedly based on. Rags-to-riches stories do happen, of course. We know that author J.K. Rowling (net worth $1 billion, give or take) lived on welfare while she wrote the Harry Potter books, and we are also aware that many people with very humble beginnings head major companies. Howard Schultz, CEO of Starbucks, grew up in a housing project, as did Ursula Burns, who is now CEO of Xerox. And, of course, the entertainment, sports, and music industries are stuffed with people like

Jay-Z (net worth $500 million), who grew up poor and became very rich.[30]

But these super-succeeders may be outliers. For the average person, it is now more difficult to go up a few income rungs during their working life than it once was. In the United States, a 2012 report for the Congressional Research Service found that the likelihood of an adult moving from their initial economic position in terms of income distribution had decreased or been unchanged in recent decades.[31]

That may not be a bad thing, in a macroeconomic sense. According to a survey by CareerBuilder.com, 36 percent of surveyed employers are now looking at employees with post-secondary degrees for positions that were historically held by high-school graduates. If you assume that university and college graduates as a group have some skills (reading comprehension, organizational skills, math abilities) that are superior to what high-school graduates have as a group, then the trend is certainly a win for the companies, and presumably for the economy. All things being equal, the shift should boost productivity for the companies and, in a larger sense, for the economy as a whole. Indeed, this is what the employers report. Seventy-six percent say they get a higher quality of work with the more highly educated group, 45 percent say they get higher productivity, and 23 percent say their revenues are higher. What this means for the lower-skilled workers, however, is that their income mobility and earnings powers are unlikely to be improved while in the workforce. [32]

So what is the solution? Perhaps the most obvious is to get everyone to a higher starting point in terms of human capital development. A highly educated population attracts high-value-added industries. Unfortunately, this raising of the bar is more easily said than done. As much as there is a need to improve the post-secondary systems, there is probably more of a need to fix things at lower levels of education. In Canada and in the United States, schools are financed out of property taxes, meaning that rich districts can fund better schools than can poor ones. Less-advantaged students automatically end up in worse schools, which intensifies the divide in their educational outcome.

But in an ideal world, the low wages at McDonalds would not be a huge issue. McDonald's employees would likely see such work as short-term, something to do until they developed new skills and moved on to a higher-paying position. If the people in North America believe that they cannot better their situation, or if indeed they really cannot, than *that* is the real problem and one that should be addressed by policy. After all, in the best possible world, the most routine tasks associated with McDonald's jobs would have been taken over by automation and those who were employed would have been selected and trained to be high-productivity workers. And in nirvana, those workers would not replace the old, lower-skill workers, since everyone would have higher skills and wages would be high. Clearly, this is not the world that exists right now, but perhaps it is a vision that can be moved a little closer to reality over the next two decades.

(ENDNOTES)

[1] The OECD consists of 34 members comprising Australia, Austria, Belgium, Canada, Chile, the Czech Republic, Denmark, Estonia, Finland, France, Germany, Greece, Hungary, Iceland, Ireland, Israel, Italy, Japan, Korea, Luxembourg, Mexico, Netherlands, New Zealand, Norway, Poland, Portugal, the Slovak Republic, Slovenia, Spain, Sweden, Switzerland, Turkey, the United Kingdom, and the United States.

[2] United States Census Bureau, "Historical Income Tables, Income Inequality: Table H-3: Share of Aggregate Income Received by Each Fifth and Top 5 Percent of Households (All Races)." Retrieved from http://www.census.gov/hhes/www/income/data/historical/inequality/.

[3] Human Resources and Skills Development Canada, "Financial Security—Income Distribution/Indicators of Well-Being." Retrieved from http://www4.hrsdc.gc.ca/.3ndic.1t.4r@-eng.jsp?iid=22.

[4] Organisation for Economic Co-operation and Development, "Divided We Stand: Why Inequality Keeps Rising," OECD 2011. Retrieved from http://www.oecd.org/els/soc/49170768.pdf.

[5] Paris School of Economics, "The World Top Incomes Data Base." Retrieved from http://topincomes.parisschoolofeconomics.eu/#Database. Figures do not include capital gains.

[6] Sam Fleming, "Gap between rich and poor narrows… but *Hello!* effect makes well-off feel worse off," MailOnline, October 23, 2008. Retrieved from http://www.dailymail.co.uk/news/article-1079306/Gap-rich-poor-narrows--Hello-effect-makes-feel-worse-off.html.

[7] OECD, "OECD Income Distribution Database: Dates, Figures, Methods and Concepts." Retrieved from http://www.oecd.org/els/soc/income-distribution-database.htm.

[8] Ibid.

[9] Ibid.

[10] Ibid.

[11] Margaret Jacobson and Filippo Occhino, "Labor's Declining Share of Income and Rising Inequality," Federal Reserve Bank of Cleveland, Economic Commentary, September 25, 2012. Retrieved from http://www.clevelandfed.org/research/commentary/2012/2012-13.cfm.

[12] OECD, "OECD Employment Outlook 2012: How Does Canada Compare?" July 16, 2013. Retrieved from http://www.oecd.org/canada/Canada_final_EN.pdf.

[13] Jacobson and Occhino.

[14] *Underemployment* refers to persons working part-time because they are unable to find full-time jobs.

[15] Andrew Sum and Ishwar Khatiwada, "Labor underutilization problems of U.S. workers across household income groups at the end of the great recession: a truly great depression amongst the nation's low income workers amidst full employment among the most affluent," Center for Labor Market Studies Publication, Paper 26, 2010. Retrieved from http://hdl.handlenet/2047/d20000593.

[16] Ibid.

[17] OECD, "Divided We Stand: Why Inequality Keeps Rising," 2011, p. 33. Retrieved from http://www.oecd.org/els/soc/49499779.pdf.

[18] OECD, "An Overview of Growing Income Inequalities in OECD Countries: Main Findings," OECD, 2011. Retrieved from http://www.oecd.org/els/soc/49499779.pdf.

[19] OECD, Divided We Stand.

[20] Emmauel Saez, "Striking It Richer: The Evolution of Top Incomes in the United States," January 23, 2013. Retrieved from http://elsa.berkeley.edu/~saez/saez-UStopincomes-2011.pdf.

[21] Rajashri Chakrabarti, Donghoon Lee, Wilbert van der Klaauw, and Basit Zafar, "Household Debt and Saving During the 2007 Recession," Federal Reserve Bank of New York, Staff Report 482, January 2011. Retrieved from http://www.newyorkfed.org/research/staff_reports/sr482.pdf.

[22] Emily Kaiser, "The Haves, the Have Nots, and the Dreamless Dead," Reuters Special Report, October 22, 2010. Retrieved from http://www.reuters.com/article/2010/10/22/us-usa-economy-inequality-idUS-TRE69L0KI20101022.

[23] Michael D. Bordo and Christopher M. Meissner, "Does Inequality Lead to a Financial Crisis?" NBER Working Paper #17896, March 2012. Retrieved from http://www.nber.org/papers/w17896.

[24] Ellen Bryon, "As Middle Class Shrinks, P & G Aims High and Low," *Wall Street Journal*, September 12, 2011. Retrieved from http://online.wsj.com/article/SB10001424053111904836104576558861943984924.html.

[25] Parijia Kavilanz, "Walmart: Our Shoppers are Running Out of Money," CNN Money, April 28, 2011. Retrieved from http://money.cnn.com/2011/04/27/news/companies/walmart_ceo_consumers_under_pressure/index.htm.

[26] Greg Quinn, "Canadians Turn Deaf Ear to Carney's Warnings as Household Debt Hits Fresh Record at 165%," Bloomberg News, March 15, 2013. Retrieved from http://business.financialpost.com/2013/03/15/canadians-turns-deaf-ear-to-carneys-warnings-as-household-debt-hits-fresh-record-at-165/.

[27] Phil Oliff, Vincent Palaciios, Ingrid Johnson, and Michael Leachman, "Recent Deep State Higher Education Cuts May Harm Students and the Economy for Years to Come," Center on Budget and Policy Priorities, March 19, 2013. Retrieved from http://www.cbpp.org/cms/?fa=view&id=3927.

[28] David Sands, "Fast Food Strike: Detroit Walkouts, Protests Continue National Movement for Higher Wages, Union," The Huffington Post, May 10, 2013. Retrieved from http://www.huffingtonpost.com/2013/05/10/fast-food-strike-detroit-protests-living-wage_n_3252944.html.

[29] Conference Board of Canada, "How Canada Performs: Income Inequality." Retrieved from http://www.conferenceboard.ca/hcp/details/society/income-inequality.aspx.

[30] Kevin Smith, "Jay-Z Calls Out Rappers Who Lie About How Much Money They Actually Make," *Business Insider*, July 11, 2013. Retrieved from http://www.businessinsider.com/jay-z-thinks-rappers-lie-about-net-worth-2013-7.

[31] Linda Levine, "The U.S. Income Distribution and Mobility Trends: An International Comparison," U.S. Congressional Research Service, November 29, 2012, p. 15.

[32] Linda Nazareth, "Better-educated workers are starting at the bottom—but is that so bad?" *Globe and Mail* Economy Lab, March 28, 2013. Retrieved from http://www.theglobeandmail.com/report-on-business/economy/economy-lab/better-educated-workers-are-starting-at-the-bottom-but-is-that-so-bad/article10457015/.

PART

3

New Realities, New Attitudes

A Reversal of the Downward Slide in Commodity Prices

Global population is expanding, and that population is getting richer: together the two forces guarantee an increased demand for the Earth's resources. How that increased demand manifests itself over the next few decades will depend on management, technology, and perhaps a bit of luck.

The positive case is one where there is "enough" for everyone, at a price that is considered acceptable to most. Alternatively, there could be shortages—meaning less availability and most definitely higher prices for resources than the developed world takes for granted at present. How things play out could make a big difference to consumer behavior and choices in both the developed and developing world.

The 20th century saw remarkable economic development in much of the world, driven by hard work, technology, and new manufacturing processes. Wealth was created and a large part of the developed world got richer and acquired more luxuries. But there was a hidden subsidy, so to speak, to the new prosperity: it was aided by the fact that prices for key commodities in the world were low and, in many cases, on the decline. People could live in suburbs and drive their cars 50 miles to work because gas prices were affordable. They could spend money on vacations because the cost of food was taking up a smaller share of their budgets. And they could fill up their swimming pools because water was never in short supply.

As we head into the 2020s and beyond, that downward slide in commodity prices is going in a different direction—one that is going to be more expensive for consumers and for businesses. In some countries, this will mean scrambling for resources, with scarcities periodically becoming a way of life. It could also mean social unrest, as higher prices put basic commodities out of reach for some. In the developed world, higher resource prices may not threaten anyone's survival, but they could make a big difference to decision-making, with cost considerations forcing people to move or to choose different patterns of consumption. Or perhaps—in the best scenario of all—the push to increase commodity availability could herald the advent of new technologies that make production easier and keep prices lower.

Demand, Supply, and Prices—The Good Old Days and the Days to Come

It is almost a hidden history, since so few know of it, but commodity prices were on a downward slide over the entirety of what now seems like a long-ago century. One composite measure of commodity prices, the McKinsey Global Institute's Commodity Price Index (a composite of prices including energy, metals, and food), fell by almost half during the 20th century, in inflation-adjusted terms. Keep in mind that this occurred at a time when the world's population quadrupled and the world's output was up by 20-fold, meaning that resource demand was up somewhere between 600 and 2,000 percent.[1]

You could take apart the factors affecting dozens of commodities, but two resources have really been key to the history of the economy of the last century: food and energy. Looking at their past and future gives you an idea of the bigger picture. Let's start with food. Imagine you lived in a U.S. city in 1913 and wanted to pick up some groceries. You'd face prices like eggs for 34.1 cents a dozen (prices are averaged over 51 U.S. cities), coffee at 30 cents a pound, and butter at 35.9 cents a pound.[2] It all sounds like a bargain, right? Except that you cannot actually compare prices from 1913 to prices today. To use a food analogy, it would be like comparing apples to oranges. To put the 1913 prices into current dollars means you have to adjust for inflation, so let's do that.[3]

Using the inflation calculator from the U.S. Bureau of Labor Statistics, the 1913 price of butter in 2011 dollars come to $7.97—in the real 2011, butter sold for $3.67 a pound. Coffee, adjusted to 2011 dollars, was $6.68 a pound, although you could actually buy it for $5.65. As for the eggs? They were a lot more expensive in 1915, in relative terms. They adjusted to $7.59 a dozen in 2011 terms—a year in which you could pick them up for $1.95.[4]

Why the big decrease in food prices over the last century? Most of it was driven by

From improvements in fertilizers and chemicals through to machinery, a host of developments have lifted the productivity of agriculture over the past century, and, in particular, over the last half-century. According to the United Nations, the world's cropland grew 12 percent between 1961 and 2009, but food productivity rose by a whopping 150 percent.

productivity gains that simply meant farms could produce more per square foot. From improvements in fertilizers and chemicals through to machinery, a host of developments have lifted the productivity of agriculture over the past century, and, in particular, over the last half-century. According to the United Nations, the world's cropland grew 12 percent between 1961 and 2009, but food productivity rose by a whopping 150 percent.[5]

At the same time that prices were on the decline, the growth in the U.S. economy meant that wages were on the increase; in fact, they doubled six times in the 20th century.[6] The net result was that food took up a smaller and smaller portion of household budgets, a phenomenon that was mirrored in Canada and other developed countries. According to a report from the U.S. Bureau of Labor Statistics, in 1900 the typical American household spent 43 percent of its budget on food. By 1950 this had declined to 30 percent; by 2003, it was down to 13 percent.[7]

The effect of the decline in food prices on consumer spending patterns has been every bit as dramatic as the decline in prices itself. Over the past hundred years, there has been a lot more room in family budgets, particularly in North America, for expenditures on things besides groceries. To a large degree, this has led to a rise in home ownership and a larger share of income spent on housing (23 percent in 1903, and 33 percent in 2003), but it has also meant more money available to spend on what would once have been considered "frills." In 1901, families in the U.S. could allocate only 20.2 percent of their income to discretionary rather than essential goods. By 2003, this had risen to 49.9 percent. Discretionary goods include things like cars (unknown to the average family in 1901), entertainment, and travel, not to mention things like computers, televisions, and iPods.[8]

Low energy prices have impacted the economy in a slightly different way. Although food prices actually dipped in real terms, oil prices have been low in real terms for the past century, and that has acted as a built-in subsidy on anything that uses energy. Low oil prices have boosted economic growth directly: energy is used in homes, but it is also used to power machines for industrial production, and to transport goods over vast distances. So, industrial expansion has been possible at what now looks like a modest cost.

Again, the key is to look at inflation-adjusted oil prices so that you can compare the "real" price of oil over time.[9] Doing so shows that oil prices were actually pretty flat (at a rate of about $20 a barrel in inflation-adjusted terms) from the end of World War II through to the early 1970s. That was when the world was hit by the actions of the Organization of the Petroleum Exporting Countries (OPEC), a cartel of oil-producing countries that controlled supply in such a way as to cause prices to rise. The net result was that by 1979, world oil prices were around $100 a barrel in real terms. That turned around in the 1980s, however, when overproduction was combined with lower consumption and prices fell accordingly. Prices were around $30 a barrel in the 1980s, although high demand caused them to spike to over $40 by 1990. Another recession in the early 1990s sent them down once again.

That link between recessions and oil prices is an important one, particularly as it relates to the United States. In periods where oil prices are low, economy activity soars. At some point, this causes energy prices to spike, which acts as a brake on economic activity and frequently causes it to grind to a halt. Economist James Hamilton analyzed the vulnerability of the United States to rising oil prices and found that 10 out of 11 of the country's post–World War II recessions were caused or exacerbated by rising oil prices.[10] When recession ensues, demand for oil declines and prices also fall.

Low food prices, low energy prices, low prices for scores of other commodities: these factors have caused the global economy, and, in particular, the North American economy, to boom over the past century, but the days of low resource prices are ending, and the future is one where most commodities will cost more. We have already seen the beginnings of this, of course. In the years before the Great Recession, oil prices in particular were starting to climb (which in turn triggered the downfall of the U.S. economy, to some extent). In the summer of 2008, prices climbed to close to $100 a barrel in nominal terms, and there was much talk of how the world would cope with a new era of expensive oil. The world was "saved" from that, so to speak, when the global economy collapsed and prices were driven lower. That recession is over, however, and the overriding trend is for prices to rise over the next two decades. Indeed, oil prices have risen since the end of the recession, even at a time when many feel that the U.S. economy in particular is still sluggish.

In fact, the over-riding trend is for almost all commodity prices—from food to metals to energy—to rise because of higher demand. What we know for sure is that the world is becoming more crowded. From 3 billion people on the planet in 1960, the world has reached a population of over 7 billion as of 2013. Within a couple of decades—the United Nations estimates that it will happen by 2025—there will be 8 billion people on the planet, and 9.6 billion of us by 2050.[11]

But it is not just a growing population that will create the demand for resources—wealth will play a part as well. We are fairly certain that we will see a rising world "middle class" over the next couple of decades, as well as an increase in the number of people living in urban areas (see chapters 5 and 3, respectively). The pace of global industrialization is rapid. According to McKinsey, during the years that the United Kingdom was industrializing, in the 1700s and 1800s, it took about 154 years for the country to double per capita incomes. When the U.S. did so in the 1800s, it took about 53 years. More recently, it took China 12 years, and India 14.[12]

This rapid rise in wealth will be positive in many ways, particularly for the people involved. Just as the rise in U.S incomes gave consumers there more leeway in their spending, higher incomes in the developing world will also mean more freedom, and more luxuries too—and that's where the problems begin. As countries become more developed, what was one an unattainable luxury (like heat in the winter and coolness in the summer) rapidly becomes a necessity. And with more and more people wanting that necessity—well, demand goes up, a lot.

In the case of food, the sheer increase in the world population is going to send demand through the roof. Projections by the U.S. Department of Defense suggest that the world's demand for food will rise by 35 percent by 2030.[13] Looking a little further out, a report by the Food and Agriculture Organization of the United Nations suggests farmers are going to need to produce fully 70 percent more food than they do today if they are to meet the demands of a population that will top 9 billion by 2050.[14] That is easier said than done in a world where the competition for arable land is intensifying. Cities are getting bigger and spreading out further, and even where land is available, food production is facing competition from biofuel production.

That "food versus fuel" debate is an important one. The issue is complicated and hotly debated on both sides, but what we do know is that there are resources—such as maize (corn) and vegetable oil—that can either be used as they have traditionally been used (as food), or can be used in the production of biofuels. In fact, about 40 percent of the United States' stock of corn is used to make ethanol.[15] Over the past few years, the U.S., along with countries such as the United Kingdom, France, and Germany, has supported ethanol production through tax credits, with the idea of providing alternatives to fossil fuels. The unintended consequence has been a drop in the land available for agriculture.

There is also the fact that a wealthier planet typically has different tastes than one with more income constraints. Lower-income populations eat rice and grains, while higher-income ones want more meat. You can see this playing out in China, where consumption of beef has already risen, and is expected to rise by 24 percent on a per capita basis over the next decade.[16] More beef means a higher demand for grains to feed cattle, and it also means higher demands for water to grow the grains—and so the cycle goes.

Energy demand—and prices—are also going to be hit hard by the needs of the world's rising middle class: research suggests that in countries that improved the living standards of the poor, an increase of 1 percent in gross domestic product leads to a 1 percent or higher increase in total energy consumption.[17] Putting that into the broadest terms—adding up all the power needed for new freezers bought in India, or new cars driven in China—suggests frighteningly high increases in the amount of total energy that will be demanded by the world. According to the baseline 2012 forecast from the International Energy Agency, global energy demand is expected to rise by over one-third through 2035. Almost all of the demand is expected to come from emerging economies. Although demand from the developed world is only expected to rise 3 percent over the period, the developing world is expected to make up the difference.[18]

Just how much you think that this is going to impact energy prices depends on what you believe about oil supply. At one point, that centered around the idea of peak oil, and an imminent exhaustion of oil supplies, but that is less of a concern these days as hydraulic fracking technology increases the North American oil supply.[19] In fact, the United States is now producing so much oil that it is likely to be the largest global oil producer before 2020, and a net exporter of oil a few years after.[20] And fracking will no doubt make a big difference to oil price hikes in the years ahead, and will certainly limit any price volatility that the United States may have been exposed to had they continued to be dependent on imports. Still, oil prices are set on world markets, and whether North America can be totally shielded from demand-side pressures is unknown.

However you look at it, we live in a world of finite resources and rising demands—and unless something changes, that will mean rising prices.

THE POSSIBLE SOLUTIONS

Is there a solution to the resource crunch we are likely to face? As with so many other things in economics, the situation can be turned around if we get productivity correct. After all, this is what happened over the 20th century, and for centuries before that. The political economist Thomas Malthus wrote about the shortages caused by overpopulation in 1798, and fretted that famine was an inevitability given how quickly the planet was becoming populated.[21] That did not come to pass—at least not on a global level—despite the fact that the world's population did increase to a level Malthus could barely have imagined. Instead, technological improvements have allowed the world to produce more of everything (Malthus would have had trouble imagining that too). So can we not do that again? And if technology is not going to be the fix, is there another way to handle the issue of lots of buyers and a limited supply? There are, indeed, some things that can make a difference.

Technology and Productivity

The only real way to keep prices low is higher productivity—basically, squeezing more out of every bit of resource extraction and every acre of land farmed. If that could happen, it would be the magic bullet—but it will not happen without political will, business investment, and a significant amount of money flowing toward a problem that is just becoming a problem.

In agriculture, a clutch of ideas could increase productivity. Consider "vertical farming," the creation of skyscrapers filled with vegetation. This potential solution was outlined a couple of years ago by a professor at Columbia University named Dickson

Despommier in a book called *The Vertical Farm*.[22] The thinking behind the idea is similar to the thinking that once advocated building skyscrapers to house hundreds of families in big cities. If adopted it could mean a lot more food grown close to where people live, although there are some drawbacks, most notably the cost of the electricity it would take to power such structures.

There is also increasingly talk of using "big data" to create "smart farming." For example, in Silicon Valley, companies are forming partnerships with farmers in order to use sensor and mobile technologies to improve operations. Farmers are using soil sensors that monitor moisture levels using their iPads, which could be miles away.[23] A report done for the Australian agriculture sector recommended a mix of initiatives to encouraged smart farming, including connecting farms to broadband-enabled senior networks.[24] As in every industry, technology is being used to improve productivity and efficiency. Some of the new methods might endure and others will be replaced with ever-evolving technologies, but whatever measures are implemented, there will be some catching up to do: global productivity gains in agriculture have fallen from 2 percent between 1970 and 2000 to 1.1 percent today. By some estimates, they are still declining.[25]

In energy extraction, the big productivity improvement these days is hydraulic fracking. This is actually not a particularly new technology—it was developed in the 1940s—but it has been used with increasing frequency over the last couple of decades (most notably in the Canadian oil sands). The process of fracking involves drilling into the ground and injecting water, sand, and chemicals into shale rock, which in turn frees trapped hydrocarbons. Fracking inspires pretty strong emotions, and is either the greatest thing since sliced bread or the work of the devil, destroying the environment in the name of saving a few pennies. To be sure, there are environmental issues that go along with fracking, and these need to be monitored and improved. However, it is a method of resource extraction that allows us to tap into previously untapped resources, which is a gotta-have in a world with expanding demand.

Government Policy and Investment

Is there a role for government in dealing with the coming commodity price hikes? If there is, it should be before a crisis happens, not after. Those with long memories can recall the disastrous attempts governments made in the 1970s to deal with the "energy crisis"— attempts that sent gas prices through the roof. In the U.S., there were price controls as the Nixon administration decided that oil companies were not allowed to fully pass on the higher cost of imported oil to consumers. But at the lower, regulated price, the companies found it made sense to supply less oil, and cut back on imports to the point where they could supply only their own franchises. Ultimately, the lower price led to a gas "shortage," and long lines at the pumps.[26] Canada also experimented with a price ceiling on oil during the early 1980s, and went as far as creating a government-owned oil company, Petro-Canada. These measures were subsequently abandoned: not only did they come close to destroying an industry, but by regulating prices, the government gave consumers a disincentive to change their consumption habits.

Where government *can* play a role is in encouraging the exploration of alternative sources of energy, perhaps by giving research and development tax credits or direct subsidies. Unfortunately, these measures, and others like them, may be a difficult "sell" given that governments around the world are under pressure to control their deficits and debts. And that will be a hallmark of the coming decades as well: the need for good choices in terms of public sector policies, and the reality that government fiscal situations mean that the private sector will be, for better or worse, increasingly on its own. And perhaps that is simply how it should be: the private sector is going to need to bear the brunt of R&D expenditures going forward.

Conservation

If countries cut back on resource use, the impacts could be dramatic. That is probably most true for energy. As well as its baseline economic scenario, the International Energy Agency has also come up with an "Efficient World Scenario," in which, as compared to their baseline scenario, growth in primary energy demand is half of what it would have been by 2035. It's a nice idea, but the world is not even close to that level of conservation.[27] The most effective way to achieve true progress on the conservation front is to simply let prices rise, or maybe to help the process along by implementing taxes on use.

> The International Energy Agency has come up with an "Efficient World Scenario," in which, as compared to their baseline scenario, growth in primary energy demand is half of what it would have been by 2035. It's a nice idea, but the world is not even close to that level of conservation.

The problem of food scarcity is a different dilemma. According to scientists from Oxfam, producing animal-based food takes five to 10 times more water than producing a vegetarian diet. At the extreme, some believe the world will have to become vegetarian in order to continue feeding the planet. At present, humans derive about 20 percent of their protein from animal-based products. That may need to drop to 5 percent by 2050 in order to feed the extra couple of billion people who will be around at that time. Also at issue is whether there will be enough water to produce the food for the expanded population.[28]

Of course, going vegetarian is not the only solution. Part of the problem is that there are inefficiencies in the way food is sold and traded between countries. Even now, shortages of food in Africa could potentially be eliminated through more effective trade practices. A report from the World Bank in 2012 showed that just 5 percent of Africa's cereal imports were being provided by African farmers, thanks to food-trade barriers that stopped farmers from trading more easily with each other, as well as high transportation costs and a lack of infrastructure.[29] All of these things can be fixed through better polices and better international cooperation, although change in this area does not come easily (as is abundantly clear to those who have tried to change things).

Letting the Market Decide

Technology and policy and the rest of it can make a big difference, but the absolute best way to allocate resources efficiently is through the price system. Higher prices solve a lot of problems. For a time, people will resist making changes to their behavior, believing that, as always, any rise in prices must ultimately be reversed. But when people wake up to the idea that there is not going to be a decline in prices, they will change their consumption patterns, perhaps substituting grains for meats or shopping more consciously for foods produced close to consumption rather than those produced farther away. And yes, they will even go back to the energy-conservation behaviors that pop up every time North America experiences a hike in oil prices.

High prices can spur innovation as well. The higher the prices are, the bigger the payoff will be to those who find a way to produce something at a lower price. And so the race will intensify: Can someone come up with a way to dig deeper, grow more, produce more efficiently? The company or individual who manages to do that will become a big winner in monetary terms, and sometimes it is money the spurs the innovation race.

A MORE EXPENSIVE FUTURE

If we are very lucky, and if extraordinary measures are taken, we should be able to stem some of the coming increase in commodity prices—but not all of it. Although we have previously managed to keep the world going with enough food and nicely priced oil, things are different this time around. The coming increase in population will not just be sharp, which indeed it has been for the past 40 years; in the next decades, we will be adding people with spending power and a thirst for what commodities can do for them. That will be new to us.

Productivity and other measures may go some way toward bridging the gap between what is available and what is needed, but there is nothing revolutionary enough on the horizon to go the whole way. The price system will need to make up the difference, allocating things by who is able to pay. McKinsey notes that, historically, when a resource is in short supply, either the public or private sector comes up with an innovation that increases the supply. That suggests that there is hope—that as prices go higher we will perhaps see more and more technologies that help bring them down.[30]

In actual fact, however, prices are just going to be higher for most things. That means it will cost more to drive your car and heat your home, but it will also cost more to buy a house or to outfit your child in his or her back-to-school wardrobe. Energy costs are "input" into everything, but we also have to remember that virtually all inputs will be more expensive. Although food and energy are the prime examples, we are talking about a world in which everything, from lumber to cotton, will cost more thanks to demand increasing more quickly than supply.

Higher prices will also mean a lower standard of living for most people, although there might be some interpretation as to what that means. Whether we are talking about developing countries or developed ones, the portion of the population at the lowest income levels will be most vulnerable to high prices. An analysis based on U.S. census data estimates that in 2012, households with incomes under $10,000 a year were spending 78 percent of their after-tax income on energy costs, as compared to 9 percent for those with incomes over $50,000.[31] In the case of food, in 2011 the lowest 20 percent of U.S. households, income-wise, spent 16.1 percent of their annual expenditures on food, while the highest 20 percent spent 11.6 percent.[32] If you judge poverty on how much of one's budget people must spend for essential services, we could be heading into a world where the absolute number of poor will be on the rise. That will beget the need for more social spending, particularly if high resource prices leave the broader economy sluggish and make well-paying work difficult to find.

For those at higher income levels, the result of higher commodity prices may not be as disastrous, but if those prices go high enough they will lead to some difficult choices. In a sense, the situation will be like an unwinding of the forces that made it possible for families to choose to spend on holidays as well as on groceries. If food prices take an increasing share of the budget, and it costs more to heat the house and drive the car, the increase must come from somewhere else. Where possible, it will come from substitutions. The nice thing about the price system is that it is something of a self-correcting mechanism. If prices of beef go higher, people think about eating more chicken, or maybe about having a vegetarian meal or two a week. If it costs a ton to drive to work, people look at more cost-efficient ways of getting there, or possibly even consider living closer to their place of employment. When energy prices do rise dramatically, we will likely see an extra push to allow telecommuting.

On the business end of the equation, companies will need to be able to adapt to rising prices for their inputs. This may mean substituting materials where possible, but it may also simply mean having a business plan that allows for scenarios with multiple prices for commodities: even if the trend in pricing is for prices to move higher, it will not be a smooth progression, and volatility will be the name of the game over the next two decades.

Of course, the simplest thing for companies to do will be to pass on the input price increases, and we will see some of that as well—perhaps a lot of that. To some extent, the increases in prices will be in the markets where demand rises the most sharply—a global brand may impose higher prices in Beijing than it does in Chicago, for example—but inevitably there will be price increases that get shared by all consumers.

The larger question is whether the coming price inflation will prompt a policy response from central banks such as the U.S. Federal Reserve. History has shown us how destructive it is to have an ongoing cycle of rising commodity prices, rising prices, and workers demanding rising wages just to keep up. To break the cycle, it is possible that central banks will resort to tighter monetary policy and higher interest rates. When (and if) that happens is almost impossible to predict: a lot will depend on how much economic activity rises or falls with the higher commodity prices. But keep in mind that the next couple of decades will be a time when capital—another commodity, so to speak—is also in high demand and tight supply, thanks to demands from the emerging world; it is not hard to construct a scenario in which it will cost more to borrow money.

For investors, does the fact that commodity prices are headed higher make it a good sector in which to invest? As much as that should be a slam-dunk, there are a lot of other things in question besides the global price of commodities. Consider, for example, the fact that the U.S. is moving to energy self-sufficiency. This raises issues about the profitability of companies that have traditionally filled the need for U.S. energy imports. There are also implications for those countries that have traditionally exported oil to the U.S., a list that includes many in the Middle East, but Canada as well.

Investors also need to brace for more volatility in future. That will be true for the commodity sector as well as for the broader market. With higher commodity prices, the overall profitability of companies will depend on careful planning and an ability to absorb price hikes as they come. Given that none of this will happen in a smooth way, the equity markets will be in for a protracted bumpy ride—although the opportunities for big gains will also be there for those who have the acumen to find them.

THE PATH TO THE FUTURE

Forecasting anything out 20 years is fraught with risk, and forecasting commodity prices is no exception. So how can we be so sure that the trends are headed in an expensive direction? Mostly because the overriding trend is driven by demographics, and demographics is the one thing we *can* forecast pretty accurately. We know which countries' populations are growing, and we know (pretty much) how quickly. Add to that what we know about the economic direction being taken by the major parts of the world and you get a good picture of where prices are going. We may not know exactly how much those eggs or that gallon of gas will cost in 15 or 20 years, but we know that unless something changes, it is going to be a price that siphons off purchasing power from households, and has a dampening effect on consumer spending for anything that is not deemed "essential."

The thing that might prompt the most innovation and action in terms of commodity supply is simply the voice of the people who want the product. That could happen through initiatives from the public and private sectors. Governments cannot fix anything alone, but widespread support for spending on research and development, and the right policies to encourage it, could go some way toward making things happen.

The rising wealth and power of consumers in developing countries is not just creating a demand for food, it is also breeding a political voice. For now, this voice might be used to protest against the building of football stadiums in Brazil at a time when social services are inadequate, but it could easily be extended to a demand for not just more food or energy availability, but for more availability at lower prices. In the case of developed countries, the voices are likely to be even louder. In the past, the demands might have resulted in ultimately unsuccessful actions such as gas rationing or government-regulated gas prices, but hopefully lessons have been learned from those experiences.

Ultimately, the problem of a more expensive future must be solved with innovation. It has happened before and it can happen again—but it might take a leap of faith to get from here to there: for awhile, at least, we need to let the chips fall where they may. That means letting the price system operate, and making it clear that, in the absence of any change, high prices are here to stay. When that happens, there will be a clamoring for any kind of invention, big or small, that can reduce gas prices at the pump or tomato prices at the checkout line. The profit motive is a powerful one, and has traditionally been pretty effective in bringing new innovations to the fore.

(ENDNOTES)

[1] Richard Dobbs, et al., "Resource Revolution: Meeting the World's Energy, Materials, Food and Water Needs," McKinsey Global Institute, November 2011. Retrieved from http://www.mckinsey.com/insights/energy_resources_materials/resource_revolution.

[2] All prices are averaged over 15 U.S. cities. Source: U.S. Bureau of the Census, U.S. Bureau of Labor Statistics. Retrieved from http://www.infoplease.com/ipa/A0873707.html#ixzz28ptPJw00.

[3] To adjust any series into current dollars (or to "deflate" it), divide the current price into a price index such as the Consumer Price Index. The adjusted series is then in "constant" dollars (the constant year being whatever year the consumer price index is benchmarked to).

[4] The year 1915 was chosen as the starting point since it matches the first year for which data on the inflation calculator is available. Source: Bureau of Labor Statistics inflation calculator, http://www.bls.gov/data/inflation_calculator.htm.

[5] Associated Press, "UN: Farmers Must Produce 70% More Food by 2050 to Feed Population," November 28, 2011. Retrieved from http://www. theguardian.com/environment/2011/nov/28/un-farmers-produce-food-population.

[6] Derek Thompson, "How America Spends Money: 100 Years in the Life of the Family Budget," *The Atlantic*, April 5, 2012. Retrieved from http:// www.theatlantic.com/business/archive/2012/04/how-america-spends-money-100-years-in-the-life-of-the-family-budget/255475/.

[7] U.S. Bureau of Labor Statistics, "One Hundred Years of Consumer Spending." Last revised 2006. Retrieved from http://www.bls.gAov/opub/uscs/

[8] Ibid., p. 68.

[9] Data is for average crude oil prices as measured by Illinois Crude, and has been adjusted for inflation using the consumer price index as presented by the U.S. Bureau of Labor Statistics. Source: http://inflationdata.com/ Inflation/Inflation_Rate/Historical_Oil_Prices_Table.asp.

[10] James Hamilton, "Oil Shocks and Recessions," Econbrowser, April 25, 2009. Retrieved from http://www.econbrowser.com/archives/2009/04/ oil_shocks_and_1.html.

[11] United Nations, "World Population Prospects: The 2012 Revision," June 13, 2013, p. 2. Retrieved from http://esa.un.org/wpp/Documentation/pdf/ WPP2012_Press_Release.pdf.

[12] Dobbs et al.

[13] Matthew Burrows, "Global Trends 2030: Alternative Worlds," U.S. National Security Council, December 9, 2012, Kindle edition location 69.

[14] "2050: A Third More Mouths to Feed", Food and Agriculture Organization of the United Nations." Retrieved from http://www.fao.org/news/story/ en/item/35571/

[15] Colin A. Carter and Henry A. Miller, "Corn for Food Not Fuel," *New York Times*, July 30, 2012. Retrieved from http://www.nytimes.com/2012/ 07/31/opinion/corn-for-food-not-fuel.html?_r=0.

[16] R.J. Whitehead, "China Can't Keep Up With Demand for Beef, Exporters Line Up to Fillet," Food Navigator-Asia.com, August 23, 2013. Retrieved from: http://www.foodnavigator-asia.com/Markets/China-can-t-keep-up-with-demand-for-beef-exporters-line-up-to-fillet.

[17] Catherine Wolfram, "Rising Middle Class Fuels Global Energy Surge," www.bloomberg.com, January 17, 2012. Retrieved from http://www. bloomberg.com/news/2012-01-17/rising-middle-class-fuels-global-energy-surge-catherine-wolfram.html.

[18] International Energy Agency, "World Energy Outlook 2012 Factsheet," November 2012, p. 1. Retrieved from http://www.iea.org/publications/freepublications/publication/English.pdf.

[19] The idea of "peak oil" was first floated by M. King Hubbert, a geologist for Shell Oil, who predicted in 1956 that the oil output in the lower 48 states of the U.S. would peak by 1970 (a premise that was pretty much correct at the time) and conjectured that at some point the world had to reach a point of "peak oil," after which oil production would have to fall. Some put that time at the year 2005, at which point oil production did start to tail off. However, since then production has risen, and actually hit a record in 2012.

[20] International Energy Agency, p. 2.

[21] Thomas Malthus, "An Essay on the Principle of Population" (New York: Oxford University Press, 1998).

[22] Dickson Despommier, *The Vertical Farm* (New York: Thomas Dunne Books, 2010).

[23] April Dembosky, "Silicon Valley Links with Salinas Valley to Make Farming 'Smart'," *Financial Times*, June 28, 2013. Retrieved from http://www.ft.com/intl/cms/s/0/55656cf2-dff4-11e2-bf9d-00144feab7de.html#axzz2byHR4umj.

[24] CSIRO, "The Future of Farming," June 21, 2013. Retrieved from http://www.csiro.au/Organisation-Structure/Divisions/ICT-Centre/Smart-Farm-project.aspx.

[25] Matthew Burrows, "Global Trends 2030: Alternative Worlds," U.S. National Security Council, December 9, 2012, location 1242.

[26] Jerry Taylor and Peter Van Doren, "Time to Lay the 1973 Oil Embargo to Rest," Cato Institute, October 17, 2003. Retrieved from http://www.cato.org/publications/commentary/time-lay-1973-oil-embargo-rest.

[27] International Energy Agency, p. 3.

[28] John Vidal, "Food Shortages Could Force the World Into Vegetarianism," *The Guardian*, August 26, 2012. Retrieved from http://www.theguardian.com/global-development/2012/aug/26/food-shortages-world-vegetarianism.

[29] World Bank, "Africa Can Feed Itself, Earn Billions, and Avoid Food Crises by Unblocking Regional Food Trade," October 24, 2012. Retrieved from http://www.worldbank.org/en/news/press-release/2012/10/24/africa-can-feed-itself-earn-billions-avoid-food-crises-unblocking-regional-food-trade.

[31] American Coalition for Clean Coal Electricity, "Energy Cost Impact on American Families, 2002–2012," February 2012. Retrieved from: http://

www.americaspower.org/sites/default/files/Energy_Cost_Impacts_2012_
FINAL.pdf.

[32] U.S. Bureau of Labor Statistics, "Consumer Expenditures 2011," News
Release, September 25, 2012. Retrieved from http://www.bls.gov/news.
release/cesan.nr0.htm.

TREND # 8

Work Is Not a Place

In today's world, technology allows many people to work many places—a situation that sounds good on the surface but nevertheless seems to be greeted with suspicion by a large swathe of employers, employees, and would-be employees. Some employers see the benefits of allowing telecommuting and the like, while others definitely do not. Some employees like the idea of becoming freelancers, while others see it as a decision that would come with big economic repercussions. In terms of economic efficiency, the jury is still out as out as what the best practices really are.

But the time has come to make the call, and the next two decades will see it being made. The old model—in which everyone heads to work in an office at the beginning of the day and heads home at the end—is in the process of breaking down, and that will be a (mostly) good thing.

Work used to be a place—a place that people went to every day. They got up in the morning, got into some form of transportation (cars, buses, trains, subways), and made their way to the office. They stayed in the office for a regulation eight-hour day, or maybe a lot more than that, then headed home again. The next day, they did it all again. They ate at their desks, and they saw more of their office mates than their families, and they were okay with that, at least most of the time. Their employers were okay with it too, and if they were not, they fired the workers they had and got different ones.

As most of us know, this little fable is not describing something that happened in the distant past. It's a scenario that still plays out for a large number of North American workers—although not all. In fact, it happens for a lot fewer workers than ever before, and if the trends continue, it will be the paradigm for a much smaller number still.

Yes, work used to be a place. Now, however, work is changing into something that is all about getting the job done. This is a luxury that technology has given us: many jobs (although certainly not all) can be done anywhere somebody has a laptop computer, whether that's in a corporate office, a home office, an airport, or a coffee shop. This simple fact is a game changer, and its implications go well beyond worker convenience. Where people work, and how they do their jobs on a day-to-day basis, affects everything from transportation to construction, from family life to the environment, from worker retention to worker satisfaction.

So do people really need to work together in offices? Or do people just need to work? Over the next 20 years, someone is going to make the call on this ongoing debate. Right now, work is happening via a number of different models—traditional and otherwise—but a consensus is going to emerge soon, and it is likely to involve a work world that is more fractured than in the old, homogenous model. Adapting to the new model will mean adjustments to costs and attitudes, but these should ultimately benefit both workers and employers.

THE WORK AND WHERE-TO-WORK MATRIX

The work world of the future must satisfy the needs of both employers and employees. What employers need is clear enough: to be profitable. And that will come from keeping costs down and productivity high—a delicate balance.

A whirlwind of trends is affecting the workplace right now. The global economy is in the aftermath of a wide-reaching recession, and the pressure to be cost conscious and productive is prevalent across industries. Some find a solution in minimizing the number of employees they have and making up the shortfall with freelancers; some do not want to go that route. Some are happy to save office space and have everyone telecommute; some want employees where they can see them. Some want to do away with as many workers as they can and find productivity improvements through technology.

Employers need to get the work done, and they implicitly need to pay out a level of compensation that is low enough to ensure that they turn a profit at the end of the day. They need to keep their costs down, but having staff on the payroll means high fixed costs from several channels. The first is real estate—an actual building to house employees. Then you have to add in the costs of running an office—the purchase and maintenance of desks and computers and copy machines and (maybe) a cafeteria, and that's just for starters. Salaries are expensive, but so are benefits like health care, paid vacation, and pensions or matching retirement-fund contributions.

Then again, there is an argument to be made that providing a place for all employees to be together creates intangible benefits that splitting up the work and farming it out does not. In a sense, employing workers means "owning" workers, ensuring that their loyalty is not split between clients.

What workers need is also mostly straightforward. Workers need to be compensated, and compensated in different ways. At the top of the list is direct income, or some combination of income and benefits. But when choosing between employment options, other things come into the decision-making as well. Workers choose the positions that work with their lives—with their family needs, their commuting needs, their ambitions, and their level of job satisfaction.

Some employees may prefer a permanent, on-site position; others may want to be their own boss, working on projects of their own choosing; still others may wish to work off-site, regardless of whether they are full-time, contract, or freelance. Some live in fear of layoffs, having no desire to be anything but employees with benefits and a degree of security. Others are thrilled to be free agents, selling to clients, not employers. Some prefer to leave their homes and bunny slippers behind and be in an office every day. Others think it is ludicrous to waste time commuting and find they are more productive at home, where there is no guy in the next cubicle having a fight with his girlfriend on the phone or someone burning microwave popcorn in the staff kitchen.

Should employers even care what employees want? In the aftermath of a brutal recession, it is easy to say *no*. At the moment, it would seem that employees are easy enough to find in most fields, right? Wrong. Although as of the fall of 2013, the U.S. unemployment rate was still over 7 percent, employers still report having a hard time finding the right fit in terms of appropriate employees. There is a mismatch between who is available and who is needed—and that mismatch will not improve for companies that make it difficult for workers to have some say over their hours and job practices. Radical? Maybe, but the companies who are open to radical ideas may end up the economic winners.

So it comes down to this: Will the companies of the future hire workers, or will they hire people to do projects (or "gigs")? Regardless of the type of employee they hire (full-time or temporary), will they expect them to work on-site, or will they be permitted to do their work remotely? The answers to these two questions will shape how the workplace evolves over the next two decades, but also how things evolve in a larger sense.

THE GIG ECONOMY

Working used to mean being employed by a company, maybe for a very long while. The pre–baby boomer generation aspired to "gold watch" careers: you stayed at a job for two or three or even four decades, and the company rewarded you with a gold watch. Things changed a bit for the baby boomers and the Gen Xers, thanks to gyrations in the economy. Moving on to a new job after a few years was maybe not the preferred method of doing things, but it was okay and people did it.

Now we have another shift: the shift to being a freelancer, a person who lives from gig to gig, project to project. Part a consequence of economic circumstances and part a consequence of workers wanting to have better control of their time, the "gig" economy is in full swing. The movement to non-permanent work marks a structural shift in the North American economy, one that could potentially leave both employers and employees better off.

Defining exactly what we mean by the gig economy is difficult. Very roughly, you could say that gig economy participants are basically the self-employed, but that does not necessarily provide a good accounting. For example, some of those who call themselves "self-employed" and who are willing to take gigs may actually be unemployed workers in transition, particularly given that we are still in the wake of the recession. They may be willing to

> Part a consequence of economic circumstances and part a consequence of workers wanting to have better control of their time, the "gig" economy is in full swing.

work on gigs for the short term, but would be willing to take full-time employment if and when it is offered. Then there are the "self-employed" such as doctors or lawyers, many of whom are actually running small businesses and employing others and serving clients rather than taking on "gigs." Finally, the self-employed can be tomorrow's entrepreneurs, taking on small gigs one day and employing scores of others later.

There is a blurred line between what we think of as "freelance" work, on the one hand, and a "start-up," on the other. The latter tends to denote the starting phase of a business, one that will presumably get bigger and employ others over time. A freelancer, in contrast, tends to be someone who works by himself, on various gigs or projects. There is, however, some overlap. A baker who leaves the employment of a bakery to start a custom birthday cake business is, in a sense, a freelancer, but he can also be counted as a start-up, whether or not he ends up employing anyone else in future. In contrast, someone who starts his own tech firm may be the only worker in the business in the short run, but may also have every intention of building a much bigger business and doing more than accepting small projects.

The point is that there are many variables to take into account when talking about this type of work, and that fact should be kept in mind while crunching the following numbers. According to the Freelancers Union, a U.S.-based organization, one in three workers is a freelancer—meaning that there are 42 million workers in this category in the United States.[1] That's a pretty generous estimate, however, and includes everyone who has ever taken on a freelance project or assignment. In 2013, consulting company MBO Partners did a survey on what they call "independent workers" (which include those who work at least half of the time as contractors, freelancers, or consultants) and came out with a somewhat lower total of 17.7 million—a figure that represents a 20 percent gain from the 2012 number.[2]

So, who is a gig economy employee these days? Well, there are some clear trends by industry. Using data that suggest that there are about 10 million Americans who are self-employed and calling them freelancers (again, a slightly different definition), analysts at Economic Modeling Specialists suggest that 43 percent of the self-employed are what economist Richard Florida calls the "creative class" of scientists and technologists, knowledge workers and professionals, artists, designers, entertainers, and media workers.[3]

The fact that so many of the freelancers are "creative" may suggest that they are free spirits with portable skills, but it also has a lot to do with the fact that the media companies have been hit hard by the last couple of business cycles and are looking for ways to rapidly reduce costs. Think of them as a leading indicator of the rest of the economy: it might be nice to see your staff, but when it's a matter of survival, you are happy enough to have them write from home and be paid on a piecework basis.

Part of what is causing, and will continue to cause, the wave of gig workers is the fact that it is now so easy to go that route, at least in some professions. In order to bring in business, a self-employed person has to find out where it is and make the case that they are the best person for the job. In the old—pre-Internet—days, that might have been a heavy-on-the-shoe-leather ordeal, or required a lot of cold calling. Now, however, a multitude of job sites are making it much simpler for companies to post positions, and for those looking for jobs to obtain them. The website Elance.com, for example, allows those looking to hire for projects (in things like editing, graphic design, data analysis, and many more fields) to post projects of all sizes and for interested parties to bid on them.

So, given the trend toward a "looser" definition of work, the question is: In 10 or 20 years, just how much of the North American economy will be composed of freelancers? There are various estimates, but at this point it is all conjecture. It could certainly be 30 or 50 percent of all workers, but like so many things, the answer will depend on which path will provide the higher profitability for business, and presumably the better path for competitiveness. For companies, not having people on the payroll makes for less encumbered, fleeter organizations. Hiring an employee means creating a contract that might encumber you for many years. You have to find them, train them, pay them benefits, and maybe even give them a holiday party. If you fire them, they can hit you with a lawsuit suggesting that they were wronged in some way and you'll need to pay them some kind of compensation. And human resource departments, themselves a cost center, are huge parts of organizations, dealing as they do with the revolving door of bringing people in and out.

> Hiring an employee means creating a contract that might encumber you for many years. You have to find them, train them, pay them benefits, and maybe even give them a holiday party.

Hiring freelancers can also create an international workplace. If you are a small business owner in the United States and you post a job on a website like Elance.com, asking for a graphic designer to create a brochure, you will no doubt get bids from throughout the U.S., but you will also get them from Canada, Poland, Pakistan, and beyond. You can see the other work created by those doing the bidding online, and you can also compare costs. Caution may initially lead you to go with someone close, but over time you may be more open to going farther afield. Hence, many who might have been against out-sourcing (or at least never thought about it) will slowly find themselves making use of the skills and resources available throughout the world. Is that a bad thing? Well, it does mean that U.S. graphic designers have more competition, but it also means that there is a world of opportunities available to them that might not have been there before.

Will being a gig employee become the new cool thing to do, and will traditional employees be viewed with something akin to pity by those who do not go that route? That's not a certain outcome. The whole idea of not working "for" a company tends to be viewed with suspicion on both sides, or at least it does by those who have not tried it. Corporations are routinely chastised for trying to keep some workers on contract (and thus avoid paying benefits), and many gig employees crave the security of a "real" job. Then again, some companies feel strongly that they need committed people who are willing to be "part of the team" for longer than it takes to complete a project.

However it may change in future, at the moment being a freelancer typically means having a lower income than if you were a full-time employee. A survey by the Freelancers Union found that 58 percent of their members made less than $50,000 a year, and that 29 percent made less than $25,000. Twelve percent of their members used food stamps during the recession.[4] (Keep in mind, however, that the actual membership of the Freelancers Union is slightly under 224,000, and its membership might skew toward lower-income earners).

But from the point of view of freelancers, there are benefits as well. You are your own boss, so to speak. Working for a large corporation (in a cubicle or out) means adhering to a lot of fairly tedious things. Want to take a holiday? Check with the office manager, and be prepared for a *no*. Want to do three 12-hour shifts and then take four days off? That doesn't work either. Of course, in reality, many freelancers work just as many hours as employees and have an even harder time scheduling time off, but at least they are doing it for themselves, not for a company in which they have no equity. And then there is the money part of it. A freelancer or contract employee does not get benefits, so in theory can ask for a higher per-day wage—and quite possibly get it.

There is some evidence that the latest wave of self-employed men and women are choosing to be out on their own, as opposed to being forced into it. According to a study[5] by the Canadian Imperial Bank of Commerce (CIBC), only 20 percent of those who formed businesses over the past few years can be considered "forced" self-employed, which is a markedly lower proportion than following the recessions in the early 1990s and early 2000s. They are better educated too: one in three had a university degree, double the rate seen in 1990. Now, Canada has experienced a fairly robust labor market following the Great Recession, so it is possible that the Canadian statistics do not apply to the United States or to other countries. The conclusions from the Canadian case do apply, however: in a strong economy where it would be possible to get a "real" job, people are still choosing to be out on their own.

There may also be a generational bent to rising self-employment numbers. As the baby boomers stream out of the "real" labor market and look for something else to do—particularly something that makes money—many may turn to the gig economy. In the CIBC study, baby boomers were responsible for close to 30 percent of the start-ups. A 2009 U.S. study by the Kauffman Foundation showed the same trend: in the preceding decade, the highest rate of entrepreneurial activity was in the 55- to 64-year-old age group.[6] This could be a positive development on many fronts. Boomers as a group are chronically unprepared for retirement, so having an ongoing income stream will be a big plus. In a broader sense, this trend would also serve to keep their skills in the labor force, even as they leave the corporate world.

But what about younger employees? Does the gig economy work for them too? It certainly could. Generation Y and Z did not grow up in (or, in the case of Gen Z, are not growing up in) a world where corporations are revered or looked upon as dependable sources of employment over the long term. They also understand very well the capabilities of technology. There may be a natural fit with the gig economy, although it will be interesting to see how it plays out. For many of the most successful gig economy participants, the path started with working in a more structured environment and then taking their skills on the road. Generations Y and Z may take that route, or may skip that step altogether and look for ways to be gig economy participants from the word *go*. That would be a key step in the evolution of the broader economy: if participants *choose* to be gig economy participants rather than feel they are forced into it, the trend will be a much bigger one than many had anticipated.

What are the consequences of a world of free agents? If the economy is moving to a place where more people are free agents, perhaps it is time to embrace that and to create the kind of education that gives new graduates the skills to manage being on their own, whatever their field. That means teaching time management, budgeting, bookkeeping, marketing, and other skills necessary for running a small business. (It is not a far-fetched idea: training along these lines is done quite routinely in medical schools, where graduating doctors are given at least some cursory guidance in how to manage independent practices. Perhaps this kind of "manage yourself" education needs to be given routinely in all high schools and colleges, in acknowledgment of the way that the economy is changing.)

And what about benefits, the crown jewel for many full-time, traditional jobs? Some gold-plated union positions may still offer dental care, prescription drug benefits, life insurance, and "free" massages (among other things), but for most people that kind of benefits package is no longer on the table. It can, however, still be available. Private insurance packages of all kinds already exist, although younger people have typically been unaware or uninterested in them. That needs to change. A 22-year-old recent graduate may consider it weird to be buying any kind of insurance package, but if that person eventually finds herself to be a 35-year-old freelancer with a family, she will be very glad that she did. It will be a challenge informing young graduates that they need to think along these lines, but just as grads are routinely offered credit cards and sold new cars, a business opportunity exists to teach them to think like business owners.

Telecommuters Versus On-Site Employees

It's a bit of an adjustment, realizing that work is something that you must do, not a place that you have to go to. Of course, for some people this distinction is a moot point. A doctor treating emergencies must do so in an ER, not from her bedroom while still in her pajamas. A construction worker has to be on-site, not at a Starbucks. But for many people, work can be done anywhere there is a computer. So the question becomes one of convenience and value: Does it make sense to have employees in an office, where everyone can work together and feed off each other's ideas? Or is there a greater benefit to the savings and flexibility that comes with having employees working from home? Employees and employers are both struggling to answer these questions, from their own perspectives, and there are no easy answers—at least not right now. Regardless, the debate will have a huge impact on the work world over the next two decades.

At issue is "telecommuting" (a term coined by a U.S. Air Force rocket scientist in 1973), and whether it makes sense for either employees or employers. Telecommuting typically means working for a company, but not on-site. It is a fairly widespread practice these days. According to a 2013 Harris Poll, one in 10 U.S. workers who are not self-employed work exclusively from home, 8 percent spend half their time working at home, and a further 17 percent spend some time working at home (figures do not include those who work primarily on-site but do extra work upon returning home).[7] Statistics Canada found that just over 11 percent of employees worked at home as of 2008.[8]

So, is telecommuting good for employees? There are lots of reasons why employees like to telecommute, the chief one being that it saves them the wasted time of what is often a long and tedious commute. The average U.S. worker commutes 25.5 minutes each way to work, although 8 percent commute one hour or more.[9] But the list of "pros" goes on. Telecommuting lets employees live where they want (maybe thousands of miles away from the office), perhaps in areas where real estate is less costly than near the office. They get to juggle their schedules as they see fit, perhaps working an "early shift" to allow them to see a child's school play later in the day. They save commuting costs, and they have to buy fewer work clothes and lunches out. Not surprisingly, survey after survey shows that telecommuters love their arrangements.[10]

But whether or not *employers* love telecommuting is the real question, as is whether they will love it over the next 20 years or so: after all, it is the employers who ultimately make the policies, whatever might be the desires of workers. On a straight productivity basis, numerous studies show that working off-site can facilitate getting things done more efficiently. One study, by economists at Stanford University, looked at the results of a work-at-home experiment at a NASDAQ-listed travel agency in China. Employees were randomly assigned to either work from home or in the office for nine months, and the results in terms of productivity were analyzed. The at-home workers had a 13 percent increase in performance compared to the at-work employees, and also took fewer sick days and breaks. The workers loved it so much the company gave others the option to do the same thing—

> A study by economists at Stanford University looked at the results of a work-at-home experiment at a NASDAQ-listed travel agency in China. At-home workers had a 13 percent increase in performance compared to the at-work employees, and also took fewer sick days and breaks.

and ultimately saw a 22 percent increase in total productivity when over half of its employees switched.[11]

Anecdotally, we are seeing many examples of how this works in North America. During the 2010 Winter Olympics, hosted by Vancouver, the organizers asked various companies, including Telus, to try to minimize the number of workers that had to enter the core of the city during each day of the Games. The company acquiesced and arranged to have workers telecommute. The net result? The workers loved it, and the company eventually decided that they did too—so much so that Telus is now working toward having 70 percent of its workforce telecommuting by 2015.[12] It is a money saver for them (fewer people on-site means lower overhead costs) and a proven way to retain workers.[13]

So why *not* love telecommuting? And why the backlash against it? The case study on that seems to come from Yahoo. "We need to be one Yahoo!, and that starts with physically being together," read the memo from Jackie Reses, head of human resources at the U.S. tech giant.[14] The memo was sent out in February 2013, seven months after new CEO Marissa Mayer took the helm. Mayer had already made waves by being young (37), female (a rarity in the higher echelons of the tech sector), and pregnant at the time she was chosen for her position (pretty much unheard of for CEOs). In a business sense, however, her decision on telecommuting might ultimately make the biggest waves of all.

Telling Yahoo employees to get back to the office was a big deal. Although only a couple hundred employees officially worked from home at the time,[15] many more had informal arrangements to come in and leave according to their own schedules. This was not unusual; telecommuting was an established part of the larger culture of Silicon Valley. But there were things about the work-at-home arrangements that reportedly made Mayer uneasy. Entire parking lots at Yahoo head office were supposedly empty during the day, which might have been okay if the company was doing swimmingly.

That was not the case, though, at least judging from the company's financials as compared to others in the industry. (At the time of Mayers' decision, employees at Apple were producing 6.5 times more revenue per employee than Yahoo, Facebook, three times more, and Google, double.[16]) There seemed to be a need for a dramatic—and, hopefully, effective—move by the new CEO.

"Some of the best decisions and insights come from hallway and cafeteria discussions, meeting new people and impromptu team meetings," read Reses's infamous memo. "Speed and quality are often sacrificed when we work from home."[17] Reses did not use the word *innovation*, but that is what is really at the heart of Yahoo's argument. If companies are to become profitable and if the economy is to blast through modest growth, we can't just build better mouse-traps; we must invent products that are completely different from mousetraps (or maybe convince the mice that they need tablets).

Those innovative products do tend to result when groups of people get together, rather than during independent work. The invention of the Post-it note is one example. The technology for the low-stick adhesive had been around for years without inventor 3M being able to find a particularly profitable thing to do with it. It was only when an engineer named Art Fry heard about it at a seminar in 1973 that things took off. He got the brain wave that it could be useful in stopping his bookmarks from falling out of his hymnal when he sang in his church's choir. He proposed the idea of putting the adhesive on paper and creating Post-its, and a classic was born.[18]

It is hard to argue with the fact that innovation brings in profit. Apple is the prime example of this—a company that spends heav- ily on research and development and moves through product cycles quickly, trashing and adapting as necessary.[19] Professor John Sullivan of San Francisco State University calls Apple a "serial innovator," and credits the fact that employees generally do not telecommute, but rather are forced to be together. Sullivan believes that Yahoo's decision is appropriate, and could improve profitability by 10 to 20 percent. He asserts: "Innovation will trump productivity or efficiency every time."[20] Others have observed this "water cooler effect" in other industries as well. One study, by Isaac Kohane of Harvard Medical School, examined data from 35,000 biomedical papers published between 1999 and 2003, looking at how many citations (a standard way to gauge article quality) each garnered. Those with the most personal contact between article authors collected the most citations. That is, even though scientists thousands of miles away from each other were able to communicate and write papers, the "best" papers were written by those who were geographically close to each other.[21]

But innovation isn't the only concern when it comes to telecommuting. "If you can't see them, how do you know that they are not goofing off?" seems to be a common way of thinking. In more sophisticated terms, most management structures still run on the old "face time" structure. And face time counts for employees too: for those seeking the highest rungs of the ladder in any company, showing up still matters, and the more you show up the higher you are likely to climb. In that sense, telecommuting really is not compatible with the kind of workforce culture now prevalent in North America. Working very long hours is a hallmark of many industries, including law, high-tech, and investment banking. At Facebook, managers proudly talk about putting employees on "lockdown" for five-hour meetings, or having a hammock and sleeping bags around for when employees are really "excited" about projects and want to sleep in the office.[22]

As to where telework goes from here, somewhere over the next few years the pieces have to fall into place and a consensus of sorts be reached. An early voice in the debate was Sir Richard Branson, the flamboyant founder of Virgin Group Ltd. "Old-school thinking," said Sir Richard of the Yahoo decision, bragging that Virgin did not force people to be in the office all day, and that "in 30 years' time, as technology moves forward even further, people are going to look back and wonder why offices ever existed."[23] But for every Sir Richard there is someone like Michael Bloomberg, former mayor of New York and founder and part owner of Bloomberg LLP, who calls telecommuting "one of the dumber ideas I've ever heard."[24] Others may put things in more tactful terms, but the fact is that many companies who experimented with telecommuting— a list that includes Pixar, Best Buy, Bank of America, and Google— are now ordering their employees back to work.

THE LARGER QUESTIONS FOR THE ECONOMY

If we do end up with a "fractured" workforce, what will that mean for the larger economy? There are several areas in which the new model will have a significant impact.

Overall Economic Efficiency and Competitiveness

Whether telecommuting or a gig-type economy will ultimately lead to higher economic efficiency and thus boost competitiveness is really at the crux of the matter. If so, we should be doing everything we can to encourage it; unfortunately, however, the evidence is not exactly clear.

One analysis on the subject was done by BCA Research, which looked at the economy of the United Kingdom. What they found was that in the aftermath of the recession, there was a significant increase in hours worked and employment, but not in overall economic output. The explanation, in their view, was that the work was being done by freelancers, who were putting in a lot of time and not getting a lot back for their efforts in monetary terms.[25] As a result, the value of economic output in the U.K. was lower than would have been the case had employees done the work, meaning that measured productivity was on the decline. This is in contrast to the situation following other recessions, when productivity has tended to rise. A similar pattern of low productivity can be seen across other countries (including Canada and the United States) in the post-recession period, raising some question about freelancers and whether they are ultimately effective for the macroeconomy.

It remains to be seen whether the gig economy ends up being more or less lucrative for its participants. We are still in the very early days of the transition from the more traditional economic structure. People may not be working as efficiently as they could be, and those who have been forced into the situation could still be looking for new full-time employment. Later gig workers may feel and work differently.

There has been little work done on whether telecommuting is good for the macroeconomy rather than for individual companies. If it frees up people from having to commute and use resources (such as time and gas) getting to work, it should certainly have some positive benefits. However, if it makes companies less effective and productive (which is essentially the argument being made by Yahoo and others) then that would not be the case. The eventual answer to how positive things turn out to be will depend in large part on the way companies handle the situation.

Real Estate Patterns

The whole North American urban planning network is based to some extent on people living close to their jobs. Some workers choose to live in a downtown core, close to an office (causing condos and high-rises to spring up all over the place). Others might prefer the suburbs, which in turn means having transit built and available. If people choose to live even farther out and drive in to work, it means building more and more highways. All choices require public spending to support the work model chosen by employers and the housing decisions chosen by employees.

If fewer and fewer people work in the offices of the people who are employing them, there could be a significant impact on real estate prices. In places like Paolo Alto, California (home of Yahoo), real estate is massively expensive (as of the summer of 2013, the average price of a home was $1.6 million).[26] A model that allows people to live farther away could put downward pressure on prices—although allowing them to do so and then changing your mind would have the opposite effect.

Of course, some would make the argument that telecommuting (and perhaps the gig economy) increases "urban sprawl." After all, if you do not have to be at work in a downtown office, then you can choose a house farther away from the core but presumably still within an hour or two from where your company is likely located. Although there has not been a lot of work done on that subject, it was first raised in a paper by Jack Nilles in 1991, when he conjectured that there was likely going to be a connection between the two. Nilles updated his research again in 2013, concluding that the effect had ended up being a "wash," and that while some telecommuters moved closer to work, others moved farther away.[27] As this next wave of telecommuting takes place, however, it will be interesting to see if the historical patterns hold.

And what of the potential impact on commercial real estate? Fewer people commuting and fewer people working on more than just a project at a time will translate into a much smaller demand for office space, and, in particular, for downtown office space. That could have big implications for rental prices, as well as for the construction industry.

The Environment

The work world as we know it is bad for the environment in a lot of ways. There is the amount of gas used to get to work, and there is everything that goes along with building and heating and running offices. The carbon footprint associated with an "everybody in the office" model is very high compared to having more people off-site. A study by Global Workplace Analytics found that half-time telecommuting could reduce carbon emissions by over 51 million metric tons a year—about the same as the savings from taking all of New York's commuters off the roads.[28] Another study, this one from the National Resources Defense Council, found that a modest expansion of telecommuting could save Americans a total of $1.9 billion annually and reduce oil demand by 20 million barrels per year[29]—the latter being a pretty significant consideration for a nation that wishes to achieve oil self-sufficiency.

Given all of that, is there a role for either government policy or social pressure to allow for more off-site and telecommuting? The facts at least frame the debate in a different way than is usually the case. Very often, telecommuting is seen as a "family-friendly" policy, a frill that is good for employees but not for companies and certainly not for the economy as a whole. When you add in the environmental considerations, however, you see that this is not the case at all, and that, in fact, from a macroeconomic perspective there is a reason to support telework—and perhaps to even tax the companies who do not promote it.

Labor Force Participation Rates

The prospect of a less rigid labor force might have its drawbacks, but if it is appealing to those who might have dropped out of the workplace otherwise, it could go some way to solving another labor force problem—declining participation rates and labor shortages.

Admittedly, those problems are not widespread in the aftermath of a brutal recession, and it seems that companies are okay with implementing policies—such as a requirement that all workers be on-site—that might not be optimum in terms of employee satisfaction. But even if labor shortages are not expected across all industries, we are nonetheless heading into an era where there will be shortages in some areas. Creating an economy where a "one size fits all" policy is not in force may be a good way to increase labor force participation rates in the years ahead.

To put it in simpler terms: working and commuting is hard on parents, and telecommuting can make a whole lot of difference as to whether they (and mothers in particular) want to work for a specific company, or work at all. In the past few years, we have seen a kind of "brain drain" of highly educated women who throw in the towel and leave the (inhospitable) workplace all together. It is a problem for the companies who have trained them, but it is a larger problem for an economy that will increasingly need to retain high-quality labor in the face of baby boomer retirements. If allowing people to work at least part of the time at home would go some ways to remedying that situation, this is yet another reason to encourage the policy.

Monetary Policy

A sustained movement to a gig-type economy could pose significant challenges in the setting of monetary policy. For the past several years, the U.S. Federal Reserve and other central banks have closely monitored the unemployment rate, formally or informally targeting a level that is consistent with "enough" jobs. Only when the economy gets to that point, or close to it, can they stop tailoring interest rate and monetary policy to send economic activity purposely higher. But what happens when employment is not the best metric to use, because a large proportion of people do not have a single employer? Including self-employment in the number crunching could work, but given the wide definition of the term, that might not be the best measure. It may be necessary to look at whether the jobs that exist provide incomes at or above a certain level, or to choose other benchmarks altogether.

Income Distribution

As much as a gig economy world may offer freedom and perhaps even higher incomes to some, it also raises the possibility of a worsening situation in terms of income distribution. If, say, a hospital likes the gig formula and choose to pay per project rather than per employee, it might work out just fine for the surgeon who comes in to perform a few high-paying operations a week. It may not work out nearly as well for the janitor who is told he can be paid per shift, when available, but cannot expect to be put on a permanent payroll.

In sports, unions benefit average players more than they do the stars who can negotiate much higher salaries on their own. That's true of labor unions too. These days, unionization is not much in fashion, but just having an employment contract makes a big difference to a lot of people. It means job security and benefits and a protected way of life. Taking that away will throw many people who would prefer not to be free agents to the wolves. At any level of education and income, those without good management and sales skills will find the new world harder to navigate. At the lower end of the skills pool, things will be particularly difficult, and intense income disadvantages could result.

Government

And yes, there is a role for government in all of this. Canada's socialized health network and initiatives like "Obamacare" in the U.S. actually work quite well in a world where employers will increasingly be checking out of the benefits business. It is a matter of public debate to decide just how big a role government should play.

A NEW KIND OF WORK WORLD

In a changing work world, what is likely to become of that traditional model, the gold-watch job that comes with benefits, a regular paycheck, and a degree of security? It will still exist—in some form, for some people—but not everyone will want or be able to access that model. We are moving into an era of at-arm's-length relationships with our employers (at best), or perhaps even to becoming a world of freelancers. There is no doubt that this will change the world as we know it. But will those changes be good, bad, or a mixture of both? Only time will tell.

(ENDNOTES)

[1] Freelancers Union. http://www.freelancersunion.org.

[2] MBO Partners, "The State of Independence in America," Third Annual Independent Workforce Report, September 2013. Retrieved from http://www.mbopartners.com/state-of-independence/independent-workforce-index.html.

[3] Richard Florida, "The Geography of America's Freelance Workers," *The Atlantic Cities*, February 25, 2013. Retrieved from http://www.theatlanticcities.com/jobs-and-economy/2013/02/geography-americas-freelance-economy/4118/.

[4] Steven Greenhouse, "Tackling Concerns of Independent Workers," *New York Times*, March 23, 2013. Retrieved from http://www.nytimes.com/2013/03/24/business/freelancers-union-tackles-concerns-of-independent-workers.html?pagewanted=all&_r=0.

[5] Benjamin Tal, "Start-Ups—Present and Future," *In Focus*, CIBC, September 25, 2012. Retrieved from http://www.freelancersunion.org/http://research.cibcwm.com/economic_public/download/if_2012-0925.pdf.

[6] Dane Stangler, "The Coming Entrepreneurship Boom," Ewing Marion Kauffman Foundation, June 2009, Retrieved from http://www.kauffman.org/uploadedFiles/the-coming-entrepreneurial-boom.pdf.

[7] Rick Hampson, "The work-from-home tug of war," *USA Today*, March 11, 2013. Retrieved from http://www.usatoday.com/story/news/nation/2013/03/11/the-work-from-home-tug-of-war/1979457/.

[8] Martin Turcotte, "Working at Home: An Update," *Canadian Social Trends*, Statistics Canada, Catalogue Number 11-008-X, December 7, 2010. Retrieved from http://www.statcan.gc.ca/pub/11-008-x/2011001/article/11366-eng.htm.

[9] Larry Copeland, "Americans' Commutes Aren't Getting Longer," *USA Today*, March 5, 2013. Retrieved from: http://www.usatoday.com/story/news/nation/2013/03/05/americans-commutes-not-getting-longer/1963409/.

10 For example, a 2013 survey by Staples Inc. found that when telecommuting was allowed, 75 percent of business decision-makers noticed happier employees, and 37 percent reported less absenteeism. Retrieved from http://staplesadvantage.newshq.businesswire.com/press-release/staples-advantage/survey-shows-telecommuting-provides-better-worklife-balance-benefits.

11 Nicholas Bloom et al., "Does Working from Home Work?: Evidence from a Chinese Study," Stanford, February 22, 2013. Retrieved from http://www.stanford.edu/~nbloom/WFH.pdf.

12 Omar El Akkad and Suzanne Bowness, "Telework or Teamwork? Yahoo and the Evolution of the Office," *Globe and Mail*, February 26, 2013. Retrieved from http://www.theglobeandmail.com/report-on-business/careers/the-future-of-work/telework-or-teamwork-yahoo-and-the-evolution-of-the-office/article9099573/.

13 For a discussion on how companies including Cisco and Best Buy have used telecommuting to retain workers, see Joel Kotkin, "Marissa Mayers' Misstep and the Unstoppable Rise of Telecommuting," *Forbes*, March 26, 2013. Retrieved from http://www.forbes.com/sites/joelkotkin/2013/03/26/marissa-mayers-misstep-and-the-unstoppable-rise-of-telecommuting/.

14 El Akkad and Bowness.

15 Claire Cain Miller and Nicole Perlroth, "Yahoo Says New Policy Is Meant to Raise Morale," *New York Times*, March 5, 2013. Retrieved from http://www.nytimes.com/2013/03/06/technology/yahoos-in-office-policy-aims-to-bolster-morale.html?pagewanted=all&_r=0.

16 John Sullivan, "How Yahoo's Decision to Stop Telecommuting Will Increase Innovation," www.ere.net, February 26, 2013. Retrieved from http://www.ere.net/2013/02/26/how-yahoos-decision-to-stop-telecommuting-will-increase-innovation/.

17 El Akkad and Bowness.

18 Daven Hiskey, "Post-it Notes Were Invented by Accident," www.todayIfound out.com. Retrieved from http://www.todayifoundout.com/index.php/2011/11/post-it-notes-were-invented-by-accident/.

19 For more discussion, see http://www.mercurynews.com/breaking-news/ci_16703362?nclick_check=1&forced=true.

20 John Sullivan, "How Yahoo's Decision to Stop Telcommuting Will Increase Innovation," February 26, 2013, www.ere.net. Retrieved from http://www.ere.net/2013/02/26/how-yahoos-decision-to-stop-telecommuting-will-increase-innovation.

21 Debra Bradley Ruder, "The Water Cooler Effect," *Harvard Magazine*, May-June 2011. Retrieved from http://harvardmagazine.com/2011/05/water-cooler-effect.

22 David Zax, "How Facebook Survived 34 Intense Days of 'Lockdown' to Build Grap Search," *Fast Company*, January 29, 2013. Retrieved from http://www.fastcompany.com/3005165/how-facebook-survived-34-intense-days-lockdown-build-graph-search.

23 Richard Branson, "One Day Offices Will be a Thing of the Past," virgin.com blog, March 4, 2013. Retrieved from http://www.virgin.com/richard-branson/one-day-offices-will-be-a-thing-of-the-past.

24 "Mayor Bloomberg Agrees with Marissa Mayer, Says Telecommuting is Dumb,"nbcnewyork.com, March 1, 2013. Retrieved from http://www.nbcnewyork.com/news/local/Bloomberg-Telecommuting-Dumb-Marissa-Mayer-Yahoo-Working-from-Home-194318371.html.

25 Buttonwood, "Go Freelance and Work Harder: But Will You Work Better?" Buttonwood's notebook, *The Economist*, July 15, 2013. Retrieved from http://www.economist.com/blogs/buttonwood/2013/07/work-and-growth.

26 "Palo Alto market trends," trulia.com. Retrieved from http://www.trulia.com/real_estate/Palo_Alto-California/market-trends/.

27 Jack Nilles, "Urban Sprawl Revisited," JALA Thoughts, July 29, 2013. Retrieved from http://www.jalahq.com/blog/?p=448.

28 Joel Kotkin, "Marissa Mayer's Misstep and the Unstoppable Rise of Telecommuting," *Forbes*, March 26, 2013. Retrieved from http://www.forbes.com/sites/joelkotkin/2013/03/26/marissa-mayers-misstep-and-the-unstoppable-rise-of-telecommuting/.

29 Justin Horner, "Telework: Saving Gas and Reducing Traffic from the Comfort of Your Home," NRDC, March 2011, Retrieved from http://www.mobilitychoice.org/MCtelecommuting.pdf.

Challenging Financial Markets

The bull markets were fun, the roller coaster was scary, and the bear market—if that's what it is—is not a blast either. The financial markets have gone from a place where people could relatively easily take care of their futures to one where it seems pretty challenging to make any money. Over the coming decade things will continue to be challenging, but you can make gains in any market as long as you have the correct knowledge regarding the ways that the world is changing.

An understanding of demographics is one tool for dealing with the financial markets; an understanding of the broader global environment is another. Putting those things together can go a long way toward helping investors feel that they are in control of their financial future, rather than at the mercy of circumstances beyond their control.

"The United States has developed a new weapon that destroys people but leaves buildings standing," joked comedian Jay Leno. "It's called the stock market." The audience laughed, but it probably wasn't all that funny to a lot of them. Leno made his joke in October 2008, a particularly tumultuous time for the markets, but hardly a month in isolation. Since the official end of the Great Recession, in 2009, there have been many weeks in which a roller-coaster ride in the financial markets has left many wary, or maybe more like terrified. After all, it was not that long ago (as recently as 2007, actually) that you could put your money into a government savings bond and get a return of at least 4 or 5 percent. Alternatively, you could put your money into the equity market and, for your extra risk, have a good prospect of making decent returns, perhaps for your retirement. Rationally or not, at the moment, a lot of people are now wondering whether any of these things will be true again.

The good news is that people can and will be able to make money in whatever kind of financial markets are ahead. What it will take to do so, however, is a more specialized knowledge base that comes from understanding the big picture and continuously learning about the changing environment. The shifting demographics of North America and of the developed world mean a challenging investment landscape, but not an impossible one: the gains may not be as easy to achieve as they once were, but the potential is still there, even in twisted financial times.

THE PATH OF INTEREST RATES

In the years following the Great Recession, the developed world has gotten used to bargain-basement interest rates. In fact, interest rates are so low, and look to remain low for so long, that a kind of complacency has set in in many areas. In the United States, the benchmark federal funds rate targeted by the Federal Reserve was 5.25

percent at the end of 2006; in a bid to prop up a weakening U.S. economy, it was cut to 3.25 percent by the summer of 2008. Then, following the collapse of Lehman Brothers in 2008 and the prospect of an economy that could rapidly spiral downward, the Federal Reserve cut the rate to effectively zero within a few months. As of 2013, it seemed in no hurry to put it back to "normal" levels. Many parts of the world, including Canada, the United Kingdom, Europe, and parts of Asia, have also felt the need to maintain generationally low interest rates even years after "recessions" have officially ended.

On the plus side, a low cost of capital encourages investment and risk taking, which is ultimately positive for any economy. Of course, there is such a thing as too much of a good thing: the dot.com bubble of the late '90s and the housing-market bubble in the years following are each arguably the result of leaving interest rates too low for too long. As well, low interest rates are typically seen as a negative by those investors who want to take minimal risks. Socking your money away in a U.S. Treasury bond may make sense from a risk minimization standpoint, but it does not give you much of a return when a five-year Treasury bond yields close to zero.

Arguably, central banks have played the largest role in driving interest rates down to the lows seen in recent years. As the economic crisis deepened from 2008 onward, central banks continuously cut their target interest rates as a way to keep economic activity going. With the weakness persisting throughout the global economy, it seems as if it will be years before interest rates move higher.

However, central banks can only do so much to influence interest rates. Market interest rates are set when securities are bought and sold. For example, a country can float bonds in the market to try to finance its borrowing needs but it cannot set the effective rate that investors are willing to pay for its bonds. We saw this recently when European countries, like Greece, tried to issue debt in 2011 and 2012. Although the European Central Bank rate was close to zero at the time, countries within Europe frequently had to pay double-digit returns to get lenders interested in buying their securities.

Before we get to where interest rates are likely to go in future, let's back up a bit and look at how interest rates have moved over the past few decades. In fact, world interest rates have been moving down for decades, and it has had nothing to do with the world being in recession. "Real[1]" interest rates in the G7 countries peaked in the early 1980s and have basically been on a downward trajectory ever since.

On the supply side, one explanation that has often been given for the low rates is the theory of the "global savings glut." U.S. Federal Reserve Chairman Ben Bernanke coined the phrase in a 2005 speech.[2] Discussing how the U.S. was able to finance a very large current account deficit (the difference between everything bought by the U.S. and everything sold by the U.S.), he gave credit to the fact that there were countries in the world with aging populations and high savings rates, and that capital was able to offset the low savings pool in the United States.

To an extent, the facts bear him out. American consumers were not saving much (at the time of Mr. Bernanke's speech, the personal savings rate in the U.S. had actually headed into negative territory)[3], and nor was the U.S. government, which was firmly in the red. Corporations, however, had started to hoard cash. Worldwide, there was also a lot of money sloshing around. China, in particular, was experiencing a huge investment boom, and a surge in commodity prices was filling the coffers of commodity-producing countries, including Canada, as well as oil producers such as Saudi Arabia and Russia. So there was cash in the world available to finance capital projects.

Other analyses dispute the fact that there ever was much of a savings glut, and instead make the argument that the low interest rates were the result of weak global demand for capital. An analysis by the McKinsey Global Institute, for example, suggests that the developed nations have seen such a drawdown. According to their calculations, the investment rate (investment as a share of gross domestic product, or GDP) of mature economies has plummeted since the 1970s.[4] That fits with what we know about economic history. During the 1950s and '60s, the U.S. and other developed countries had to invest heavily to deal with the loss of infrastructure following World War II. In addition, North America and Europe had young and growing populations that needed infrastructure, schools, and commercial buildings. Over the last 40 years or so, however, demand has largely slowed. According to McKinsey's calculations, the demand for capital would have been $20 trillion less if the investment rate had stayed stable.[5]

Given all of that, what is the likely path of interest rates? Let's start with the supply side of things. We know that the developed world is aging, as is much of the developing world. If the usual behaviors hold, this means that there will be fewer "savers" in the world, and a small pool of savings. That suggests that there will be a smaller pool of capital worldwide, which in turn means higher interest rates. North America can get a sneak peek into the future by looking at Japan, or at countries in Europe, several of which are ahead on the aging curve. As Japan's population has aged, the private savings rate (expressed as a percentage of gross domestic product) has declined from 8 percent in 1991 to 3 percent as of 2009.[6]

Despite the low savings rates in the developed world, a high savings rate in China could keep the global pool of savings relatively high. As of 2008, Chinese households had a 23 percent savings rate, while government, businesses, and households also had positive net savings. In fact, in 2008, nearly one in every four dollars saved worldwide came from China.[7] The country is rapidly industrializing and spending on investment, to the point that it has accounted for 40 percent of its GDP in recent years.[8] It has long been a necessity for households to save at that rate: unlike the situation in other more developed countries, China has not had a social safety net to cover such things as pensions and health. Those things are in the works, however, which means that the imperative to save is being diminished. In addition, although China's growth has to date largely come through exports, there is now a push to make it more domestically oriented. In turn, this will be another reason for Chinese savings to fall—and for the world supply of capital to go with it. There is a similar situation in India, where the young population and rapidly growing middle class are a potential source of capital, but not an unlimited one.

On the demand side, a new appetite for capital from the developing world is going to be a major issue. Despite the expected decline in China's savings rate, it is likely that the country's demand for capital will only increase. As mentioned above, China has already moved forward with a massive push to improve infrastructure (partly as economic stimulus following the global crisis) as well as a gigantic building program. But China is not done with the investments and will continue to spend heavily for years to come. India, another country with huge potential but weak infrastructure, will also try to move forward, as will other emerging countries. To some extent, this push for more capital may be offset by weaker demand from the developed countries as they move into a lower growth trajectory, but it will not be enough to completely offset the higher demand from the developing world.

So when will the supply of capital be inadequate to satisfy the demand? The Organisation for Economic Co-operation and Development (OECD) calculates that until about 2030, the global savings rate will remain about constant, meaning that there will not be a fall in the quantity of global capital.[9] From that point on, however, the trend will reverse and world's capital supply will fall.

The net effect? Higher demand means higher prices, which in this case means higher real interest rates. The demand pressures for capital emanating from the developing world will be similar to the higher demand expected for resources such as oil and wheat and copper. Countries that were decidedly poor are developing a middle class, and that middle class is demanding more of the things that typically go with the "good life." That could mean air conditioning in the summer or a diet that includes more protein, but it could also mean capital to finance home purchases or to finance new businesses. In many ways, this will be a positive thing. For one thing, higher economic activity in the developing world will create a market for products and services from the developed world. But the supply and demand trends are fairly easy to understand, and they point to a higher cost of capital for households around the world.

> The demand pressures for capital emanating from the developing world will be similar to the higher demand expected for resources such as oil and wheat and copper. Countries that were decidedly poor are developing a middle class, and that middle class is demanding more of the things that typically go with the "good life."

The final wildcard when it comes to interest rates is inflation. As a way to kick-start their economies, central banks throughout the world have kept interest rates at historic lows and expanded their monetary bases. We know that such actions have historically led to inflation, which shows up as a component of interest rates (as it did, notably, in the 1970s and '80s). The way to guard against this would be to let interest rates rise gradually, but with the labor markets in the United States and Europe (and, to a lesser degree, Canada) still quite weak, the banks seem happy to move cautiously. Their reluctance to raise rates may indeed be the correct economic decision. They may rejuvenate their respective economies without triggering any price pressures and then let interest rates rise slowly over a period of time. If, however, it looks like the inflation genie is out of the bottle, the banks may be forced to raise rates much more aggressively and over a shorter period of time.

If we are looking at a 20- or 30-year time horizon, it is wildly speculative to talk about exactly where interest rates are going. But here's what we do know: the interest rates that North Americans have enjoyed over the past few years are the result of a perfect storm of factors that is slowly but surely reversing. In the short term, interest rates will rise as central banks reverse policy from one of crisis to one more compatible with modest growth. In the longer term—the period after 2030, give or take a few years— interest rates will rise further because there will be a major pull on capital and an inadequate supply. Will there be many gyrations in the interim, sending rates up, down, and everywhere in between? Absolutely. But if you are taking a look at the long-term picture, it may be helpful to know that real interest rates have about a decade and a half where the bias is to stay low; after that point, the will bias will be toward going higher.

EQUITIES—TREATING DEMOGRAPHICS AS A TOOL, NOT DESTINY

In an ideal world, there would be strong economic growth everywhere, which in theory would lift the equity markets. After all, an economy in which gross domestic product is rising rapidly is by definition one in which there is a lot of spending and a lot of activity. In that kind of situation, you could assume that companies—the ones that own the stores where people buy things and the restaurants where they eat; the ones that make the cars they drive or import the toys their kids play with—are also doing well and making profits. High profits presumably translate into higher stock prices. And, of course, the reverse would also be true: an economy with lower economic growth would have a bias toward lower stock prices. That's why many people look at a world where North

America may be stuck in a slower growth trajectory and worry that the equity markets cannot escape a downward bias as well.

In truth, the situation is more complicated than that, and there is in fact considerable evidence to suggest that a growing economy is not actually required for a return on equities to be strong. One study, by Dimson, Marsh, and Staunton,[10] looked at stock market returns for 16 countries for a full century—1900 to 2000—and found that there was actually a negative correlation between growth and returns. Contrary to what one might expect, the researchers found that stronger growth led to lower market returns. The study was updated through 2002[11] with basically the same conclusion: markets can go up even if gross domestic product goes down.

What's behind this the counterintuitive relationship between economic growth and market returns? For one thing, when economies are hot, investors pile in pretty quickly, meaning that it is hard to get a bargain and, hence, hard to get high returns. Developing markets, after all, have posted brilliant growth rates in recent years, but valuations have been so high that many investors have been disappointed with their returns. Second, the stock market may be a proxy for the larger economy, but it may not be a complete one. Equity markets reflect publicly listed companies only, not all parts of the economy, meaning that they can overstate or understate actual growth. Finally, companies can have great results without any benefit to shareholders if, for example, the money is paid out in executive salaries or is diverted in some other way.[12] Indeed, the profitability picture over the post-recession period has actually been fairly good, despite sluggish economic growth overall, even if the markets have not always reflected that reality. Going forward, businesses may be challenged to do well against a backdrop of strained governments and stretched consumers, but it is not an impossible task.

Growth aside, one thing we do know is that demographics play a role in the financial markets. Households spend and save differently at different points of their lives, and the sum total of their actions affects the economy and the markets. For example, households in their 20s and 30s do not tend to be big savers. These are typically the years when people buy their first house, start a family, get a start on paying back their student loans, and generally act like consumers. As they hit their 40s, however, things change a bit. Retirement is looming and they start to think more about accumulating assets; maybe they acquire a financial advisor or start learning about the markets on their own. Once past 65, people start to draw down on their savings and investments rather than adding to them.

These are broad generalizations, of course, but the data seems to bear them out. The U.S. Federal Reserve does a comprehensive study of family finances every couple of years, the most recent of which is the 2010 Survey of Consumer Finances.[13] As of that year, the Federal Reserve found that 52 percent of all U.S. families did save money. However, of those families with a head aged between 35 and 44, 47.6 percent saved, while for those with a head between 66 and 64, 51.4 percent did so. The median holdings of financial assets for all families was $30,200. Again, however, there was considerable variation by age. Families with a head under 35 had median holdings of $7,100, while for those aged 55 to 64, the median was $77,200. And for those with a head aged over 75, it was $43,500. Canadian data also show a similar pattern.[14]

Analysts have been constructing doomsday-for-stocks scenarios based around the aging population for years now, and we are getting to the point where the theories are about to be put to the test. Scores of baby boomers are currently opening birthday cards that have the number 6 on them, and not as a second digit, either! As a generation, more and more boomers are becoming sixty-somethings; soon, some will become seventy-somethings. That does not spell happy news for equity investors. Then again, having demographics as a planning tool is potentially a huge bonus. Much of the volatility in the equity markets in recent years came out of nowhere, and would have been pretty much impossible to predict. Having said that, much of the long uptrend in stocks that started in the 1970s was actually possible to model using demographics—and some of the future path of equities is also possible to predict using demographics.

So, accepting that people have different financial habits at different points in their lives, there are a couple of ratios that are helpful in determining the way that financial markets may move as the population ages. Let's examine those in more detail.

The Middle-Young Ratio

The middle-young (MY) ratio is basically what it sounds like: a ratio of those in their 40s relative to those in their 20s. Rather than looking at the mass of people who might be drawing down on their savings, it concentrates on two groups with different agendas.[15] A high proportion of forty-somethings to twenty-somethings should correlate with high market returns, while the reverse is also true.

The forty-somethings, after all, are the big savers; they are right at the age when they are making important moves up the career ladder and reaching their highest income levels, or at least the highest income levels that they have managed to date. The twenty-somethings are the big spenders and are a lot less likely to be socking large amounts away. If they are saving, the bulk of it is likely to be for a down payment on their first home, not trying to make a killing on Wall Street or Bay Street.

Empirically, there seems to be a nice fit between the way that the MY ratio and financial markets in North America have moved together over the past two decades. Comparing the MY ratio for the United States to the price-earnings ratio on the S&P 500, you can see that the two have basically trended together through the period from 1960 to 2010 (see the following figure).

THE MIDDLE-YOUNG RATIO AND U.S. STOCKS

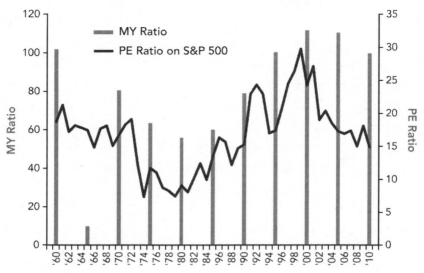

Source: United Nations Population Database, Bloomberg (PE ratios are for year-end), Author Calculations.

Of course, there have been gyrations in equities over the period, although these have generally been attributed to economic factors. For example, the stock market slump in the early 1970s is generally thought to have been caused by the collapse of the Bretton Woods system[16] and the oil shock of 1973 and so on—but perhaps there was more to it than that. During that period, the baby boomers were spending money, not investing, and the group in their 40s at the time were the "Depression Babies," a very small group. Hence, the middle-young ratio was low, and the markets were naturally going to be sensitive to economic events. Similarly, in the period around 2000, perhaps it was not just the promise of dot.com riches that drove the markets. The chance of getting great returns on tech stocks was obviously a draw for a lot of people, but clearly there was also the capital available from the now-forty-something boomers to back up those tech sector dreams. In fact, from the mid-1980s through to the beginning of the 2000s, there was something of a demographically driven bull market at play. Lots of money was being thrown into the markets, and valuations got shoved higher.

You can see a similar trend in the Canadian market.[17] The pattern is a bit less smooth—which can partly be explained by the dominance of commodity companies, the prices for which tend to move with much more volatility than other equities—but the evidence of a demographically driven bear market is easy to see. As with the U.S., it is clear that the global economic crisis hit at a particularly bad time. Even without bad economic news, there would have been a bias toward decline for the equity markets. After all, all but the youngest boomers were moving out of their 40s and perhaps veering to lower-risk investments than equities. With the extra threat of a long recession, of course the financial markets were hit hard.

THE MIDDLE-YOUNG RATIO AND CANADIAN STOCKS

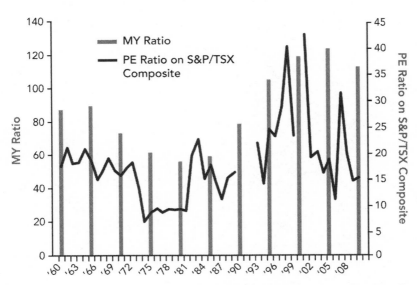

Source: United Nations Population Database, Statistics Canada
(PE ratios are for year-end), Author Calculations.

> The baby boomers are moving out of their "middle" years and the generation that followed them is much smaller in numbers. This means that the middle-young ratio will decline until around 2020, signaling a demographically driven bear market.

Then again, that is the past. What about the future? Unfortunately, the MY ratio is not a particularly hopeful indicator when it comes to the direction of the equity markets. The baby boomers are moving out of their "middle" years (only the very last wave of the boomers, born in the mid-1960s, was still in its 40s as of 2013) and the generation that followed them is much smaller in numbers. This means that the middle-young ratio will decline until around 2020, signaling a demographically driven bear market. Keep in mind that that is quite aside from any decline in stocks caused by economic events.

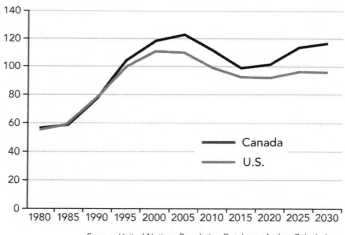

LOOKING FORWARD: THE MIDDLE-YOUNG RATIOS

Source: United Nations Population Database, Author Calculations.

The Middle-Old Ratio

Another ratio that may be useful in predicting the direction of stocks is the so-called middle-old (MO) ratio.[18] First formulated in a Federal Reserve Board of San Francisco study, the MO ratio looks at the ratio of those aged from 40 to 49 to those aged 60 to 69. The idea is that the real wildcard for the markets is going to come from the way that the aging boomers act in terms of liquidating or holding on to their assets, something that is not captured by the MY ratio. Implicit in using the MY ratio as a predictor is the assumption that those over 60 are not actively affecting the markets through asset purchases, or that if they are making purchases they are being equally offset by the sales of assets. If, all of a sudden, boomers start to sell their equities, then prices would go down.

THE MIDDLE-OLD RATIO AND U.S. STOCKS

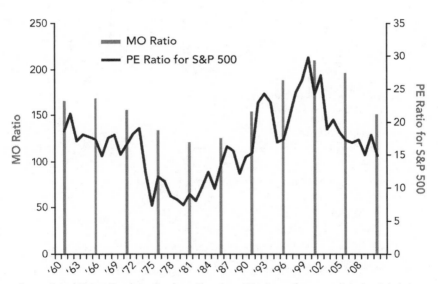

Source: United Nations Population Database, Bloomberg (PE ratios are for year-end), Author Calculations.

Using U.S. data from 1954 through to 2010, the Federal Reserve study found that there was a statistically significant relationship between the middle-old ratio and price-earnings ratio on the S&P 500. Although that study used a formal economic model to fit the two series, just graphing the two series shows the fit between the two: clearly, the U.S. demographics supported the dot.com years and, equally clearly, they have become somewhat less supportive since. The same relationship is visible for the Canadian data, although here again the caveats regarding the volatility of the price-earnings ratio on the S&P/TSX also hold.

THE MIDDLE-OLD RATIO AND CANADIAN STOCKS

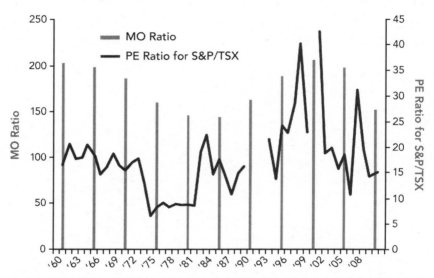

Source: United Nations Population Database, Statistics (PE ratios are for year-end), Author Calculations.

All things being equal, this predictor also indicates a long-term secular bear market in stocks caused by demographics and quite separate from anything that might or might not affect the economy.

It's worth noting that you have to temper these findings with your expectations about how people will act in future, rather than in the past. There are reasons to believe that boomers will not rush to sell their equity holdings. Chief among these is the fact that their portfolios are in many cases worth less than they had expected them to be, meaning that even those who had planned to sell in the immediate future are more likely to hold on to their stakes. In truth, though, it is only the earliest boomers who have reached their post-working years, and given the pattern of births in Canada and the United States, the number of people turning 65 each year will peak around the mid-2020s. If the markets have not reached pre-recession levels by the time that group gets to their retirement years, those boomers are likely to throw in the towel and give up.

Whether or not boomers pull assets out of their portfolios sooner or later depends on their overall wealth, not just their financial wealth. For most people, the major source of asset holdings is in their homes. A household with a highly valued, mortgage-free house is a lot less likely to liquidate their savings than one with negative equity in their house and maybe a mortgage too. The first household could sell their house, downsize to something smaller, and still have cash left over; the second does not have that option. Sadly, given the huge correction that has been seen in the U.S. housing market over the past years, the number of households in the second category has climbed stratospherically. If housing goes up in value before boomer retirements peak, that would lessen the risk of boomers needing to tap into their financial market portfolios. Unfortunately, that seems unlikely to happen in a way that will be large enough to mitigate the losses, so there is indeed the potential for a big rush on equities as boomer retirements start to take hold.

The prospect of a liquidation of equity holdings by the boomers seems more likely than it did prior to the recession. One argument against this type of liquidation is that there are fairly good public and private pensions in place in North America, meaning that many households do not have an immediate need to tap into their investments too quickly. In fact, figures from the U.S. Bureau of Labor Statistics show that only 18 percent of private sector households had a defined benefit pension in place, down sharply from 35 percent in the early 1990s.[19] Public sector workers had a much higher rate (78 percent), but as governments at all levels look to pare back expenses, everything is now on the table, including what used to be locked-in-stone pension agreements. So the bias is going to be for an earlier liquidation of savings by boomers than was true in previous generations.

LOOKING FORWARD: THE MIDDLE-OLD RATIOS

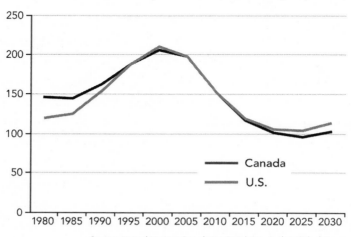

Source: United Nations Population Database, Author Calculations.

HELP FROM ABROAD?

Even if a decline in investable capital in the developed world is going to put downward pressure on stock prices, could that not be off-set by an inflow of cash from other countries? After all, countries like India and China are rapidly industrializing and creating new middle classes. Those newly wealthy households are going to want good returns on their money, and increasingly they will look out-side their own borders. It would be a bit of a reversal from the situation that exists as economies are developing. Right now, money flows into China looking for returns; later, it might flow into Canada or the United States.

Despite the aging populations in other parts of the world, the demographics still suggest growing pools of investors in many countries. Western Europe has very poor demographic fundamentals for investment. The MY ratio shows no improvement at all through to at least 2030. China, India, and Latin America, however, all have much better investment profiles. Given that they are further behind on the aging curve than North America, their bulge of middle-aged investors will be looking for returns in the next 10 years or so. If their money comes into North America, it could provide a nice support to the markets. Or, conversely, North American money could look for returns in foreign markets. Either scenario, however, would require a substantial amount of risk taking, as well as appropriate capital flow regulations.

Interestingly, the middle-old ratio for these same countries is less hopeful than the middle-young ratio. That is because the growth in the forty-something population is actually going to be more than offset by growth in the sixty-something population. As an indicator of the health of the domestic markets in the countries in question, this statistic does not bode well. Indeed, given that the pension systems in countries like China and India are not nearly as comprehensive as they are in North America, there is considerable potential for a liquidation of assets and a decline in those markets.

LIVING IN DIFFICULT TIMES

Do we know what is going to happen in the financial markets tomorrow or next week? That's a bit difficult to predict. Next year? Still hard. Further out than that, however, there are clear trends coming from demographics and from what we know about the long-term path of the global economy. That means we are not peering into the future with no guidance at all.

Let's not call any market "good" or "bad": after all, the label really depends on which side of the equation you are on. Take long-term interest rates, for example. We know that they are going to have a tendency to rise from about 2030 onward, which is not going to be a positive development for Generation Z (those born post-2000). That generation will be buying houses and taking out mortgages in the 2030s, and will no doubt be grumbling about the fact that they are facing higher interest rates than did their Generation X and Y parents. Generation X and Y, however, might be happy enough that they are getting decent returns on their guaranteed investments. After finally paying off their student loans and starting to think about retirement savings, they may be pleased to put their money into a government bond rather than trying their luck in the stock market, if they so choose.

And for those who do want the returns that come from equity investing? That's fine too, although they should understand that they will have to work for them. The demographic signs point to markets that will give tepid gains for years to come, and probably produce a great deal of volatility. Making money in the years ahead is going to require investors to be simultaneously more active and more educated, but forewarned is forearmed. For some, this might mean relying more on financial advice, whether that comes through an advisor or through efforts at self-education.

And yes, the demographics point to a bear market for stocks in North America for the next decade or so. This may mean that blindly buying and holding stocks is not a great idea, but it does not mean that there are not gains to be made in portfolios that are knowledgably managed. We know a lot about the world ahead and about its demographics. Choosing companies that cater to the trends—or to the population and its needs—will be a giant step toward ensuring returns.

(ENDNOTES)

[1] Any interest rate has two components—the "real" return and the expected rate of inflation. If a lender is making a loan at a time when the anticipated inflation rate is 3 percent, then to get a "real" return of 5 percent, the nominal interest rate (the total rate) rate has to be set at 8 percent.

[2] Ben Bernanke, "The Global Savings Glut and the U.S. Current Account Deficit." Remarks at the Sandridge Lecture, Virginia Association of Economists, Richmond, Virginia, March 10, 2005. Retrieved from http://www.federalreserve.gov/boarddocs/speeches/2005/200503102/.

[3] Chris Isidore, "The Zero Savings Problem," CNN Money, August 3, 2005. Retrieved from http://money.cnn.com/2005/08/02/news/economy/savings/.

[4] Richard Dobbs, Susan Lund, Charles Roxburgh, Alex Kim, Andreas Schreiner, Riccardo Boin, Rohit Chopra, Sebastian Jauch, Hyun Kim, Megan McDonald, John Piotrowski, "Farewell to Cheap Capital." McKinsey Global Institute, December 2010, p. 9. Retrieved from http://www.mckinsey.com/insights/global_capital_markets/farewell_cheap_capital.

[5] McKinsey, p. 9.

[6] International Monetary Fund, *Japan Sustainablity Report (G20)* (IMF, November 2011). Retrieved from http://www.imf.org/external/np/country/2011/mapjapanpdf.pdf.

[7] Mauricio Cardenas and Jeff Frank, "Lower Savings in China Could Slow Down Growth in Latin America," The Brooking Institution, opinions, February 11, 2011. Retrieved from http://www.brookings.edu/research/opinions/2011/02/11-china-savings-cardenas-frank.

[8] Chong-En Bai, Chang-Tai Hsi and Yingyi Qia, "The Return to Capital in China." National Bureau of Economic Research Working Paper #12755, National Bureau of Economic Research, 2006. Retrieved from http://www.nber.org/digest/jul07/w12755.html.

[9] OECD, "Looking to 2060: A Global Vision of Long-Term Growth," Economics Department Policy Note #15, p. 5. Retrieved from http://www.oecd.org/eco/outlook/2060policynote.pdf.

[10] Elroy Dimson, Paul Marsh, and Mike Staunton, "Lower Your Expectations to the New Normal," *Financial Times*, April 17, 2013. Retrieved from http://www.ft.com/intl/cms/s/0/be436e04-9de6-11e2-9ccc-00144feabdc0.html#axzz2cVjeXyOt.

[11] Jay Ritter, "Economic Growth and Equity Returns," *Pacific Basin Finance Journal*, August 2005.

[12] For a complete discussion, see Buttonwood, "The Growth Illusion," *The Economist*, August 28, 2009. Retrieved from http://www.economist.com/blogs/buttonwood/2009/08/the_growth_illusion.

[13] Board of Govenors of the Federal Reserve System, Survey of Consumer Finances, 2013. Retrieved from http://www.federalreserve.gov/econresdata/scf/scfindex.htm.

[14] The most recent data in that case comes from Statistics Canada's Survey of Financial Security, last compiled in 2005. Interestingly, Canadians who had financial assets had more at every age than Americans, although the numbers are not calculated in exactly the same way as they are in the American study. The key thing, however, is that the life-cycle pattern is approximately the same for the two countries: people hold more in their stock portfolios in their 50s than they do in their retirement years. In the Canadian case, those aged 55 to 64 held $252,457 in financial assets (defined as private pensions assets plus other assets) while those aged 65 plus held $178,613.

[15] See John Geanakoplos, Michael Magill, and Martine Quinzii, "Demography and the Long-Run Predictability of the Stock Market," Cowles Foundation Paper #1099, 2004, for the original analysis and a complete discussion of the theory.

[16] For more on the collapse of the Bretton Woods system of fixed exchange rates, see International Monetary Fund, "The End of the Bretton Woods System, 1972–81" http://www.imf.org/external/about/histend.htm.

[17] Given the number of commodity companies listed on the Toronto Stock Exchange, price-earnings ratios tend to be extremely volatile compared to other major exchanges. To get a better idea of how stocks have traded over time, the graph of Canadian MY ratios excludes price-earnings ratio data for the years 1991, 1992, 1993, and 1999.

[18] Zheng Liu and Mark M. Spiegel, "Boomer Retirements: Headwinds for U.S. Equity Markets?" Federal Reserve Board of San Francisco, August 22, 2011.

[19] Monique Morrissey, "Private Sector Pension Coverage Fell by Half Over Two Decades," Economic Policy Institute Blog, Economic Policy Institute, July 2013. Retrieved from http://www.epi.org/blog/private-sector-pension-coverage-decline/.

Searching for the Second Act

They have always set trends and they are doing so again: baby boomers in North America have moved through their primary careers and are now looking for their "second act." Believe it or not, that might mean working—and working for a long while: boomers are a workaholic generation, and, at any rate, many need the money.

Still, whether they choose to retire at the first opportunity, or when it is forced upon them, boomers will be leaving the labor force in droves over the next two decades. As they do, they will look for "meaningful" ways to spend their time.

Yes, we are still talking about the baby boomers. They are unique and plentiful and influential, and what they do matters for everyone else—for good and for ill. As they reach the end of their working lives and spill over into the retired portion of the population, they are showing themselves to be a diverse group, albeit one with some commonalities. Whatever their wealth and income status, they are increasingly looking to spend their time in ways that are more meaningful than sitting in a cubicle. Trouble is, many have not had time to do much else besides the work they were paid to do, and figuring out exactly what to do with the rest of their lives is a bit of a struggle.

Here's a shock wave that's about to reverberate through society: boomers will actually have far fewer choices, in some domains, than they expected. Although boomers were a fairly indulged generation—one that had more luxuries than their parents—they are going to be a fairly poor generation in income terms. More than any economic cycle, the reduced circumstances of the boomers is going to impose a kind of culture of thrift upon North America's economy.

But if many do not have the money they hoped they would have, they will have more time. And, in a way, time is the ultimate luxury good. For scores of baby boomers, time has been a most precious commodity, and many have made their economic choices accordingly. As they retire (kicking and screaming, if need be), they will find that the palette of choices available to them is completely different than when they were working, and the choices they make in terms of spending their time and money will cause ripples through the economy.

RETIREMENT IS A DIRTY WORD—AND ANYWAY, I NEED THE MONEY

In Canada and the U.S., boomers comprise about 30 percent of the respective populations, a high enough figure to ensure that their actions matter. The boomers have always been influential—*Newsweek* figured that out back in 1948, when it ran a cover story entitled "Babies Mean Business!"[1] And indeed, they did. Meeting boomer demand meant creating a whole new world of products—from the Barbie doll and Play-Doh when they were tiny, through to minivans when they had their own kids. In the 1970s and '80s, the boomers wanted convenience. They lived in households where everyone was working, and they wanted to get things done more quickly. Companies obliged by selling pre-made Jell-O and sheets that did not need to be ironed.

As the boomers retire, new changes will flow through the economy. From being a continent where the majority of people are in the workforce, North America will shift to one where "leisure" (defined by economists as meaning "not working for pay," as opposed to "leaning back in a deck chair") is increasingly important. It doesn't necessarily mean that anyone wants to go back to ironing their sheets, but it does mean that there will be time for things other than work.

Of course, tell a boomer that we are turning into a "leisure economy" and you'll likely get a negative response. Many boomers take pride in the fact that they are time-crunched: their proud call, over so many decades, has been "I'm *soooo* busy!" The word *retirement* is not one that they like very much. "We need a new name," read the final line of a Canadian Association of Retired Persons article describing the ways that boomers' retirements will be different than those of previous generations. "How about the Canadian Association for Remarkable People?"[2]

Let's separate the myths from the realities. First of all, many of the parents of the baby boomers would chafe at the idea that they did "nothing" during their own retirements, or set some kind of example that boomers would prefer not to emulate. For the pre-boomer generation (sometimes called the "Silent Generation," the "GI Generation," or the "Greatest Generation"), born between the mid 1920s and mid 1940s, the pattern was pretty set. Most married, and did so early, and children came early too. Most did not divorce. The labor force participation rate of women was low, and men typically worked in one or two jobs for their whole careers. Retirement age was 65, and most did retire on schedule. Some moved to Florida, some stuck around to play with the grandkids, some went to quilting groups, some played golf, and some got involved in their churches. By and large, retirement incomes were modest, but this was a generation used to being parsimonious.

Then you've got the boomers. As a generation, they have been very different from their parents. They've come through some scary business cycles, and many are intimately acquainted with unemployment. Job-hopping has pretty much been the norm: according to a study by the U.S. Bureau of Labor Statistics, later-wave boomers (those born between 1957 and 1964) held an average of 11.3 jobs between the ages of 18 and 46.[3] Boomers have also had a very different pattern of family life. Not only are they less likely to have had enduring marriages, but their propensity for getting divorced also seems to be continuing into their retirement years. And that is financially disastrous: whatever retirement savings have been accumulated must be split in half, and living expenses have to be almost doubled.[4]

But what about retirement? In actual fact, boomers *do* intend to retire, at least from their primary jobs. According to a 2013 study by Del Webb, a residential construction company focused on adults over the age of 55, 57 percent of still-working boomers aged 50 to 60 planned to leave their full-time careers by the age of 65. That is not actually much different from the reading in 1996, when the median age of retirement was expected to be 63. Still, retirement apparently does not mean a complete exit from labor force activity. According to the same survey, 79 percent of boomers anticipate working in some capacity post-retirement, with about 51 percent expecting to be on the job full-time.[5]

The reality is that the vast majority of people will retire eventually. For the boomers, however, both sentiment and the economy may be getting in the way. Baldly put, you can separate the baby boomers into two streams: those with enough money to retire and enjoy life, and those with inadequate resources who are terrified of retirement but might have to accept it anyway.

Income—or, more accurately, wealth—inequality among the boomers has many causes. In some cases, it is the result of the amount of money earned when working, but that is not nearly the whole story. Some boomers who earned a modest salary throughout their working lives are managing to retire with nice pensions and tidy savings. Others with higher salaries have gotten caught in the fallout from any number of unfortunate circumstances or bad decisions (long bouts with unemployment, housing market collapses, marital collapses, et cetera) and now find themselves retiring with insufficient pension income or assets. During their working lives, it might have been difficult to separate the haves from the have-nots. What will separate them now, however, is the ability to retire when they choose.

When it comes to that decision, mortgage debt is the biggest issue. According to a survey by Securian Financial Group, of those boomers now close to retirement, 67 percent expect to carry mortgage debt with them into retirement. That is up sharply from the 30 percent tallied in Securian's 2009 study.[6] It gets worse, however: according to a survey by the MetLife Mature Market Institute, as of 2013, 8 percent of U.S. baby boomers did not just have a mortgage to contend with—they owed *more* than the value of their homes. The situation is a little better in Canada (which had

> Baldly put, you can separate the baby boomers into two streams: those with enough money to retire and enjoy life, and those with inadequate resources who are terrified of retirement but might have to accept it anyway.

a less severe recession and avoided a housing market bubble), but even so, one-quarter of Canadian boomers aged 50 to 59 planned to carry some debt into retirement.[7]

What about that ace-in-the-hole baby boomer planning strategy—inheriting bucks from their parents when they pass away? The great transfer of wealth from the boomers' parents to the boomers has been a hot topic for decades now, with estimates of how much money will change hands in the United States ranging anywhere from about $10 to $30 trillion.[8] After all, the pre-boomer generation had a pretty lucky break in terms of the real estate market. They bought decades ago—back in the years when the boomers were born, from the 1950s through the 1970s—and even with a recent correction they have seen gigantic gains in the value of their properties. Some bought stocks in those decades, too, and recent market gyrations have not erased substantial gains. Are they rich? Not exactly. The parents of the boomers are not a particularly wealthy generation, but many bought and paid off their homes, meaning that there are tidy amounts in real estate. Then again, with life spans increasing, much of that wealth might be tapped into by the time any inheritance actually takes place. The leading edge of the boomers, the ones who have already gotten those inheritances, are proof of that. A survey by Investors Group asked Canadians who were expecting an inheritance how much they thought they would receive. Fifty-seven percent said "more than $100,00." However, when Canadians who had already received an inheritance were asked how much they got, the figure was $57,000.[9]

The fact is, many baby boomers cannot afford to retire, and are taking what they can get to stay in the labor market. According to a 2013 survey by the Conference Board, 62 percent of those aged between 45 and 60 in 2012 felt that they would have to delay retirement, compared to 42 percent in 2010.[10] The trend is reflected in labor force participation rates as well: according to U.S. census data, 21 percent of those aged over 65 were in the labor force in

2010, compared to 18.4 percent 10 years earlier. For the group aged over 75, 8.6 percent were in the labor force, an increase from 8.0 percent in 2000.[11] No doubt the data is skewed by the fact that more older women are in the workforce than ever before, but it nevertheless illustrates the fact that the boomers are not exiting the workforce particularly quickly.

Baby boomers who stay in the labor market are causing two different phenomena that parallel what we are seeing in the wider economy. Boomers with high skill levels have the ability to leave their established careers and pursue second act positions that play to their passions. Boomers with less education (and generally more financial stress) are accepting lower paid, often part-time work. Each choice has an impact on the non–baby boom population.

Although the first trend gets the most attention, more baby boomers are likely to find themselves working to bring in some cash, rather than seeking meaningful second careers. The shape of things to come may be illustrated by a story that appeared on Bloomberg Business News in 2013. The article profiled a 77-year-old pre-boomer gentleman named Tom who was once vice-president of marketing for a major consumer brand but who currently makes a living demonstrating meatballs at Sam's Club, flipping burgers, and cleaning up at a golf club. He worked all his life, paid off his mortgage in full, and saved some cash for retirement—but not enough. The rule of thumb is that you need 10 to 20 times your working income to retire comfortably. Not only had Tom not put away that much, what he had put away was partially lost during a couple of bad investment cycles. No big drama and no reckless spending was involved, but at the end of the day he needed more money than he had available, and his job choices no longer included executive ones.[12]

Project Tom's experience onto a large chunk of the boomer generation and you'll get an idea of how things are likely to shake out. An analysis on U.S. pre-retirees from the Schwartz Center for

Economic Policy Analysis, based on data from the U.S. Census Bureau, states it very plainly: 59 million Americans aged 50 to 64 in 2011 will not have enough retirement assets to maintain their standard of living when they retire. In fact, many near-retirees in the U.S. have *no* retirement accounts or investments. Perhaps not surprisingly, 77 percent of those surveyed are in the bottom income quintile; however, the results also include 22 percent of those in the top quintile.[13]

The second trend—the one we've heard the most about in the media—has those who might have simply retired seeking meaningful second careers instead. For some, that will mean becoming entrepreneurs. According to the Kauffman Foundation, boomers are far more likely to start businesses than are members of younger generations. During the years from 1996 to 2010, boomers between the ages of 55 and 64 had a higher rate of entrepreneurial activity than did Generation Y (aged 20 to 34).[14] The reasons are likely varied: they want to do something meaningful and interesting; in many cases the recession made it difficult for them to hold on to corporate jobs; and perhaps most importantly, they are hoping to make some money to subsidize their retirements or semi-retirements.

Other boomers include working with non-profits or philanthropic organizations in their definition of "meaningful" work. In some cases, this might mean working with no pay, although in others it could mean accepting a position at perhaps a lower level of pay than they might have earned in the past. According to the non-profit group Encore.org, which tracks boomer careers, as many as nine million people in the U.S. are now engaged in work that relates to their personal passions and combines those with a social purpose; another 31 million are interested in making the leap into doing so.[15]

But whether we are talking about meaningful work or just work to pay the bills, we must look at the wider implications. A lot of those "interesting" positions in non-profits that boomers are willing to take for pin money might once have gone to younger workers. The U.S. unemployment rate for 20- to 24-year-olds was a hefty 13 percent in August 2013, compared to just 5.1 percent for those 55 and over.[16] The more wide-ranging effect, however, seems to come when baby boomers take "ordinary" jobs, the kind that once would have gone to teen workers. A study by the Canadian Imperial Bank of Commerce found that the jobless rate among Canadians aged 15 to 18 was 20 percent in 2013, the highest on record, and that employment among this group was down 22 percent since 2007, compared to a 4 percent drop in their population. For all categories of typically "teen" jobs—retail sales, food and counter help, cashiers—they found big drops in youth employment and big increases in employment for other age groups.[17]

CHANGING THE VIBE

The baby boomers have unquestionably been behind a number of cultural trends. One of the most significant, however, may be the creation of the "time-crunch economy." Evidence of this shows up in the statistics on the ways that people use their time at various points in their life.[18] Data from the American Time Use Survey shows that, on average, those aged 15 and over have 5.4 hours of what can be deemed "free" time per day (that is, hours not specifically earmarked for work, transportation, housework, education, and the like). However, this free time varies from a low of 4.27 hours for those aged 35 to 44, through to a high of 7.1 hours for those aged 65 to 74.[19] And that makes sense: people in their 30s and 40s are in the thick of child-raising and career-building. Older people, particularly if they are retired, have far fewer demands on their time.

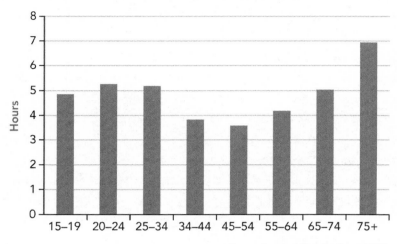

TIME-CRUNCHED

*Hours spent by Americans on leisure
and sport on weekdays, by age*

Source: American Time Use Survey, 2012.

Now think about how old the boomers were in the 1970s, '80s, and '90s. As a group, they were squarely in their time-crunch years. So, there were virtually decades when the amount of leisure time across North America was on the decline: every year, the continent got a bit more time-crunched. No wonder, then, that golf course operators grew frustrated at how few people had time to play 18 holes, and the fabric sections of department stores quietly closed and gave way to more space for manufactured clothing. Meanwhile, companies focused on creating "convenience" products that would make life easier for those in a hurry. Who had time to play golf or sew or cook anymore? Of course, there were other factors at work as well—over the same time period, the price of imported clothing fell as young populations in Asia staffed factories more efficiently—but there was a definite trend in place.

Now the golf courses are getting crowded again, and there may be more time to do crafts and cook. More than that, there will be new trade-offs between time and money. At one point, boomers had absolutely no time but some money; a decade from now, almost all boomers will have more time, and some will have a lot less money. At some point in the past, it made sense to buy vegetables pre-cut and Jell-O pre-made. Now, it might make more sense to actually make the Jello-O; after all, if you are not rushing to work, there is time for it to set.

The time-versus-money trade-off will certainly have an impact on the larger economy. We do know that older people tend to consume somewhat less than younger ones, and have been expecting the aging of the population to have an impact on consumer spending. The thing with the boomers, however, is that they have always been enthusiastic consumers of services as well as goods. If circumstances force them to slam the brakes on that type of spending, the economic impact could be particularly pronounced.

Leaving aside for a moment the impact on the economy, let's consider what happens to the boomers themselves when the time-crunch problem isn't such a problem anymore. Once work is done, or at least cut back, many baby boomers may be faced with the problem of "getting a life." For a long time, boomers didn't need to think too hard about how to fill their time, or where to find friends or make connections. Their work life was very likely their full life—or at least a significant chunk of it. So what now? In a 2013 Age Wave/Merrill Lynch survey, boomers were asked what they thought they would miss most about their jobs when they retired. The most common response, cited by 38 percent of respondents, was that they would miss the steady paycheck. However, when retired boomers were asked what they actually did miss most, the most common response (cited by 34 percent) was "the social connection."[20] This is something we may see boomers pursuing in retirement—ways to make social connections that do not involve participation in the workforce.

For many, there may also be a disconnect between what they want to do in retirement and what they can afford to do. According to 2010 survey by Allstate Financial, baby boomers have a clutch of activities that they want to pursue in retirement (from travel through to home renovations), and most figure that they will need $10,900 per year to cover those costs, plus another $30,000 for basic expenses. Unfortunately, boomer savings are probably not up to the task. To cover that $40,000-plus, boomers need approximately $1.2 million in retirement savings; in reality, the average surveyed boomer has more like $120,000.[21]

Those boomers who can spend more will do so, but at every income level boomers will be more concerned about spending on experiences rather than on things. They do not need more "stuff," but they will have time to do all kinds of things that they were not able to do before. There will be some trial and error, but the boomers will undoubtedly find a mix of what they want to do and what they can afford to do. Here are just some of the ways this could play out.

The Search for Meaning

Workaholic or not, many boomers are now looking for "meaning," however that may be defined. You hear it from people switching careers (either voluntarily or because they have been laid off); they talk about pursuing their passion at their next jobs, rather than just following the straight line they'd set out for themselves at another stage in their lives. Those who have the luxury of avoiding financial panic may want to do something different, something meaningful, perhaps something that gives them more control.

Although the baby boomers have not embraced traditional religion, once retired, they may get more involved with a religious institution with which they already have an acquaintance. In his book *God Is Alive and Well: The Future of Religion in America*, Frank Newport argues that people get more religious as they age.[22] Given the size of the baby boomer generation, their religious rebirth could lead to a wider surge in religious activities.

For other boomers, however, the search for meaning will manifest as a search for some kind of spirituality. That might translate into seeking out new-age retreats or holistic healing, or making a "bucket list" and ticking off the various items, whether that means learning to skydive or traveling to exotic places.

Civic and Business Involvement

As the baby boomers age, they will have a larger and larger impact on the societies in which they live. The most basic way this will manifest itself is in an increase in voter participation. In the 2010 U.S. presidential election, 61 percent of those over the age of 65 voted, compared to just 44 percent of those aged 25 to 44.[23] Of course, this data relates to the first wave of the boomers as well as to an earlier generation, but it seems reasonable that this trend will be carried through to the rest of the boomers as well. The reversal of the time-crunch is a factor here too: showing up at the voting booth is easier when it does not have to be done on the way home from the office or on the way to soccer practice.

Along with the desire to vote comes an interest in political issues. Not surprisingly, the political agenda is likely to be increasingly dominated by issues about which boomers feel passionate. With their "real" careers behind them, some will run for political office, either as a lark or because of a genuine desire to affect change. Others will lobby for the causes that directly affect them. That does not mean that issues for younger families will be pushed off the agenda, but they will certainly have plenty of competition for funding and political attention.

One interest, or perhaps obsession, among boomers in retirement will be checking their investments. This could, in turn, mean getting more heavily involved in the decisions of the companies in which they are shareholders. In the pre-retirement years, that might mean monitoring media articles and returning forms for proxy votes, but post-retirement, it could be a whole different ball game. Going to shareholder meetings won't just be a way to pass the time; it will also be a way in which to take an active role in affecting a much-needed investment portfolio. It may not be welcome by the companies involved, however: a bunch of boomers showing up to eat all the Danish pastries and ask uncomfortable questions will not be seen as the ideal way to keep things moving.

> Going to shareholder meetings won't just be a way to pass the time; it will also be a way in which to take an active role in affecting a much-needed investment portfolio. It may not be welcome by the companies involved, however: a bunch of boomers showing up to eat all the Danish pastries and ask uncomfortable questions will not be seen as the ideal way to keep things moving.

Volunteering

The volunteer sector is just starting to see the benefit of boomers' interest, and there is plenty of scope for further engagement— maybe. In theory the baby boomers are excellent candidates for volunteer work. They are the most-educated generation ever, and men and women alike have honed their skills during long careers. The problem, however, may well be to find the right fit for the flood of workers who have skills to offer, and to offer them volunteer opportunities that fit with their post-work lives.

Many baby boomers feel that they don't know enough about the kinds of volunteer experiences that are available to them. According to a 2010 Canadian study, surveyed boomers noted that while many organizations provide retirement seminars, the focus is always on financial planning, with little information or mention of volunteer opportunities.[24] And that makes sense, given that the organizations that use volunteers are only starting to figure out ways to best use boomers and their specialized skill sets. Boomers want to feel engaged in the causes they are supporting, and they want to have their time respected.

According to a recent blog post for a United Way branch in Michigan,[25] organizations are increasingly targeting boomers with "skills-based volunteering" opportunities, or jobs that would typically have a market value of $40 to $500 an hour. Traditional volunteer opportunities, in contrast, typically pay $18 to $20 an hour.

Another issue that has frequently plagued the fit between baby boomers and volunteer activities is travel. Boomers in retirement typically plan to travel, meaning that they may not be able to make the commitment that some organizations are looking for. An organization that's looking for volunteers to commit twice a week for a year may not be pleased to hear that a potential volunteer is planning to take three months off to tour Asia.

Philanthropy

When you think of fastest-growing industries of the future, what comes to mind? Environmental technologies, robotics, e-learning, maybe? How about philanthropy? If the word conjures visions of elderly rich people doling out dollars to museums, you might need to rethink your assumptions.

As a group, baby boomers now give more than any other generation. According to a study commissioned by Blackbaud (a company that provides software to non-profits), not only do boomers comprise the largest group of charitable givers (34 percent), they also give 43 percent of the total (or $61.9 billion).[26] While there are no doubt boomers who give proportionately less—the pulls on their incomes and the need to save for retirement have an impact on what many are able to give—another, wealthier strain is giving generously. For that group, the next decade or so will be when they make some decisions about how best to transfer their wealth. It could be a new "golden age of philanthropy," similar to the years between 1895 and 1915, when Andrew Carnegie and his contemporaries made big fortunes and followed up with significant philanthropic works. More likely, although there are certainly latter-day

Carnegies out there (Bill Gates comes to mind), the boomers' impact will come via a lot of moderately rich people choosing their projects.

So philanthropic organizations, non-profits, and foundations are going to see an injection of cash, but it may come with strings. Boomers are notorious for wanting to be involved in the projects for which they write checks, which could mean a subtle but significant change in the way many organizations are run.

Education

Thanks to the boomers, the biggest growth industry of the next two decades could well be education, but it will be education very broadly defined. Boomers with time on their hands will look for ways to learn things—from how to make holiday decorations out of yarn to finally finishing that Ph.D. This desire, in turn, will provide strong opportunities for those who can provide learning experiences.

Within the arts, the opportunities to teach boomers will multiply each year. For example, right now, music studios are crowded after schools and on Saturday mornings, prime time for kids to take their piano or guitar or voice lessons. The next two decades will provide the opportunity to bring in the kids who quit several decades ago, and who are now in the sixth and seventh decades of their life. Few may harbor plans to be concert pianists, but all will wish to challenge themselves and possibly hold off on the dementia that is more likely if you do not. So, for the schools that make an effort to entice this new generation of students, the hours during the elementary school day could be pretty busy.

Traditional educational institutions could be very busy places as well. One factor that has been shown to influence the increase is early education. If you attended an educational institution earlier in your life, you are more likely to be comfortable attending one when you are older.[27] The boomers' status as the most educated generation up to now suggests a trend toward higher participation in future. At present, less than one-third of today's U.S. residents aged 70 to 74 have some college education; that percentage will rise to 50 percent by 2015.[28] That means there will be a large group of people with time on their hands, and who are not afraid of post-secondary institutions—and hence will be more than likely to further their studies, albeit after what might have been a pretty long gap.

BUILDING CHARACTER?

If a large swathe of the population suddenly has more time and less money on their hands, a societal shift seems likely. From being big spender to looking for thrifty fun, from being a workaholic to finding out what people do when they do not work—these will be transformational years for the boomers. As they morph from one thing to another they will change the economy as well, and companies will need to respond with different offerings. That means more than just stocking more reading glasses (at the supermarket as well as at the optician); it may mean offering different pricing to those who need things right away (a traditional boomer hallmark) and to those who want to save a little money by waiting for service (a new boomer hallmark). The boomers were always about change—and whether this coming change is good or bad, the next act is in already in progress.

(ENDNOTES)

1 "Population: Babies Mean Business," *Newsweek,* August 9, 1948.

2 CARP, "Boomers Retire? That's Just Not Happening...," Canadian Association for Retired Persons website. Retrieved from http://www.carp.ca/2013/06/13/boomers-retire-thats-just-not-happening/.

3 U.S. Bureau of Labor Statistics, "Number of Jobs Held, Labor Market Activity, and Earnings Growth Among the Youngest Baby Boomers: Results from a Longitudinal Survey Summary," July 25, 2012. Retrieved from http://www.bls.gov/news.release/nlsoy.nr0.htm.

[4] For more on baby boomers and divorce, see Susan Brown, "The Gray Divorce Revolution," Bowling Green University Working Paper, http://ncfmr.bgsu.edu/pdf/working_papers/file108701.pdf.

[5] "Del Webb Survey Shows Boomers Looking to Retire Sooner," *Wall Street Journal*, January 11, 2013. Retrieved from http://online.wsj.com/article/PR-CO-20130611-906396.html.

[6] Krista Franks Brock, "Baby Boomers Plagued by Mortgage Debt as They Enter Retirement," DSNews.com, April 30, 2013. Retrieved from http://www.dsnews.com/articles/baby-boomers-plagued-by-mortgage-debt-as-they-enter-retirement-2013-04-30.

[7] "CIBC Poll: Canada's Boomers Not Interested in a Modest Retirement," Canada Newswire, September 21, 2011. Retrieved from http://www.newswire.ca/en/story/1039943/cibc-poll-canada-s-baby-boomers-not-interested-in-a-modest-retirement.

[8] Dan Kadlec, "Wealth Transfer? Boomers Banking on a Mirage," *Time*, June 12, 2012. Retrieved from http://business.time.com/2012/06/12/wealth-transfer-boomers-banking-on-a-mirage/.

[9] Raffi Anderian, "Baby Boomers Set to Inherit $1 Trillion," *Toronto Star*, February 12, 2012. Retrieved from http://www.thestar.com/business/personal_finance/retirement/2012/02/20/baby_boomers_set_to_inherit_1_trillion.html.

[10] Chad Levanon and Ben Cheng, "Trapped on the Worker Treadmill," The Conference Board, January 2013. Retrieved from https://hcexchange.conference-board.org/blog/post.cfm?post=1455.

[11] Braedyn Kromer and David Howard, "Labor Force Participation and Work Status of People 65 Years and Older," U.S. Census Bureau, American Community Survey, Janaury 2013. Retrieved from http://www.census.gov/prod/2013pubs/acsbr11-09.pdf.

[12] Carol Hymowitz, "At 77 He Prepares Burgers Earning in Week His Former Hourly Wage," *Bloomberg Business News*, September 23, 2013. Retrieved from http://www.bloomberg.com/news/2013-09-23/why-100-000-salary-may-yield-retirement-flipping-burgers.html.

[13] Schwartz Center for Economic Policy Analysis, *Fact Sheet*, 2013. Retrieved from http://www.bloomberg.com/news/2013-09-23/why-100-000-salary-may-yield-retirement-flipping-burgers.html.

[14] Martin Zwilling, "Boomers Are Driving a New Entrepreneurship Boom," *Forbes*, February 2, 2011. Retrieved from http://www.forbes.com/sites/martinzwilling/2011/02/07/boomers-are-driving-a-new-entrepreneurship-boom/.

[15] Sharon Epperson, "Retired Boomers Find Second Acts in Encore Careers," CNBC, August 10, 2013. Retrieved from http://www.cnbc.com/id/100952275.

[16] U.S. Bureau of Labor Statistics, "Labor Force Statistics from the Current Population Survey," Series ID: LNS14000000 Retrieved from http://data.bls.gov/timeseries/LNS14000000.

[17] Avery Shenfeld, "Why Tyler and Chloe Can't Get a Job," *CIBC Insights*, September 5, 2013. Retrieved from http://research.cibcwm.com/economic_public/download/eisep13.pdf.

[18] The data from Canada's General Social Survey and the U.S. Use of Time Survey inevitably has people remarking that they do not have anything close to the amount of free time that statistical agencies claim. Whether or not this is a valid point—and the results come from surveys, so they must have some validity—the fact remains that they show that time use varies over a lifetime, so are thus a reasonable guide for comparison.

[19] U.S Bureau of Labor Statistics, "American Time Use Survey 2012," June 20, 2013. Retrieved from http://www.bls.gov/tus/#tables.

[20] Merrill Lynch Wealth Management, "Americans' Perspectives on New Retirement Realities and the Longevity Bonus," Merrill Lynch, 2013. Retrieved from http://wealthmanagement.ml.com/publish/content/application/pdf/GWMOL/2013_Merrill_Lynch_Retirement_Study.pdf.

[21] Ernie Zelinski, "Top-Ten Activities to Pursue When You Are Retired," Retirement Café. Retrieved from http://www.retirement-cafe.com/Top-Ten-Activities-When-You-Are-Retired.html.

[22] Frank Newport, God Is Alive and Well: The Future of Religion in America (Washington, D.C.: Gallup Press, 2012).

[23] See Emily Brandon, "Why Older Citizens Are More Likely to Vote," *U.S. News and World Report*, March 19, 2012. Retrieved from http://money.usnews.com/money/retirement/articles/2012/03/19/why-older-citizens-are-more-likely-to-vote.

[24] Volunteer Canada, "Bridging the Gap," 2010. Retrieved from http://volunteer.ca/content/bridging-gap.

[25] Emily Ferstie, "Volunteer Engagement: Reaching Out to Boomers," United Way for Southeastern Michigan Blog Post, May 2012. Retrieved from http://liveunitedsem.org/blog/entry/volunteer-engagement-reaching-out-to-boomers.

[26] Deborah L. Jacobs, "Charitable Giving: Baby Boomers Donate More, Study Shows," *Forbes*, August 8, 2013. Retrieved from http://www.forbes.com/

sites/deborahljacobs/2013/08/08/charitable-giving-baby-boomers-donate-more-study-shows/.

[27] Linda Nazareth, *The Leisure Economy* (Toronto, ON: John Wiley & Sons Ltd., 2007, p. 219.

[28] Civic Ventures, "Fact Sheet on Old Americans." Retrieved from http://www.civicventures.org/publications/articles/fact_sheet_on_older_americans.cfm.

Ladies First

Women are making economic strides worldwide, and over the next two decades will change their economic positions in both the developed and developing world. Still, the economic progress of women is proceeding rather slowly. A faster pace would help the world recover from the economic slowdown and keep it in higher growth mode in the decades ahead.

If there is a topic out there that invites confusion, it is the place of women in the global economy. In North America, we hear frequently about the "end of men"! This phenomenon is supposedly in full swing because women are, for example, entering law and medical schools in larger numbers than men. Globally, we hear that women are making strides toward economic parity with men in many countries, although obviously not all. There are nuggets of truth in each of these characterizations.

Still, as much as there have been changes—many of them induced by the last, traumatic business cycle downturn—men and women are certainly not changing places as economic power brokers. Women remain a fairly untapped economic resource in much of the world—including in North America. Although the choice to keep women out of the labor market may sometimes be a matter of social preference, in a world that is facing economic malaise there are larger issues at play. Women do not just hold up "half the sky"[1]: they are going to have to hold up a big chunk of the global economy over the coming decades if we are to keep economic activity going at a steady pace.

THE WORLD OVER: THE GENDER GAP AND ITS COSTS

Any way you measure it—and anywhere—there is a substantial gap between the economic place of women and men. And although the issue sometimes gets muddled in North America (where the debates bog down over the issue of who can "afford" to stay home), in a global sense it is very much a positive to have women fully participate in the economy. Women who earn money are generally healthier than those who do not, and economies that fully utilize their human resources—male and female—are typically healthier than those that fail to do so.

Let's look at the positives first. Throughout the world, there are examples of women moving forward, to the extent that consulting company Ernst & Young refers to women as the "largest emerging market in the world." By their estimation, between the years of 2012 and 2017, the global incomes of women will grow from $13 trillion to $18 trillion, with the incremental $5 trillion representing almost twice the growth in gross domestic product (GDP) expected from India and China combined. By the year 2028, Ernst & Young expects to see women control close to 75 percent of spending worldwide.[2]

Nice as these expected signs of progress may be, there is also plenty of evidence to suggest that there remain sizable gaps between men and women in terms of economic and even health status in most countries of the world. One of the most comprehensive ways to explore this is through the Gender Gap Index, a measure developed by the World Economic Forum (WEF) that contains separate components on annual education-, political-, and health-based criteria for 135 countries. This measure does not just look at how well women are doing in absolute terms (women in the United States certainly earn more than women in many parts of the world, for example, which would automatically give the U.S. a high score), but also explores how they are doing in relation to men in their country (a measure that, in the U.S., would produce a lower score).

Since 2006, the year that the Gender Gap Index debuted, there have been big improvements in women's status. Between that time and 2012, on average over 96 percent of the global gap in health outcomes in the world has been closed, as has 93 percent of the gap in educational attainment, 60 percent of the gap in economic participation, and 20 percent of the gap in political empowerment. No country has closed the gap entirely, although in the case of the top-ranked countries—Iceland, Finland, Norway, and Sweden— the composite gap (including each sub-index) is between 80 and 86 percent closed.[3]

One sub-component of the Gender Gap Index, the "Economic Participation Index," deserves special attention. This is the measure that looks at the percentage of women who participate in the labor force in a given country compared to the participation of men. The results show that in 2012, Mongolia (a land-locked country of about three million people in central Asia) ended up with the highest score, besting not just Canada and the United States but also the Nordic countries that dominated the overall list. The Economic Participation Index, rather than measuring the size of the pieces, shows how much of the entire pie women access. In those 2012 results, Mongolia was followed by the Bahamas, Burundi, Norway, Malawi, Lesotho, Luxembourg, and, finally, the United States (which took eighth place, four spots ahead of Canada).[4]

So why does all of this matter? If people are making the choices they want to, what difference does it make if they participate in the labor market? Forget any social arguments about women's rights and opportunities; there are macroeconomic reasons to want to see a closing of the gender gap. The gap between male and female participation rates is a deficit that has an impact on economic growth.

When you look at growth in an economy, it is typically composed of two things: first, growth caused by people working; and second, growth that comes from productivity (i.e., getting more out of each person who is working). The labor force participation rate is a measure of the people in any group who are either working or looking for a job as a percentage of all of those in the group. A society with more people—male and female—in the labor force is likely to produce more than one with a lower participation rate. And an economy operating at a higher speed produces higher incomes, which in turn produces other benefits. In a piece written in 2013, Goldman Sachs called this a "virtuous cycle as higher female disposable income trickles down to increased spending on education and healthcare, but also triggers a multiplier effect as women influence others to participate in the economy and invest in ideas."[5]

In an aging developed world, there is certainly a need to raise the labor force participation rate of women in many countries. In Japan, for example, the population is aging so rapidly that growth depends on having the kind of labor force growth that can be driven only by women being enticed to work outside the home. Christine Lagarde, the managing director of the International Monetary Fund (IMF), has actually gone as far as to say that "women could actually save Japan," citing the fact that the female labor force participation rate in Japan is only 50 percent (compared to 80 percent for men).[6] It is certainly a possible solution—one would think—for a country with an aging population that desperately needs some kind of an economic miracle.

The consulting firm Booz and Company takes these types of calculations one step further and looks at what they see as the perceived gross domestic product "cost" of not fully including women in the labor force. According to their math, if the female labor force participation rate were as high as the male rate, virtually every country in the world would have a higher gross domestic product. In the United States, for example, the level would be 5 percent higher; in Japan, 9 percent. In the developing world, where female participation rates are still very low compared to male rates, the increases would be staggering. For example, if the participation rates of women rose to the same levels as those of men in the United Arab Emirates, GDP would rise by 12 percent. If the same were to happen in Egypt, GDP would rise by a staggering 34 percent.[7]

There is also a close correlation between the overall gender gap and economic competitiveness. The WEF also publishes the World Competitiveness Index, which ranks countries on various measures of economic efficiency and competitiveness. When that index is graphed against the Gender Gap Index, there is close correlation, and for good reasons. If a country does not use half of its available talent, it cannot hope to be close to the top of its economic potential.

So what happens once women are enticed into the labor force? The next step is having them achieve positions of power. In the wake of the Wall Street–driven financial crisis in 2008, numerous articles asked whether the whole thing could have been avoided if more women—who as a group seem less prone to risk-taking behavior—had been at the helm of Wall Street firms.[8] Others have suggested that had British Petroleum (BP) had more senior-level women, the 2010 Deepwater Horizon oil spill that dumped 210 U.S. gallons of oil into the Gulf of Mexico might never have happened.[9] While we will never know for sure about those particular events, there is in fact ample evidence to show women do lead differently than men.

Studies show that having women on corporate boards can head off trouble. According to an article published in the *International Journal of Business Governance and Ethics*, of 624 board directors polled in Canada, women were more likely than men to use "cooperation, collaboration and consensus building" when dealing with complex issues. The study also found that women were more likely than men to take into account the interests of multiple stakeholders.[10] In 2012, a study by the U.S.-based Committee for Economic Development (CED) declared that the lack of women on corporate boards in the U.S. (women made up just 12 percent of board membership at the time) was a detriment to economic competitiveness.[11]

THE SITUATION IN NORTH AMERICA

Whatever the situation internationally, we have been led to believe that North America is different. The message is simple: women do better in North America. In 2010, "the end of men" became a popular catchphrase, thanks to a popular book of the same name by journalist Hanna Rosin. "At this unprecedented moment," she wrote, "women are no longer merely gaining on men; they have pulled decisively ahead by almost every measure."[12] Although

Rosin's book explored the situation around the world, her main examples came from the United States, where she surveyed states gutted by the worst recession in decades. In her observation, the survivors and "thrivers" were primarily women. Often, these women worked in well-paid service jobs and were married to men who had not fared well during the economic devastation.

To be sure, there is evidence that the economic gap is closing. And in some ways, this recent recession has been much worse for men than for women—so much so that it has sometimes been termed a "mancession." But this is not nearly as true as sometimes portrayed. Consider the statistics on employment. In the spring of 2008, before the economy really lost any ground, the "employment ratio"—the proportion of working-age population that has a job—was slightly above 69 percent for men. It then sank to a level of 63.3 percent by end of 2009, before recovering somewhat to 64.5 percent in 2013.[13] In contrast, although the women's participation rate went down a little less, from 56.6 percent to 53.5 percent, it has not reversed, and as of mid-2013 was sitting at 53.3 percent.[14] In Canada, the employment-to-population rates also declined over the business cycle. In 2008, the ratio for men was 68.0 percent; this fell sharply to 65 percent in the following year and had only recovered to 65.8 percent by 2012. For women, the rate went from 59.1 percent to 57.9 percent over the same period.[15] So although men might have been hit earlier and perhaps harder in certain sectors, women also lost some of their economic footing as a result of the recession.

There is no big mystery as to why men got hit harder than women during the early part of the recession. Male employment has traditionally been in the construction and manufacturing sectors, and these areas tend to be vulnerable early in economic downturns. During the 2008–09 downturn, the United States went through a protracted housing crisis—a double whammy in terms of male employment.

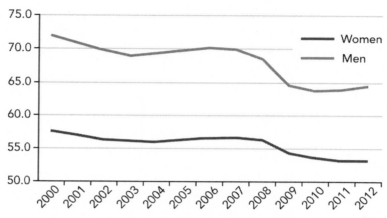

LESS LIKELY TO BE WORKING

Employment-to-population ratio, U.S.

Source: St. Louis Reserve (FRED database), U.S. Bureau of Labor Statistics.

In contrast, women tend to be disproportionately represented in service industries, particularly those in health care, social services, and education. Those areas were relatively untouched during the recession (although they are increasingly being hit as governments reduce budgets). The recession only exacerbated a trend away from high pay for jobs that require physical strength and minimal education and toward those that value softer skills. It has been happening for years: high-paying jobs that require only a basic education (for example, in manufacturing) are declining, and higher paying jobs that require a college level education (notably in finance) are increasing.

At the top of the economic pile, the visuals suggest that women are doing better, and making inroads that would not have been imagined a couple of decades ago. Perhaps the best example comes from Silicon Valley, where in 2012, 37-year-old Marissa Mayer was named president and CEO of search-engine Yahoo—despite the fact that she was seven months pregnant at the time. There are a handful of other women at the helm of major corporations these days too, including Meg Whitman (Hewlett-Packard), Denise Morrison (Campbell Soup Company), Rosalind Brewer (Sam's Club), Indra Nooyi (PepsiCo), and Virginia Rometty (IBM). When these women (the oldest of whom was under 60 in 2013) were in college 40 years ago, the sum total of women on a similar list would have been zero.

Still, despite the phenomenal progress of some, the overall statistics are still only "okay" in terms of what they say about women's progress in the corporate world. According to the research group Catalyst, as of 2012 women made up 14.3 percent of the ranks of executive officers in the Fortune 500. That's up a bit from 13.5 percent in 2009. If you look at the Fortune 500 board seats held by women, there is a bit more progress. In 2012, women held 16.6 percent of the seats, compared to 9.6 percent in 1995.[16] In Canada, women held 18.1 percent of senior/corporate officer positions in the Financial Post 500 in 2012, up from 14 percent in 2002. For board seats, the percentage is a bit lower, with 14.5 percent of the Financial Post 500 board seats held by women in 2011, compared to a tiny 6.2 percent in 1998.[17] So progress is happening rather slowly.

One data point that has gotten a lot of media attention in the past few years is this question whether young women are earning more than their boyfriends. An article in the online edition of Slate took that question as its title, and addressed the fact that, as of 2010, women in their 20s in large American cities were earning more than men in their 20s.[18] In fact, that claim is more or less correct. According to marketing research firm Reach Advisors, a survey of median earnings of childless women and men aged 22 to 30 working full-time in the largest

> A survey of median earnings of childless women and men aged 22 to 30 working full-time in the largest American cities revealed that the women earned 8 percent more than the men.

American cities revealed that the women earned 8 percent more than the men. On the surface, this sounds like an indicator of shifting fortunes for men and women, but there is more to the data than meets the eye.

Typically, the women employed in cities these days are in higher paying service sector occupations, while men could be in either those or in blue-collar occupations. That says nothing at all about whether women in the same professions as men are earning a premium—that is, there is nothing in the study to say that female law interns were earning 8 percent more than male ones (and, in fact, it is highly unlikely that they were). Still, it is significant that even a statistically biased survey could reach a conclusion such as this one. Thirty years ago, there would have been no way to sort the data to reach the conclusion that twenty-something women make more than twenty-something men, but things have changed over the decades. Think about the typical occupational categories for young city workers. While the categories for men may not have changed much over the years (law interns and construction workers), the categories for women have (law interns and retail workers today, secretaries and retail workers in years past).

So what comes next for women in economic terms? Well, the best place to start on that is by looking at the characteristics that will bring economic success, and that clearly means higher education or at least the acquisition of high-value-added skills. If you look at unemployment rates by education level, the spread between those with more and less education has only gotten wider in recent years. In 2012, the overall unemployment rate in the United States was 6.8 percent. For those with a bachelor's degree it was lower, at 4.5 percent, while for those with only a high-school degree it was 8.3 percent, a fairly significant spread. Even for those who do have a job, the income split is pretty pronounced by education level. In 2012, median weekly earnings in the U.S. were $815 a week; those with a bachelor's degree earned $1,066, and those with a high-school degree $652.[19] Given all that, you would think that young men would be clamoring into the doors of post-secondary institutions. Unfortunately, the data suggests otherwise.

According to data from the U.S. Department of Education (DOE), women have been earning more degrees than men since 1978. By 1987, women were earning more master's degrees than men, and by 2006 they earned more doctorates. In fact, since 1982, U.S. women have earned almost 10 million more college degrees than men. As of the 2013 graduating year, the DOE estimates that women will get 62 percent of all associate's degrees, 57 percent of bachelor's degrees, 60 percent of master's degrees, and 52 percent of doctoral degrees.[20] The Canadian figures—and the figures for a host of other developed countries—are not much different.

So why are men not getting these degrees? Apparently, because they are not applying to the schools in the first place. There is even evidence to suggest that men are not getting into schools *despite* the fact that administrations are holding them to lower standards than women: as of 2010, men made up 44 percent of the applicant pool for colleges in the United States.[21] A 2006 piece in the *New York Times* by Jennifer Delahunty Britz, dean of admissions at the U.S. liberal arts school Kenyon College, shocked some readers when Britz lamented "all the girls I've rejected," basically admitting that because Kenyon got fewer applicants from young men, they were more valued and by extension did not need to be as accomplished as young women in order to get an acceptance.[22] Other schools, including the University of Richmond, have also acknowledged that they look for a 50-50 gender-balance on campus, which means men are more likely to get a "yes" to their admissions than women. (It is impossible to know whether the smaller pool of male applicants is actually more qualified than the larger pool of women. If this were the case, it would make their higher acceptance rates "fair." However, since no school has come out and suggested that this is the case, it is perhaps not.)

The fact that men seem to be choosing to put themselves at an economic disadvantage is not really good news for anyone, but it does suggest that the next generation is shaping up to be a place where women have a systematic advantage over men in the form of more education. While that may not hold every man back or give every woman a fast-pass into the executive suite, the education gap between men and women is likely to close some of the pay gap that currently exists (albeit partly for the wrong reasons). For now, this trend is showing up as the "women make more than their boyfriends" phenomenon. Within a decade, it will increasingly manifest as "women make more than their husbands."

SO WHO WANTS TO "OPT OUT"?

Of course, there are other trends at play. One is that a number of very well-educated women are deciding to forgo working and become stay-at-home mothers. In 2003, *New York Times* journalist Lisa Belkin put a name to the phenomenon when she dubbed it the "Opting Out Revolution."[23] A decade later, figures show that there is an opt-out effect in existence, although perhaps not to the extent that the media sometimes portrays.

In 2009, the U.S. Census Bureau published a very comprehensive study on the labor force participation of women with young children. Using data for the period from 2005 to 2007, the researchers found that there are two kinds of women who tend to leave the workforce when they have young children. The first is women whose earnings are so low that they cannot afford child care, which is straightforward enough. The second group is women whose household earnings (generally meaning their spouse's earnings, but also perhaps income from investments and inheritances) made it possible to not work. Those women who had husbands in the highest 20 percent of earners had a 5.9 percent decrease in their labor force participation rates between 1994 and 2005.

Further evidence of the fact that highly educated women are opting out comes from research by Vanderbilt University professor Joni Hersch.[24] Hersch caught up with women who graduated from what she calls U.S. "Tier 1 schools" a decade after graduation, and compared their experiences to women who did not attend those schools. The gap varied between professions, with physicians and educators who graduated from the Tier 1s pretty much as likely to be employed as those who attended the other schools. MBA graduates from the "top" schools, however, were 16 percentage points less likely to be employed than the other women. Presumably, the women who went to the "best" schools were more likely to be married to men who also went to those schools, and were hence the most able to leave the labor force if they wanted to.

The question of why people—male or female—are choosing to opt out in higher numbers deserves closer attention. Is it because these individuals really do not want to work outside the home? Or is it because working outside the home in the highest-paying careers is deemed to be so difficult that anyone who has a choice would bail on trying to make it work? Arguably, a reason for the big split between men and women is that the corporate workforce does not make it worthwhile, in economic terms, to put in less than what in corporate parlance is called "110 percent."

And the evidence is that "face time" still matters and is probably hurting female economic progress. According to an article from the *Harvard Business Review* based on a special tabulation of U.S. census data, the percentage of American mothers who worked more than 50 hours a week in 2011 was a paltry 9 percent, compared to 29 percent of fathers. For individuals who have a college degree, the gap was even wider, at 14 percent of women compared to 37 percent of similarly educated men.[25] The article implied, no doubt correctly, that the gap between the number of hours worked goes some way toward explaining why there is still a gap between male and female executive achievements. Of course, we do not know for sure that the extra hours being put in by men automatically make them more efficient, nor do we know that the women who are not in the office are not on their laptops late at night making up the time. However, it probably would not matter if they were; even with the ability to work elsewhere that technology provides, the optics still matter at the end of the day.

IMAGINING THE IMPLICATIONS OF "LADIES FIRST"—ON MEN

Opting out aside, through their educational choices many North American women are putting themselves in a place where they will have high earnings potential. And we are talking about a different generation of women than we have seen previously—these are Generation Ys and Zs who believe that anything is possible, both socially and through the powers of technology. But if women are indeed going to take more positions of power over the coming decades, what does it mean for men? For example, if a man decides to take some time out of the labor force while his wife works, he is going to have different financial planning needs than would a man in a more traditional set-up. Or, if men increasingly find themselves with more sporadic work rather than in full-time pensionable jobs, they are going to have to plan their futures differently. Women have always had more patchwork careers, and have been only partly successful in making life decisions around them. For men it will be a whole new ball game, and one for which many will not be prepared.

> Women have always had more patchwork careers, and have been only partly successful in making life decisions around them. For men it will be a whole new ballgame, and one for which many will not be prepared.

When the 1983 film *Mr. Mom* was produced—telling the story of an executive (played by Michael Keaton) who loses his job and decides to do a stint as a stay-at-home dad—the idea was novel enough that it was automatically funny. Dad doing the laundry? Dad trying to make dinner? Hilarious. Thirty years later, while stay-at-home dads are still the exception rather than the rule, their numbers have expanded steadily. The actual number of men who identified themselves as "stay-at-home-dads" in the United States is still small (189,000 as of 2012), as of the spring of 2011, approximately 18 percent of preschoolers—nearly one in five—were regularly cared for by their fathers during their mother's work hours.[26] If, as the data suggests, women married to top earners are apt to "opt out," might we see more men married to top earners making this same choice in future? That is certainly a possibility, if indeed women are headed to the executive suite in higher numbers.

MAKING THE CHANGES—FOR EVERYONE'S SAKE

To be sure, women already have a lot of economic influence, some of which is not well-recognized. For example, in the United States, consumer spending—which comprises about 70 percent of the U.S. economy at present—is already powered by women, given that women control about 60 percent of household wealth and drive 80 percent of all consumption.[27] But as much as they drive spending, women's influence on the larger macroeconomic agenda is not yet at a point that would maximize economic output.

If the economy would benefit from the fuller participation of women, then should public policy not encourage it? In the developing world, the way forward on this issue is perhaps simplistically easy, if only in theory. Women must be given much fuller educational opportunities, which in turn will quickly change women's economic status. Unfortunately, getting to the point where education for women is a given means first changing societal attitudes, which is an extremely difficult thing to do indeed.

You do not need to look further than developed countries like Canada and the United States to see that attitudes change slowly. It has long been known that there are specific things that can be done to encourage women to enter and stay in the workforce. The providing of parental leave (not just leave for mothers) is at the top of that list, as are child-care and daycare subsidies, flexible work hours, the ability to telecommute, and part-time work (with prorated benefits) in the case of professional careers. Some of these things are available to some women (and men), but in a recession-ravaged, soft-economy world, where workers are easy to find, many of these "frills" have slipped off the corporate table. However, in a world where productivity is waning and a wave of baby boomers is nearing retirement, these "frills" may very well become necessities.

As the world gets reshuffled, just a bit, it will be interesting to see what the cohorts of Generation Y and Z men want from the labor force. Empowered by the possibilities of technology, will they want to telecommute? Will they ask for parental leaves for themselves? Will they want eldercare leaves to take care of their aging boomer and Generation X parents? If policies that support work-life balance were about all workers rather than simply women workers, it would go a long way toward moving forward an agenda that might ultimately benefit society in general.

It remains to be seen what women and men will put on the corporate negotiating table and obtain in the years ahead. Right now, high unemployment rates through much of the world as well as crushing student debts in much of North America are causing no one to ask for much of anything. Things change, however, and as labor supply growth starts to wane, the opportunities may change too.

WOMEN: THE WILDCARD POSSIBILITY FUELING GROWTH

Any long-term economic forecast can be thrown off by a wildcard, although when people make that observation it is usually to explain some negative factor that has sent growth spiraling downward. Women, however, are an economic wildcard that could actually send growth a whole lot higher. In an everything-held-constant future, the speed limit on world growth will be uncomfortably slow. The old superpowers are facing unfavorable demographics, and even the superstars of recent years (China, Brazil) are hitting a slower growth trajectory. There are new players that will do well, but not well enough to lift the world into higher gear. Women, though—women could indeed lift the world to a new level, economically. In fact, they could lift growth to exceptional heights— if they are allowed *and encouraged* to fully participate in the labor market.

Where will things be two decades from now? Hopefully not with disillusioned men and burned out women across North America, or with stalled progress elsewhere in the world. Forget social change: if things are going to improve significantly in an economic context, human resources need to be fully employed. That means employing men and women to the best of their abilities.

(ENDNOTES)

[1] Nicholas Kristof, *Half the Sky: Turning Oppression into Opportunity for Women Worldwide* (New York: Vintage, 2010).

[2] Ernst & Young, "High Achievers: Recognizing the Power of Women to Spur Business and Economic Growth"(Ernst & Young Limited, 2013). Retrieved from http://www.ey.com/Publication/vwLUAssets/Growing_Beyond_-_High_Achievers/$FILE/High%20achievers%20-%20Growing%20Beyond.pdf.

[3] Ricardo Hausmann, Laura D. Tyson, Yasmina Bekhouche, and Saadia Zahidi, "The Global Gender Gap Index 2012," World Economic Forum.

Retrieved from http://www3.weforum.org/docs/WEF_GenderGap_Report_2012.pdf.

[4] Ibid.

[5] Goldman Sachs, "Women's Work: Driving the Economy," Issue 53, April 25, 2013, p. 1. Retrieved from http://www.goldmansachs.com/our-thinking/focus-on/investing-in-women/womens-work-driving-the-economy.html.

[6] Mariko Oi, "Japan's Women: Can They Save the Country's Economy?" BBC News Onlne, October 24, 2012. Retrieved from http://www.bbc.co.uk/news/business-20053254.

[7] DeAnne Aguirre, Karin Sabbagh, Christine Rupp, and Lela Hoteit, "Empowering the Third Billion: Women and the World of Work in 2012," Booz & Co., October 15, 2012. Retrieved from http://www.booz.com/global/home/what-we-think/third_billion.

[8] See, for example, Marie Wilson, "In Women We Trust: How Wall Street Could Have Avoided Our Economic Meltdown," *Huffington Post*, September 23, 2008. Retrieved from http://www.huffingtonpost.com/marie-wilson/in-women-we-trust-how-wal_b_128727.html.

[9] The highest-ranking woman at BP actually "retired" (at age 48) less than a year before the disaster. See C.V. Harquail, "Could BP Have Avoided the Gulf Oil Spill if it had more Women Executives," www.authenticorganizations.com, May 26, 2010. Retrieved from http://authenticorganizations.com/harquail/2010/05/26/could-bp-have-avoided-the-gulf-oil-spill-if-it-had-more-women-executives/.

[10] Chris Bart and Gregory McQueen, "Why Women Make Better Directors," *International Journal of Business Governance and Ethics*, 8:1, 2013. Retrieved from http://www.boarddiversity.ca/sites/default/files/IJBGE8-Paper5-Why-Women-Make-Better-Directors.pdf.

[11] Committee for Economic Development, "Fulfilling the Promise: How More Women on Corporate Boards Would Make America and American Companies More Competitive" (Washington, D.C.: CED, Committee for Economic Development, June 6, 2012). Retrieved from http://www.ced.org/pdf/Fulfilling-the-Promise-Executive-Summary.pdf .

[12] Hanna Roisin, "*The End of Men* media kit," www.hannaroisin.com. Retrieved from http://hannarosin.com/the-end-of-men/media-kit/.

[13] U.S. Department of Labor, Bureau of Labor Statistics, "Table A-1: Employment status of the civilian population by age and sex." Retrieved from http://www.bls.gov/news.release/empsit.t01.htm.

[14] Ibid.

15 Human Resources and Skills Development Canada, *Indicators of Well-being in Canada*, "Work—Employment Rate." Retrieved from http://www4.hrsdc.gc.ca/.3ndic.1t.4r@-eng.jsp?iid=13.

16 Catalyst Knowledge Center, "2012 Catalyst Census: Fortune 500," December 11, 2012. Retrieved from http://www.catalyst.org/knowledge/2012-catalyst-census-fortune-500-women-board-directors.

17 Ibid.

18 Heather Boushey, "Are Young Women Earning More Than Their Boy-friends?" *Slate*, September 7, 2010. Retrieved from http://www.slate.com/articles/double_x/doublex/2010/09/are_young_women_earning_more_than_their_boyfriends.html.

19 Data refers to highest degree earned. United States Department of Labor, U.S. Bureau of Labor Statistics, "Employment Projections." Retrieved from http://www.bls.gov/emp/ep_chart_001.htm.

20 Mark J. Perry, "Stunning College Degree Gap," *AEIdeas*, May 13, 2013. Retrieved from http://www.aei-ideas.org/2013/05/stunning-college-degree-gap-women-have-earned-almost-10-million-more-college-degrees-than-men-since-1982/.

21 Ashley Hennigen, "Missing Men: Addressing the College Gender Gap," Higher Ed Live. Retrieved from http://higheredlive.com/missing-men/.

22 Jennifer Delahunt Britz, "To All The Girls I've Rejected," *New York Times*, March 23, 2006. Retrieved from http://www.nytimes.com/2006/03/23/opinion/23britz.html?_r=0.

23 Lisa Belkin, "The Opt Out Revolution," *New York Times Magazine*, October 26, 2013. Retrieved from http://www.nytimes.com/2003/10/26/magazine/26WOMEN.html.

24 Joni Hersch, "Opting Out Among Women with Higher Education," Vanderbilt Law and Economic Research Paper #13-05, April 25, 2013. Retrieved from http://papers.ssrn.com/sol3/papers.cfm?abstract_id=2221482.

25 Joan C. Williams, "Why Men Work So Many Hours," *Harvard Business Review* blog, May 2013. Retrieved from http://blogs.hbr.org/cs/2013/05/why_men_work_so_many_hours.html?utm_source=Socialflow&utm_medium=Tweet&utm_campaign=Socialflow.

26 United States Census Bureau, "Profile America: Facts for Features," April 18, 2013. Retrieved from http://www.census.gov/newsroom/releases/archives/facts_for_features_special_editions/cb13-ff13.html.

27 Goldman Sachs, p. 2.

The Age of Innovation— Hopefully

The 20th century was remarkable—and we are going to need another remarkable century to follow it. Innovations over the past hundred years have changed the path of human progress and allowed billions of us to live on a crowded planet. In the process, these same innovations have provided at least some of us with prosperity.

The people are still coming—but will the growth and prosperity? It could—and, frankly, it needs to if our overall standard of living is not to decline. The key? A burst of innovation—not impossible, but also something that needs to be nurtured through policy and a cultural shift that embraces new ideas and processes.

I t was the story of 2010: the rescue of 33 men who had been trapped inside a Chilean mine for 10 weeks. It had all the makings of a movie thriller, some great human interest stuff (one miner sang like Elvis to keep everyone entertained), and a happy ending too: everyone got out alive. So, with all the happy news, it was easy to miss the intriguing sidebar. If it had not been for innovation—defined by the Merriam-Webster dictionary as "the introduction of something new"[1]—the miners might have not made their escape.

As a story in the *Wall Street Journal*[2] chronicled at the time, there were a host of innovations that allowed the rescue to take place. These ranged from a special drill bit made by a company in Pennsylvania to a fiber optic communications cable from Japan, from high-strength German cable to hold the capsule together to special "copper fiber" socks made in Virginia. They were the right products at the right time, and they saved lives.

So the miners are fine—but will the forces of innovation be enough to save the global economy? Because—let's be clear—the global economy is going to need saving. We have an aging population in the developed world, and a world population that is growing at an amazing clip. We are also crumbling under the weight of the debt assumed during the recession-era stimulus. A push for innovation could compensate for these and a host of other problems, and make a huge difference to the future of both the developed and developing world. But is this push going to happen? That's far from a sure thing.

INNOVATION AND PRODUCTIVITY—THE MAGIC BULLETS

Let's start with some definitions. When we talk about "economic growth," we are usually talking about two separate things. One is the expansion in the economy that comes about because there are people working. The other is the expansion in the economy that comes about as a result of how productive those people are. If a guy starts a lawn mowing business with a small, manual lawn mower, he maybe gets 10 lawns mowed a week. If he uses a large riding mower, he'll get maybe 50 lawns done, and, as a result, make a lot more money. Assuming he is paying taxes on all of it, contributions to the economy will show up in the gross domestic product (GDP) of the country he lives in. The larger mower increases his productivity, and hence the economic potential of the country. So where does innovation fit in? In a world where ideas are allowed to flourish, you can invent a riding lawnmower, or maybe something even better.

If you want to get an idea of how innovation has worked its magic, you have to start with Thomas Malthus, the guy who warned about the limits of the earth's largesse back in 1798. Malthus did the math, as he saw it at the time, and figured that the world would eventually be done in by famine and disease. As it turns out, he was wrong about just what the limits were. Thanks to innovations in everything from energy extraction to food production, Earth ended up being able to provide for far more people than he, or anyone else who lived in his time, could possibly have imagined.

If you look at the history of the economy for the past couple hundred years, the remarkable progress we have seen can be explained pretty squarely by innovation. New ideas and new processes have catapulted the world into a place where things get done bigger, better, and faster than could ever have been imagined decades, let alone centuries, ago. How does this work? The equation is fairly simple: innovation leads to productivity leads to growth. Which is to say, new ideas lead to new ways of doing things, which means doing things more effectively, which means growing the economy and raising standards of living.

It might be helpful to put some numbers to all of this. Just how important has technology (which effectively stems from innovation) been to the economy up to now? A couple of economists have attempted to calculate an answer. One of the most famous tabulations was by Nobel Prize winner for economics Robert Solow, who measured the growth in the U.S. economy relative to the growth of the inputs going into it (capital and labor). What he found was that 85 percent of the growth experienced by the U.S. between the late 1800s and the mid-20th century could *not* be accounted for by input growth. Rather, the "residual" 85 percent was about technology.[3]

So now let's take a quick tally of the things that have, literally, changed lives. The story actually starts around 1750, which is more or less the beginning point of what is sometimes called the First Industrial Revolution. If you go back much farther, you won't find a lot in terms of industrial innovation or productivity or economic growth; but from 1750 onward it was a different story, at least for awhile. From that point on, and in rapid succession, the world was introduced to what are sometimes called "disruptive" technologies, such as the steam engine, the cotton gin, and machine tools, all of which showed up over a period of about 50 years. The Second Industrial Revolution (so-called by economist Robert Gordon) came a little later, in 1890, and went all the way through to 1972. Those were the years when the world was treated to electricity, the internal combustion engine, running water, indoor toilets, communications, entertainment, chemicals, and petroleum.[4] It is a pretty remarkable list, and between the two industrial revolutions the world managed a pretty remarkable growth trajectory.

After the early 1970s, the world slowed down growth-wise and productivity-wise. Plenty of explanations have been offered for the slowing, including the energy crisis and a shift in demographics that forced inexperienced managers to take the helm.[5] However, much as other things may have contributed, there is certainly a case to be made that the developed world had gotten all it could out of earlier innovations, and that there were diminishing returns to what was being offered. Electricity changed the world, after all;

offering the first coffee percolator with an automatic drip process (Sunbeam introduced the Mr. Coffee in 1978) could not hope to compete.

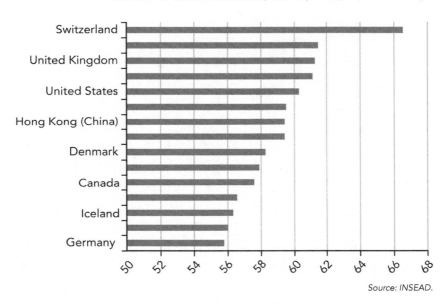

HOW THEY RANK

Global Innovation Index 2013, Score (1–100)

Source: INSEAD.

There was a third industrial revolution, which started in the 1980s and was caused by the proliferation of information technologies. It is debatable, however, whether this one was as important as the previous two. Computers and computing technology led to the development of all kinds of things that could never have been imagined previously—things like laptop computers, smartphones, the Internet, and mobile technology. And although these things have all changed the way that we live, some would argue that they are not comparable to the advent of, say, basic sanitation.[6] That view is more or less borne out in the figures we have on productivity; in the United States and in much of the Western world, productivity rose during the 1990s and early 2000s, so much so that some believed that the world had entered a "new paradigm," and that technology had killed old economic issues such as inflation. Since then, however, productivity has plateaued, and in the years since the Great Recession, has declined.[7] That lends credence to the argument that we have exhausted the growth benefits of the latest surge in technology.

WHY INNOVATION NEEDS TO HAPPEN NOW

If we are at the end of a technological revolution, with all that goes with it, how important is it that we have another one? Pretty important, as it turns out. If over the last few decades we used technology to live better, over the next few decades we may need some productivity improvements just to maintain what we have.

At the moment, the world has a few things stacked against it, growth-wise. They may not be insurmountable challenges, but we can hardly ignore them. The first is the aging populations are the reality in most of the developed and much of the developing world (see chapter 1). Stagnating or declining working-age populations are generally a detriment to economic expansion. Then, too, there is the fact that much of the world faces a decade or more of paying the bills that mounted up when government spent its way out of the "Great Recession" of 2008–09. Clearly, government spending is going to be muted for some time.

There are other challenges too. In explaining why they see innovation as key to the world's future, the Organisation for Economic Co-operation and Development (OECD) puts the emphasis on the developing world, looking at the issues that will have to be handled if people are not going to be resurrecting Malthus's theories. For one thing, global temperatures may be headed up by 3 to 6 degrees Celsius by century's end[8]; for another, it looks as if we may have three billion more people on the planet by 2060.

So, there will be more people. Naturally, some will be reasonably prosperous. But that in and of itself is a double-whammy. A surge in growth in developing countries and the creation of new middle classes around the globe certainly means higher demand is coming for everything from oil to beef (see chapter 5). Unless something changes, that will mean higher prices for all kinds of commodities—unless some way to expand supply, and expand supply at a lower production cost, is found.

All of this is going to impact the larger economy. True, higher resource prices might benefit the companies that deal in them, but *every* company is going to face higher input prices. That's an issue for anyone who is trying to make money in the equity markets, as are the demographic and growth issues facing North America. Given that an older population is more likely to sell their stocks than buy new ones, the aging of the population is not a positive for the direction of financial markets. To find decent returns, investors are going to have to pick innovative companies—assuming that they exist.

Even now, they are in pretty short supply. Ask for an example of a company known for innovation and Apple comes pretty quickly to mind. And it *is* an innovative company, a fact that has translated into handsome gains for shareholders. Indeed, it has done so well in recent years that in tallying up the gains on the Standard & Poor's 500 index these days, you often see references to "gains excluding Apple" in order to get an accurate gauge of how well *everyone else* is doing. Now, Apple's success in the equity market or as a company is not solely based on its standing as an innovation company, but it stands to reason that all companies would do better if they were more innovative. Looking out to the next decade, the demographic trends suggest that "buy and hold" is not going to be a sure-fire way for investors to make gains. This will come from investing in companies that keep posting good results, results that must be fueled by good and innovative products and by productivity gains.

Then again, the word *productivity* sometimes scares people. If companies are more productive, will they need fewer workers in future? We do know that as economies develop, old processes and jobs are often replaced by new ones. The advent of the automobile heralded a new era and lots of employment, but it also effectively killed the profession of "buggy-whip maker." In 1942, economist Joseph Schumpeter termed this process "creative destruction," suggesting the idea of destroying something in the process of creating something else.

And indeed, research by the OECD quantifies something we can see anecdotally: innovative companies create jobs while stagnant ones do not. A study by Ernst & Young asked 553 entrepreneurs how innovation had changed their workforce requirements. Not surprisingly, 74 percent said that thanks to innovation they had increased their workforces.[9] Of course, the relationship between innovation and jobs is a bit more complicated than you are likely to hear in political speeches praising the building of new research parks or factories. Companies that innovate typically do need more people (think of Apple and the development of the iPod, for example[10]), but there is no guarantee that those jobs will be in proximity to the place where the products were developed (Apple's headquarters are in California, but the iPod is manufactured in Asia). On a global basis, however, jobs and innovation do move together, as do innovation and growth.

WHERE INNOVATION IS HAPPENING

The good news is that innovation *is* happening through the world, although some countries are doing a better job of getting it done than others. To get an idea of how the world ranks in terms of innovation, we can look to the Global Innovation Index (GII) created by the business school INSEAD. The GII looks at both "innovation inputs" (measured by such things as respective countries' institutions, human capital and research abilities, infrastructure, market sophistication, and business sophistication as each relates to innovation) and "innovation outputs" (measured by knowledge and technology outputs and creative outputs).

The top 10 countries for 2013 are, according to GII rankings, Switzerland, Sweden, the United Kingdom, the Netherlands, the U.S., Finland, Hong Kong, Singapore, Denmark, and Ireland, an identical list to the 2012 ranking. But looking at the top of the pack with an economist's eye leads to a bit of confusion: several countries that rank high in terms of innovation are actually not doing well in an economic sense. Ireland, for example, is mired in a deep recession. And other countries that do not make the list (Canada, for example, is 11th, and Germany is 15th) are showing a lot of economic strength at the moment. Then again, innovation strength is a leading index rather than a coincident one, and its gains are not necessarily concentrated within national borders. [11]

Also interesting is that some of the top economic performers in recent years have not necessarily shown themselves to be top performers on the innovation scale. Looking at the BRICS (Brazil, Russia, India, China, and South Africa—the nations flagged a dozen years ago as the ones to watch in terms of growth), China ranked 35th in 2013, South Africa 58th, the Russian Federation 62nd, Brazil 64th, and India 66th. INSEAD also tagged a group of emerging economies with good innovation policies—including Armenia, China, Costa Rica, Georgia, and Hungary—as actively outperforming others in their income groups.

The INSEAD report also looked at a couple of other indicators more traditionally associated with innovation; namely, R&D spending and patent applications. What they found was that after a significant drop during the recession, countries have since started investing in the latter. This is true in the developed world, but also in rapidly developing countries such as China, India, and Malaysia, where spending has tended to be in the double digits.

The World Intellectual Property Organization (WIPO) also tracks patent applications, and reported that between 2008 and 2011, worldwide patent filings were up by 3.8 percent. There was huge variation by region, however, with China reporting a 22 percent increase in patent filings over the period, compared to a 3.3 percent increase in the U.S. and Canada, and a decline of 0.8 percent in Europe. China contributed 72 percent of the patent filings over the period, continuing what WIPO notes is a "shifting in the geography" of patent filings.[12]

The increase in innovation activity from China brings up an interesting point: it's possible that a surge in world innovation and productivity will originate in newly industrialized countries, and the benefits may spill over into the developed and developing world. The countries now experiencing the best manufacturing productivity performance in the world are Singapore, Taiwan, and South Korea. Each came out of the Great Recession with relatively low bills for fiscal stimulus and have taken a proactive role toward encouraging innovation. They spend heavily on research and development, and have highly educated workforces—all in all, a nice equation for success.

> According to a report by the U.S. Intelligence Council, the next 15 to 20 years will see a "shift in the technological center of gravity" from the West to the East and the South.

According to a report by the U.S. Intelligence Council, the next 15 to 20 years will see a "shift in the technological center of gravity" from the West to the East and the South.[13] Large corporations, of course, are already shifting their focus to places where growth is strongest, countries like China and India as well as other emerging economies. In turn, this will stimulate innovation emanating from those countries.

A ROLE FOR EVERYONE IN INNOVATION POLICY

So innovation needs to happen, and we are only partway to ensuring that it does. Whose fault is that? Well, let's just say that there is a role for everyone in taking the next step.

Government

The fact that governments all over the world are cash-strapped does not bode well for innovation. Innovation policies do not bring in tax revenues in the short term. In fact, even in the long term, successful innovation does not necessarily bring benefits to the originating country. So, heavy spending on R&D in Canada, for example, may or may not result in a surge in tax revenues in Canada; even if it does, it may take some time before they are realized. That means that a government that is counting its pennies (which describes virtually every government) may not have much incentive to support pro-innovation policies, at least unless there is heavy public support for them. So, the first challenge may be to create the buy-in for public spending to support innovation policies, even if payback is not on the immediate horizon.

Governments around the world have chosen different options to encourage innovation. From direct subsidies to R&D tax credits to support for higher education, there are a host of possibilities and no one-size-fits-all formula to create a successful climate for innovation. A 2013 report by consulting firm Pricewaterhouse-Coopers (PWC) makes this point, stating that "no single strategy or approach works for all countries." They do note, however, that the most successful countries integrate a number of different measures related to taxes, including low overall tax rates, R&D incentives, and tax breaks for investors.[14]

Then again, it's not just about the money: government policies regarding innovation are as important as public spending on it. There is an argument to be made that during earlier industrial revolutions, it was easier to get the ball rolling, so to speak, because government red tape was not nearly so onerous. Of course, there are innovations in which government does need to be heavily involved in (drugs do need to be tested and monitored), but some countries make it particularly difficult for ideas to turn into reality. From standards and pricing through to consumer education and public procurement, governments do play a role in successful innovation.

And encouraging innovation *within* the government sector can make a big difference as well. The Internet, after all, came from the U.S. Department of Defense. In 1969, the Department funded something called ARPANET, which was basically an experiment to link the department and its military contractors through "reliable networking."[15] In a similar vein, technologies originally developed by governments for military use have often ended up with much wider applications. World War II sparked the development of a long list of innovations, from pressurized air cabins through to nuclear power.

Finally, the real key to ensuring that innovation is possible and that it happens at a high level within any country is education. Innovation in the 21st century is not what it was in the 19th or even 20th century. During the first two industrial revolutions, the rock-star innovations were things that you could see and touch, like steam engines. As a report by the Brookings Institution notes, most patents inventors in days gone by were blue-collar workers; these days, innovation is coming from those with STEM-type training (science, technology, engineering, and math).[16] That's not to say that a college dropout cannot sit in his mother's garage and create something anymore: some innovation will surely originate in that way. Still, innovation is likely to come from increasingly sophisticated training, some of which will need to be supported by either the public or private sector.

A country without a skilled labor force—with high skills in math and science—cannot hope to be a country with a strong innovation culture. In these days of government budget cutbacks, it is going to be an ongoing challenge to ensure that education remains a high priority at both the lower and higher levels. It is, however, a challenge that must be met.

Business

There are a lot of things that business can do to foster innovation, but at the top of the list is changing their mindset. Innovation is not a quick fix kind of thing: developing a new technology might take years, and might not ever result in a profitable product. That means companies have to take a very long-term view if they are going to innovate, and that can be an expensive decision to make.

In many ways, however, this is a short-term economy, and it's almost as if the private sector has also realigned in a way that does not foster innovation. There might be a bit of nostalgia at play here (and perhaps we're looking at the past through an *It's a Wonderful Life* lens), but decades ago there was a combined emphasis on making money while also creating new products that would be profitable in some future period. More recently, it has been argued that a culture of rewarding shareholders has hindered spending on anything that will not goose the next set of quarterly earnings.

Economist William Lazonick has suggested that this is a case of recognizing "shareholder value" while simultaneously failing to acknowledge taxpayer value (given that the public tacitly supports corporations through public investments that benefit businesses) and worker value (given that employees often work above and beyond the level for which they are compensated).[17] Whether or not that is completely true—shareholders do bear most of the risk

> Innovation is not a quick fix kind of thing: developing a new technology might take years, and might not ever result in a profitable product. That means companies have to take a very long-term view if they are going to innovate, and that can be an expensive decision to make.

in any enterprise—it is correct that the focus these days is certainly on a fairly short horizon, and particularly on the value of a stock in the short term. If a company with a potentially innovative product gets pounded in the market because of bad earnings, the pressure will be on do something, anything, to "turn things around"—and quickly. That turnaround can mean abandoning a promising product, or it can mean bringing it to market before it is actually ready to be there. It is also clear that companies are more involved than they used to be in stock buybacks and manipulation of stock prices, rather than in longer-term investments.[18]

A second, related problem is that lending to companies is not nearly as fashionable as it used to be as a way for the financial sector to make money. It is kind of an old-time notion, actually, putting money into a company with the idea that the company will be profitable. From the 1980s onward, financial firms have made increasing amounts of their revenue from sophisticated financial instruments and trading rather than investing (which, in turn, set about some of the conditions for the Great Recession). Without that flow of capital into companies, it is pretty difficult for innovation to flourish.

Of course, even for those companies that do spend heavily on innovation, there are no guarantees. If you look at the companies that spend the most on R&D, you are not necessarily looking at a list of the companies that produce the most innovative products. Such a list for 2012 shows that one of the top spenders in the tech sector, and the company that was ranked seventh overall, was Nokia—a company that has not come up with an innovation product in years and whose earnings are so poor that its debt was cut to "junk" status in August 2013. The auto companies are also big R&D spenders—Toyota was actually the biggest spender overall—but it is hard to call the changes in product offerings in recent years particularly innovative (although the improved cup holders are certainly nice). The companies that do have innovative products—Apple, Nike, Google—typically are not the biggest spenders; they are just the ones that have the best cultures for innovation—and that cannot be bought easily with dollars and cents.[19]

As for innovation strategy, there is no shortage of ways that a company can make that successful—or fail to do so. In a 2009 piece in the *Wall Street Journal*, researchers John Bessant, Katherin Moslein, and Bettina von Stamm chronicled nine different strategies that could help companies find their "Eureka!" moment. Ranging from things as simple as "start a conversation" (setting up communications between departments) through to "building scenarios" (enlisting writers with different perspectives to come up with visions of the future), their suggestions, which were based on reviews of over 100 companies, were aimed at finding ways to get companies to think outside of the box.[20] The key step, however, may be one back: before companies think about how to encourage innovation, they first have to decide that they want to in the first place.

Society as a Whole

Governments matter, business matters, but everyone else matters too. From parents who need to encourage their kids to take math and science through to taxpayers who need to support innovation policies, everyone has a role in creating the kind of world that needs to emerge. We need to create a culture of entrepreneurship, one where people are not afraid to take risks, and we need to encourage women (who tend to be under-represented as innovators) to get into the game. A public buy-in to the need for innovation may be the final, important key to ensuring the future.

OPTIMIST OR PESSIMIST?

As we look to the future, there are reason to be optimistic about the kind of technologies that past innovations have wrought and the ways that they might counteract the negatives hitting economic growth.

Robotics, for example, might go some distance toward offsetting the labor shortages that could come with demographic change. For the last couple of decades, China has been the world's manufacturing hub, a fact that has kept prices down for a host of goods consumed in Asia and throughout the world. China was able to be such an efficient manufacturer partly because it had a plentiful youth population who could easily fill factories with workers. That is changing: partly as a result of the one-child policy implemented in the 1970s, China is a nation that is rapidly aging, a fact that threatens its status as a growth leader, and threatens to raise prices in dollar stores across North America and the world. Could robot technology help? Perhaps. According to the International Federation of Robotics (IFR), China bought 22,577 industrial robots in 2011—a 51 percent increase over their 2010 level.[21]

In fact, the statistics on robot purchases are stunning overall. According to the IFR data, global robot sales were up 38 percent in 2011, meaning that a record 166,028 robots were sold. Although China was a primary driver of growth, the U.S. and Germany were also big purchasers. In absolute terms, the biggest buyers of robots are South Korea and Japan.[22] The latter is no surprise: with the oldest population on earth, Japan is under pressure to figure out how to produce when young labor is and will continue to be in short supply.

Given the aging of the baby boom population, one of the world's biggest challenges is going to be in managing health technologies. Large and small, there are a number of initiatives now afoot that can go some distance toward making that happen. For example, there are now attempts to use social networking to make it easier for doctors to collaborate on patient care in difficult cases. There are also mobile apps that allow doctors to communicate in one language and have quick translations to patients who speak another.

And the supercomputer known as Dr. Watson (you might remember it as the contestant that beat out former champions on *Jeopardy* in 2011) is now being used at New York's Memorial Sloan-Kettering Cancer Center to help physicians better diagnose patients and recommend treatments.[23]

The problem of resource scarcity may also be partially offset by better technologies. For example, "fracking" as way to extract oil and natural gas is already increasing potential energy production in North America. The process actually has its roots in the 1940s, when it was introduced by Standard Oil. However, it has really come to the fore over the past couple of decades, both through its use in the Canadian oil sands, as well as in the United States, where it has led to a surge in the amount of domestic energy production. According to the McKinsey Global Institute, there is a 100 to 200 percent potential increase in North American oil production by 2025, driven by hydraulic fracturing and horizontal drilling.[24]

Unfortunately, it is not too difficult to take a pessimistic view of the future of innovation. Robert Gordon has been making that case lately, suggesting that in many ways we are at the height of innovation-type progress. For example, rather than making planes fly more quickly than ever, or inventing new types of planes, these days we are slowing them down as a way to conserve fuel. He also has a laundry list of negative forces that he believes cannot be offset by the positives innovation might bring; namely, a poor education system in the United States, debt repayment, global labor arbitrage, the aging population, and pollution.[25] All of these are real and present dangers to the global economy.

Then again, health is getting better in most places, and hopefully will get better still. Developing countries are in a virtuous circle of rising incomes, rising taxes, and (eventually) rising living standards. Urbanization is creating opportunities that did not exist when people were more scattered across the globe. And women are more fully participating in the economy.

What comes next? We cannot know the future until it happens. The steam engine and the telephone were marvels in their day; the idea of flying coast to coast and texting as soon as you landed was beyond anyone's comprehension even a few decades ago, but it happened just the same. Is it foolhardy to believe that the global economy will speed up because of some kind of magical innovation cycle ready to happen? It would be, yes, because we are a little lacking in economic magic here on planet Earth. If, however, we make the kind of policy and attitude changes that would facilitate creativity and innovation, we've got a whole different ball game. The future is in our hands, just as it always has been—we just need to make the right moves and be optimistic with confidence.

(ENDNOTES)

[1] Merriam-Webster online dictionary. Retrieved from http://www.merriam-webster.com/dictionary/innovation.

[2] Daniel Henninger, "Capitalism Saved the Miners," *Wall Street Journal*, October 14, 2010. Retrieved from http://online.wsj.com/news/articles/SB10001424052748703673604575550322091167574.

[3] For more see Nathan Rosenberg, "Innovation and Economic Growth," OECD, 2004, http://www.oecd.org/cfe/tourism/34267902.pdf, p. 1.

[4] Robert Gordon, "Is U.S. Growth Over? Faltering Innovation Confronts the Six Headwinds," Working Paper No. 18315, National Bureau of Economic Research, August 2012, p. 1.

[5] James Feyrer, "The U.S. Productivity Slowdown, the Baby Boom and Management Quality," Dartmouth College, June 13, 2008. Retrieved from http://www.dartmouth.edu/~jfeyrer/managers.pdf.

[6] See Robert Gordon, "Why Innovation Won't Save Us," *Wall Street Journal*, December 21, 2012. Retrieved from http://online.wsj.com/article/SB10001424127887324461604578191781756437940.html.

[7] For statistics on U.S. productivity performance, see U.S. Bureau of Labor Statistics, "Labor Productivity and Costs." Retrieved from http://www.bls.gov/lpc/prodybar.htm.

[8] Reuters, "OECD Warns of Ever Higher Greenhouse Gas Emissions," *New York Times*, March 12, 2012. Retrieved from http://www.nytimes.com/

2012/03/16/business/energy-environment/oecd-warns-of-ever-higher-greenhouse-gas-emissions.html?adxnnl=1&adxnnlx=1384020180-woFdcFposAawGXW2t9hOYA.

[9] Ernst & Young, "Global Job Creation: A Survey of the World's Most Dynamic Entrepreneurs," January 2013, p. 3. Retrieved from http://www.ey.com/Publication/vwLUAssets/2013_Global_job_creation_report/$FILE/Global%20job%20creation%202013_CY0422_final.pdf.

[10] The development of the iPod actually involved many people and the implementation of technology that Apple had previously developed. There were plenty of MP3 players on the market prior to the iPod, but Microsoft founder Steve Jobs felt that they were "crap'" and mobilized his team to create something that would work well with downloadable music. For more see Benj Edwards, "The Birth of the iPod," MacWorld, October 23, 2011. Retrieved from http://www.macworld.com/article/1163181/the_birth_of_the_ipod.html.

[11] See Soumitra Dutta, Daniela Benavente, Bruno Lavin, and Sacha Wunsch-Vincent, "The Global Innovation Index 2013: Local Dynamics Keep Innovation Strong in the Face of Crisis," World Intellectual Property Organization, 2013. Retrieved from http://www.globalinnovationindex.org/content.aspx?page=gii-full-report-2013.

[12] "World Intellectual Property indicators, 2012 edition." Retrieved from http://www.wipo.int/export/sites/www/ipstats/en/wipi/pdf/941_2012_highlights.pdf.

[13] Matthew Burrows, "World Trends 2030: Alternative Worlds," United States Security Council, 2012. Location 2803 (in Kindle downloaded copy).

[14] PricewaterhouseCoopers, "Innovation: Government's Many Roles in Fostering Innovation," August 2010, p. 4.

[15] "History of the Internet: Where Did the Internet Come From?" netgurus.com, June 3, 2005. Retrieved from http://net.gurus.org/history/.

[16] "Patenting and Innovation in Metropolitan America," The Brookings Institution, February 1, 2013. Retrieved from http://www.wipo.int/export/sites/www/ipstats/en/wipi/pdf/941_2012_highlights.pdf.

[17] William Lazonick, "The Financialization of the U.S. Corporation: What Has Been Lost and How It Can Be Regained," Institute for New Economic Thinking, July 2012, Retrieved from http://ineteconomics.org/sites/inet.civicactions.net/files/Note-7-Lazonick.pdf.

[18] Lynn Stuart Parramore, "Big Finance Is Strangling Innovation," Salon.com, July 27, 2013. Retrieved from http://www.salon.com/2013/07/27/big_finance_is_sucking_the_life_out_of_our_economy_partner/.

[19] Adam Hartuna, "Top 20 R&D Spenders—Not Good Investments," *Forbes*, November 5, 2012. Retrieved from http://www.forbes.com/sites/adamhartung/2012/11/05/top-20-rd-spenders-not-good-investments/print/.

[20] John Bessant, Kathrin Moslein, and Bettina von Stamm, "In Search of Innovation," *Wall Street Journal*, June 22, 2009. Retrieved from http://online.wsj.com/news/articles/SB100014240529702048303045741335 62888635626.

[21] International Federation of Robotics, "Industrial Robot Statistics." Retrieved from http://www.ifr.org/industrial-robots/statistics/.

[22] Ibid.

[23] Bruce Upbin, "IBM's Watson Gets Its First Piece of Business in Health-care," *Forbes*, February 8, 2013. Retrieved from http://www.forbes.com/sites/bruceupbin/2013/02/08/ibms-watson-gets-its-first-piece-of-business-in-healthcare/.

[24] James Manyika, Michael Chui, Jacques Bughin, Richard Dobbs, Peter Bisson, and Alex Marrs, "Disruptive Technologies: Advances that will transform life, business and the global economy," McKinsey Global Institute, May 2013, p. 4.

[25] Gordon, p. 2.

Conclusion: Using Economorphics to Transform Yourself or Your Organization

So the world is changing around you—does that make you powerless? Of course not. Just knowing what changes are afoot gives your tremendous power. The best way to make practical use of this knowledge is to take each one of the economorphic trends we've explored and look at how it might affect your own organization, or your life. And the best way to do that might be through the lens of a SWOT analysis—a look at your strengths and weaknesses in the context of the opportunities and threats that are coming down the road.

f you've read this far, you know that the world is shifting, and apparently will shift a great deal more in the years ahead. But what does that mean in the context of your own concerns? If you are at the helm of business, it is all very well and good to know that the demographics are against North America, but how exactly do you make use of that information? What if you run a nonprofit? Can knowing the big-picture trends help you meet your (shrinking) budget next year? And what if you are just, well ... you? What if you are trying to steer your career and your investments in the face of what looks like a never-ending bear market? Will knowledge of the economorphic trends help at all? The answer to all of these questions is *yes*—if you use the information in a systematic way and put it to its best use.

First of all, you need to remember the words of Sir Francis Bacon (if your history is fuzzy, he was the 16th-century philosopher, statesman, and scientist credited with creating the scientific method) and tell yourself that "knowledge is power."[1] The more you know, the more you can construct plans that protect you from what is happening or, better yet, allow you to profit from it. If you'd known that dot.com stocks were going to crash in 2000, would you have bought them? Of course not. Nor would you have held on to them. If anything, you could have shorted them and made some money.

Unfortunately, no book (or person, for that matter) can predict the future with 100 percent certainty, thus ensuring that you can short the market and become a billionaire. What you can do, however, is use the knowledge that you've gathered here to best strategize your future. This book came about as a result of many keynote presentations I've given to business groups in the midst of their strategic planning processes. They wanted a view of the big picture before they added in their own variables to come up with workable strategic plans. The economorphic trends presented here can work the same way for you: understand them, add what you know about your own attributes, and you will have a formula for navigating the best path to the future.

A LOOK AT THE BIG PICTURE

Before we look at ways to use the economorphic trends, let's take a step back and think about the big picture—or the macroeconomic framework, if we want to get fancy—that emerges when we put the individual trends together. In a nutshell, there are two things going on in the world: cyclical changes, and structural changes. Some of the economorphic trends fall neatly into one category or another, but for the most part they are a mix of both.

Cyclical trends are caused by the ebb and flow of the business cycle—the fluctuations in economic variables such as employment, production, trade, and spending that together determine whether the economy is in expansion or recession. In theory, at least, there is a fairly predictable pattern to the whole thing. There is a growth phase (expansion), which is followed by a "peak" in economic activity. Then there is a recession phase (followed by a trough), and finally a recovery phase. Since the end of World War II, most business cycles in the U.S. have lasted a little under a year, although these days few believe that they are predictable in either frequency or duration.[2]

North America is now years away from being in recession, so theoretically we are in an expansion phase, but few indicators would suggest that the pre-recession peak has been regained. That means that there is overall sluggishness in terms of things like employment and gross domestic product. One could argue that many economorphic trends are being affected by this sluggishness. The divide between rich and poor, for example, has surely been worsened by cyclical factors, as has the fact that men have lost their footing in the labor market.

But if the economy zoomed up over the next year or two, would the economorphic trends vanish? No. At best, some of the intensity behind the need for innovation would diminish, or perhaps there would be less shuffling of the economic deck. The demands for resources would only get more intense, however, and there would likely be an even quicker push to urbanization. Overall, however, the economorphic trends are going to be in place whatever the business cycle fluctuations.

These trends are thus also an illustration of structural changes in the economy. The things that have shifted or are shifting are going to continue to adjust no matter what happens to interest rates or a particular country's spending choices. Of course, there are ways to improve outcomes in the face of structural shifts. For example, if the problem with income disparities is happening because decent wages are only available for jobs that require specialized training, then there could be a push for governments to fund that kind of training. For the most part, however, we have to assume that the outcomes that are occurring are the result of strong market forces, and that they are not going to be reversed very easily (and, in some cases, nor should they be).

We are in the midst of a sea change, and to maximize your own particular outcome means recognizing that context, and then making your decisions accordingly. The wheel is turning, and it is only turning one way.

STRENGTHS, WEAKNESSES, OPPORTUNITIES, AND THREATS—USING SWOT ANALYSIS

A great way to take stock of your organization (or your life) and to make the best use of your new knowledge of the economorphic trends is through a SWOT analysis. SWOT stand for strengths, weaknesses, opportunities, and threats, and if you think about it, they are a pretty good benchmark for measuring where you are relative to where you would like to be.

Putting together a SWOT analysis that incorporates the econo-morphic trends can be of use to all kinds of organizations, and to individuals as well.

Government Planners (Federal, State/Provincial, or Municipal)

This is crunch time for governments: the pressure to provide a lot with what seems like a little has never been higher. The population is aging and so is the infrastructure in most places in North America. There are certainly limited funds to pay for everything from pensions and health care through to fixing bridges that seem likely to crumble without repair.

Given the competing priorities, putting together a good strategic plan (one which incorporates solid demographic assumptions) is crucial. And, although most larger levels of government do put together planning documents, the focus is often too narrow and does not incorporate enough of our knowledge about the wider trends.

Businesses (from Large Corporations through to Mom-and-Pop Businesses—and Everyone In Between)

Large companies know all about strategic planning these days: too often in the past they have been blindsided by things that they might have been able to plan around had they know they were happening. As well, many have also missed what could have been amazing opportunities had they been grasped earlier.

The economorphic trends are a solid way to look at future opportunities, but for businesses in particular they should be used as a starting point. If the economic deck is being reshuffled, does that mean that Europe is no longer a viable destination for expansion? If urbanization is happening around the globe, which cities offer the most opportunities? A SWOT analysis can identify many questions that need to be answered before a plan is implemented.

Non-Profits and Philanthropic Organizations/ Community Groups

This is a crucial time for community groups and non-profits. We are on the cusp of major demographic changes that will help (through baby boomer volunteer resources, for example) as well as hurt (perhaps through a larger volume of potential users). A SWOT analysis is an excellent starting point for devising a strategic plan, whether grandiose or modest, on how to move forward.

Individuals

What can be more important than planning your own future? If there is one thing that seems clear in this post-crisis world, it is that no corporation or government is going to make your future their priority: you are on your own. And, apparently, the financial markets are not going to do the job for you either. That's why it makes sense to take stock of your opportunities, and gain a sense of control over what comes next.

If you are a mid-sized manufacturer and you would like to expand over the next decade or so, a good starting point is to sit down and look at your own strengths and weaknesses, and assess the external environment as well. The same is true whether you are a municipal government planner, or an individual who wants to think about your future, or maybe the future of a child heading for university or college.

You can make the process of doing as SWOT analysis as simple or as sophisticated as you like, but one simple approach is to put things into a basic diagram, and fill in the boxes as you see fit:

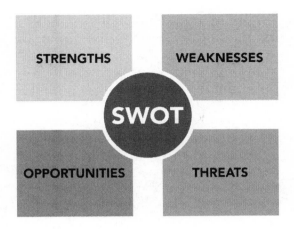

Make your initial chart and then take it one layer further by using whatever data is available on your organization, and on your industry as a whole. If possible, have someone do demographic projections to show where you will be in a few years (these should be for your user base, as well as for the community you serve, your potential volunteer force, etc.). Putting some numbers to what you are doing will serve many purposes, including making your business case should you wish to ask for government or corporate grants.

Now look at the bigger economorphic trends and pick out the ones that will have the most relevance for you. Look closely. Although you may think that some don't apply, you might find that they do. If you are running a community sports organization, for example, rising resource prices may seem irrelevant. But in fact, this could have a big impact on your bottom line in a few years. If households are squeezed financially, it could mean difficulty boosting participation numbers. In a similar vein, a rise in the middle class elsewhere in the world may mean that your sport gains popularity, which could in turn increase recognition and participation. The correlations do not have to be big or immediate, but you should start to think about the ways that the big picture will impact your reality in the short and long run.

A completed SWOT analysis can shed light on a number of things. You might find you have identified a new business opportunity, and some ways in which you can exploit it. You might find the opposite: that a staple of your business is going to be threatened, and you need to change your thinking to incorporate new opportunities. Or you might be able to make some adjustments in the short term to mitigate a problem in the long term.

Another way to use the economorphic trends and your SWOT diagram is for scenario planning. Think of that as asking a series of "what if?" questions: "What if food prices double?" "What if the majority of baby boomers decide to work until they are 70?" "What if stocks remain in a bear market for a decade?" Craft your questions to suit your industry and your goals. Scenario planning can be tacked on to your strategic plan, or it can just be something you think of casually—but as always, the more information you have about the possible future, the better.

EVERY HAND IS A WINNER

When I talk to business groups about economic and demographic trends I sometimes show dozens of slides and make dozens of points about the way the world is shifting. Then I ask a question: Based on what you know, which is the one winning trend you could pick and use to your advantage? Is it knowing that the demographic sweet spot is over in the developed world? Is it knowing that innovation is the way of the future? Is it realizing that we are headed into what might be a long bear market?

Of course, it's a trick question: just like the old song says, every hand is a winner, and every hand is a loser. But knowing what is ahead gives you the power to make your plans accordingly. And I downplay the loser part, anyway: as far as the economorphic trends go, every one is a winner as long as you put yourself on the right side of it.

The name of the song, by the way, was "The Gambler," but that should be ignored as well. If you keep up with trends affecting your future, you are the opposite of a gambler—and you can face that future knowing that you've given yourself every chance to be a winner.

(ENDNOTES)

1 Bacon argued that "deductive" reason should be replaced by inductive (scientific) reasoning. For more information see "Francis Bacon and the scientific method," Internet Shakespeare Editions, January 4, 2011. Retrieved from http://internetshakespeare.uvic.ca/Library/SLT/ideas/new%20knowledge/bacon.html.

2 "Business Cycle," Investopedia.com. Retrieved from http://www.investopedia.com/terms/b/businesscycle.asp.

Selected Bibliography

As well as other works cited in chapter endnotes, the following references were particularly instructive in the preparation of *Economorphics* and are recommended for further reading:

PART 1: TRANSFORMED DEMOGRAPHICS

Trend #1: The Demographic Window Is Slamming Shut

Bloom, David E., Axel Boersch-Supan, Patrick McGee, and Atsushi Seike. "Population Aging: Facts, Challenges, and Responses." Working Paper No. 71, Program on the Global Demography of Aging, Harvard University, Cambridge, Massachusetts, May 2011.

Bullough, Oliver. "The Russians are Shrinking!" *Wall Street Journal*, May 4, 2013.

Eberstadt, Nicholas. "Global Demographic Outlook to 2025: Risks and Opportunities for the World Economy." Lecture for the Economic Conference on Demography, Growth and Well-being, The Progress Foundation, Zurich, Switzerland, November 30, 2006.

———. "World Population Prospects and the Global Economic Outlook: The Shape of Things to Come." The American Enterprise Institute Working Paper Series on Development Policy, No. 5, February 2011.

Elliott, Dominic. "Crowd Gazing." *Wall Street Journal*, February 3, 2010.

Jackson, Richard, Neil Howe, and Keisuk Nakashima. "Global Aging and the Future of Emerging Markets." Center for Strategic and International Studies, Everest Capital, 2011.

Kasprowicz, Peter and Elizabeth Rhyne. "Looking Through the Demographic Window: Implications for Financial Inclusion." Center for Financial Inclusion, January 2013.

Kotkin, Joel. "What's Really Behind Europe's Decline? It's the Birth Rates, Stupid." *Forbes*, May 30, 2012.

Organisation for Economic Co-operation and Development (OECD). "Looking to 2060: A Global Vision of Long-Term Growth." OECD Economics Department Policy Notes, No. 15, November 2012.

Prskatwetz, Alexia, Thomas Fent, and Werner Barthel. "The Relationship Between Demographic Change and Economic Growth in the EU." Institut für Demographie, Research Report 32, July 2007.

Force #2: A World on the Move

Dumont, Jean-Christophe. "The Impact of International Migration on Destination Countries." Presentation to the OECD Directorate for Employment Labour and Social Affairs, New York, New York, June 26, 2013.

Hanson, Gordon H. "The Economic Consequences of the International Migration of Labor." NBER Working Paper No. 14490, November 2008, JEL No. F22, J61.

Jean, Sebastien, Oretta Causa, Miguel Jimenez, and Isabelle Wanner. "Migration in OECD Countries: Labour Market Impact and Integration Issues." OECD Economics Department Working Paper, No. 562, September 2007.

Kenny, Charles. "Why More Immigration, Not Less, Is Key to U.S. Economic Growth." Bloomberg Businessweek, October 28,

2012. http://www.businessweek.com/articles/2012-10-28/why-more-immigration-not-less-is-key-to-u-dot-s-dot-economic-growth.

Koehler, Jobst, Frank Laczko, Christine Aghazarm, and Julia Schad. "Migration and the Economic Crisis in the European Union: Implications for Policy." Independent Network of Labour Migration and Integration Experts, IOM Thematic Study, IOM International Organization for Migration, October 2010.

McKeown, Adam. "Global Migration 1846–1940." *Journal of World History* 15:2, June 2004, 165–89.

Organisation for Economic Co-operation and Development (OECD). "International Migration Outlook 2013." June 2013.

———. "International Migration Policies and Data: OECD Migration Databases," 2013. http://www.oecd.org/els/mig/oecd migrationdatabases.htm.

Shinn, David H. "African Migration and the Brain Drain." Paper presented at the Institute for African Studies and Slovenia Global Action, Washington, D.C., June 8, 2008.

Widmaier, Sarah and Jean-Christophe Dumont. "Are Recent Immigrants Different? A New Profile of Immigrants in the OECD Based on DIOC 2005/06." OECD Social, Employment and Migration Working Papers No. 126, Directorate for Employment, Labour and Social Affairs, OECD Publishing. http://dx. do.org/10.1787/5kg3ml17nps4-en.

Trend #3: More Urbanization (However You Define It)

Allianz Global Investors. "Infrastructure—The Backbone of the Global Economy." September 2013. https://www.allianzglobal investors.de/cms-out/kapitalmarktanalyse/docs/pdf-eng/ analysis-and-trends-infrastructure-the-backbone-of-the-global-economy.pdf.

Berg, Nate. "Exurbs: The Fastest Growing Areas in the U.S." *The AtlanticCities*, July 19, 2012. http://www.theatlanticcities.com/

neighborhoods/2012/07/exurbs-fastest-growing-areas-us/2636/.

Berube, Alan, Audrey Singer, Jull H. Wilson, and William H. Frey. "Finding Exurbia: America's Fastest Growing Communities at the Metropolitan Fringe." Metropolitan Policy Program, The Brookings Institution, Living Cities Census Series, October 2006.

Dobbs, Richard, Janna Remes, James Manyika, Charles Roxburgh, Sven Smit, and Fabian Schaer. "Urban World: Cities and the Rise of the Consuming Class." McKinsey Global Institute, June 2012.

Goldman, Henry. "Austin, Atlanta Give 'Middleweight' U.S. Cities Global Punch." Bloomberg.com, April 17, 2012.

Just, Tobias and Christian Thater. "Megacities: Boundless Growth?" Deutsche Bank Research, March 12, 2008.

"Lump Together and Like It." *The Economist*, November 6, 2008.

Manyika, James, Jaana Remes, Richard Dobbs, Javier Orellana, and Fabian Schaer. "Urban America: U.S. Cities in the Global Economy." McKinsey Global Institute, April 2012.

Romer, Paul, "Housing in China: Large vs. Small Cities." NYU Stern Urbanization Project, July 22, 2013.

United Nations Population Division. "World Urbanization Prospects: The 2011 Revision, Highlights." New York, New York, 2012.

PART 2: AN ECONOMIC POWER SHIFT

Trend #4: A Re-Shuffling of the Economic Deck

Dadush, Uri. "Europe's Long-Term Growth Prospects." Carnegie Endowment for International Peace, October 8, 2010.

Economist Intelligence Unit. "Foresight 2020: Economic, Industry and Corporate Trends." 2006.

Hawksworth, John and Gordon Cookson. "The World in 2050: Beyond the BRICS: A Broader Look at Emerging Market Growth Prospects." PricewaterhouseCoopers LLP, 2008.

Jenkins, Christine. "The 10 Fastest Growing Economies of the Next 40 Years." *Business Insider*, March 1, 2011.

McGreal, Chris. "China's Economy to Outgrow America's by 2030 as World Faces 'Tectonic Shift.'" *The Guardian*, December 10, 2012.

Toloui, Ramin. "Emerging Markets as Drivers of Global Growth and Wealth Creation." Economic Outlook, Pimco Secular Forum, June 2010.

"When Giants Slow Down." *The Economist*, July 27, 2013.

Trend #5: An Expanding Global Middle Class

Caploe, David. "New Global Middle Class Consumers: Strategies for 'Early Capture.'" Economy Watch, August 2010.

Court, David and Laxman Narasimhan. "Capturing the World's Emerging Middle Class." McKinsey Quarterly, July 2010.

Dadush, Uri and Simesle Ali. "In Search of the Global Middle Class." Carnegie Endowment for International Peace, July 2012.

Eizenberg, Alon and Alberto Salvo. "Buying Behaviors of Emerging Middle Classes." Kellogg Insight, Kellogg School of Management at Northwestern University, July 2012.

"Innovating for the Next Three Billion: The Rise of Global Middle Class—and How to Capitalize on It." Ernst & Young, 2011.

Kharas, Homi. "The Emerging Middle Class in Developing Countries." OECD Development Centre Working Paper No. 2085, January 2010.

———. "The New Global Middle Class: A Cross-Over from West to East." Wolfensohn Center for Development at Brookings Institution, 2010.

O'Neil, Shannon. "The Bright Side of the Global Economy: The Middle Class Is Growing." theatlantic.com, November 9, 2011.

Reisen, Helmut. "Emerging Middle Class Blues." OECD Insights, July 1, 2013.

Surowiecki, James. "Middle Class Militants." *The New Yorker*, July 8, 2013.

"The New Global Middle Class: Potentially Profitable—But Also Unpredictable." Knoweldge@Wharton, July 9, 2008.

Wilson, Dominic and Raluca Dragusanu. "The Expanding Middle: The Exploding World Middle Class and Falling Global Inequality." Global Economics Paper No. 170, Goldman Sachs Global Economic website, July 7, 2008.

Trend #6: The Stuck Teeter-Totter

Alvaredo, Facundo, Anthony B. Atkinson, Thomas Piketty, and Emmanuel Saez. "The Top 1 Percent in International and Historical Perspective." *Journal of Economic Perspectives* 27:3, Summer 2013, 3–20.

Bartlett, Bruce. "Labor's Declining Share Is an International Problem." *New York Times*, June 25, 2013.

———. "'Financialization' as a Cause of Economic Malaise." *New York Times*, June 11, 2013.

Greenstone, Michael, Adam Looney, Jeremy Patashnik, and Muxin Yu. "Thirteen Economic Facts about Social Mobility and the Role of Education: The Hamilton Project." The Brookings Institution, June 2013.

"Income Inequality and the Great Recession." Report by the U.S. Congress Joint Economic Committee, September 2010.

Jacobson, Margaret and Filippo Occhino. "Behind the Decline in Labor's Share of Income." Economic Trends, Federal Reserve Bank of Cleveland, February 3, 2012.

———. "Labor's Declining Share of Income and Rising Inequality." Economic Commentary, Federal Reserve Bank of Cleveland, September 25, 2012.

Levine, Linda. "The U.S. Income Distribution and Mobility: Trends and International Comparisons." Congressional Research Services, November 29, 2012.

Organisation for Economic Co-operation and Development (OECD). "An Overview of Growing Income Inequalities in OECD Countries: Main Findings." 2011.

Schmitt, John and Janelle Jones. "Long-Term Hardship in the Labour Market." Center for Economic and Policy Research, March 2012.

Van Treeck, Till and Simon Sturn. "Income Inequality as a Cause of the Great Recession? A Survey of Current Debates." International Labour Office, Conditions of Work and Employment Series No. 39.

PART 3: NEW REALITIES, NEW ATTITUDES

Trend #7: A Reversal of the Downward Slide in Commodity Prices

Dobbs, Richard, Jeremy Oppenheim, Fraser Thompson, Marcel Brinkman, and Marc Zornes. "Resource Revolution: Meeting the World's Energy, Materials, Food and Water Needs." McKinsey Global Institute, November 2011.

Erten, Bilge and Jose Antonio Ocampo. "Super-Cycles of Commodity Prices Since the Mid-Nineteenth Century." DESA Working Paper No. 110, United Nations Department of Economic and Social Affairs, February 2012.

"Food Scarcity—Trends, Challenges, Solutions." Dexia Asset Management, Sustainability Team Discussion Paper, May 2010.

"Peak Oil." *The Economist*, March 5, 2013.

"Resource Scarcity and the Efficiency Revolution." Impax Asset Management Ltd., August 2008.

Rubin, Jeff. "How Oil Prices Will Permanently Cap Economic Growth." Bloomberg.com, September 23, 2012.

"The Consequences of Costly Nosh." *The Economist*, June 20, 2011.

"World Agriculture: Towards 2015/2030: Summary Report." United Nations Food and Agriculture Organization Corporate Document Repository, 2003.

Trend #8: Work Is Not a Place

Glass, Jennifer. "It's About the Work, Not the Office." *New York Times*, March 7, 2013.

MBO Partners. "The State of Independence in America." Third Annual Independent Workforce Report, September 2013.

Moon, Nathan. "Private Sector Telework and Its Implications for Economic Development: Results of a Case Survey and Policy Assessment." Enterprise Innovation Institute and School of Public Policy's Science, Technology and Innovation (STIP) Program, Georgia Institute of Technology, Atlanta, Georgia, August 10, 2007.

Needleman, Sarah. "Negotiating the Freelance Economy." *Wall Street Journal*, November 6, 2009.

Snow, Shane. "Half of Us May Soon Be Freelancers: 6 Compelling Reasons Why." Linkedin Today, August 8, 2013. http://www.linkedin.com/today/post/article/20130808135707-7374576-half-of-us-may-soon-be-freelancers-6-compelling-reasons-why.

Sullivan, John. "How Yahoo's Decision to Stop Telecommuting Will Increase Innovation." ERE.net February 26, 2013. http://www.ere.net/2013/02/26/how-yahoos-decision-to-stop-telecommuting-will-increase-innovation/.

Zimmerman, Eilene. "Telecommuting: Steady Growth in Work-at-Home Culture, Yahoo or Not." *Christmas Science Monitor*, May 7, 2013.

Trend #9: Challenging Financial Markets

Bloch, Brian. "Demographic Trends and the Implications for Investment." Investopedia.com, March 19, 2011.

Borsch-Supan, Axel. "The Impact of Global Aging on Labor, Product and Capital Markets." Manheim Research Institute for the Economics of Aging (MEA), March 2005.

Bosworth, Barry P. "The Impact of Aging on Financial Markets and the Economy: A Survey." The Brookings Institution, 2004.

Desroches, Brigitte and Michael Francis. "Global Savings, Investment and World Interest Rates." Bank of Canada Review, Winter 2006–07.

Dobbs, Richard, Susan Lund, Charles Roxburgh, James Manyika, Alex Kim, Andreas Schreiner, Riccardo Boin, Rohit Chopra, Sebastian Jauch, Megan McDonald, and John Piotrowski. "Farewell to Cheap Capital? The Implications of Long-Term Shifts in Global Investment and Savings." McKinsey Global Institute, December 2010.

Duca, Gevit. "The Relationship Between the Stock Market and the Economy: Experience from International Financial Markets." Bank of Valletta Review, No. 36, Autumn 2007.

Geanakoplos, John, Michael Magill, and Martine Quinzil. "Demography and the Long-Run Predictability of the Stock Market." Cowles Foundation Discussion Paper No. 1380, August 2002.

Goval, Amit. "Demographics, Stock Market Flows and Stock Returns." *Journal of Financial and Quantitative Analysis* 39:1, March 2004.

Liu, Zheng and Mark. M. Spiegel. "Boomer Retirement: Headwinds for U.S. Equity Markets." Federal Reserve Board of San Francisco Economic Letter, August 22, 2011.

Loeys, Jan, David Mackie, Paul Meggyesi, and Nikolaos Panigirtzolglou. "Corporates Are Driving the Global Savings Glut." JP Morgan Research, June 25, 2005.

O'Neill, Jim, Anna Stupnytska, and James Wrisdale. "Linking GDP Growth and Equity Returns." Goldman Sachs, Monthly Insights, May 2011.

Roxburgh, Charles, Susan Lund, Charles Atkins, Stanislas Belot, Wayne W. Hu, and Moira S. Pierce. "Global Capital Markets: Entering a New Era." McKinsey Global Institute, September 2009.

Roxburgh, Charles, Susan Lund, Richard Dobbs, James Manyika, and Haihao Wu. "The Emerging Equity Gap: Growth and Stability in the New Investor Landscape." McKinsey Global Institute, December 2011.

Sandte, Holger. "Stocks Markets vs. GDP Growth: A Complicated Mixture." BNY Mellon Asset Management, July 2012.

Wade, Keith and Anja May. "GDP Growth and Equity Market Returns." Schroders, February 2013.

Trend #10: Searching for the Second Act

Achenbeaum, Andrew. "How Boomers Turned Conventional Wisdom on Its Head: A Historian's View on How the Future May Judge a Transitional Generation." MetLife Mature Market Institute, April 2012.

"Americans' Perspectives on New Retirement Realities and the Longevity Bonus: A 2013 Merrill Lynch Retirement Study." Merrill Lynch Wealth Management (in partnership with Age Wave), 2013.

Munnell, Alicia H., Anthony Webb, and Francesca Golub-Sass. "The National Retirement Risk Index: An Update." Center for Retirement Research at Boston College, October 2012, No. 12–20.

Trend #11: Ladies First

Aguirre, DeAnne, Lelia Hoteit, Christine Rupp, and Karim Sabbagh. "Empowering the Third Billion: Women and the World of Work in 2012." Booz & Co., 2012.

Boushey, Heather. "Are Young Women Earning More Than Their Boyfriends?" *Slate*, September 7, 2010.

FleishmanHillard. "Women, Power and Money: Wave 5: A Study of Women's Lives, Lifestyles and Marketplaces." Hearst magazines, July 2, 2013.

Lane, Mary M. "A Conversation About 'The End of Men.'" *Wall Street Journal* online edition, September 24, 2012. http://online.wsj.com/news/articles/SB100008723963904441800045780162334638881890.

Roisin, Hanna, *The End of Men: And the Rise of Women*. New York: Riverhead Books, 2012.

Schwab, Klaus and Saadia Zahidi. "The Global Gender Gap Index 2012." World Economic Forum, 2012.

Trend #12: The Age of Innovation—Hopefully

"2013 Global R&D Funding Forecast." *R&D Magazine*, December 2012.

"Brainbox Nation." *The Economist*, March 16, 2013.

"The Great Innovation Debate." *The Economist*, January 12, 2013.

Atkinson, Robert. "Innovation Economics: The Race for Global Advantage." The International Technology & Innovation Foundation, September 2012.

Bartlett, David. "Productivity Growth in the Developed Economies." RSM Talking Points, March 2013.

Dutta, Soumitra and Bruno Lavin (eds). "The Global Innovation Index 2013: The Local Dynamics of Innovation." Johnson Cornell University, INSEAD, World Intellectual Property Organization, 2013.

Gordon, Robert. "Is U.S. Economic Growth Over? Faltering Innovation Confronts the Six Headwinds." Working Paper No. 183315, National Bureau of Economic Research, August 2013.

Harrison, Daniel M. "Can Innovation Save the Economy?" *Washington Post*, October 2009.

Lazonick, William. "Financialization of the U.S. Corporation: What

Has Been Lost, and How it Can Be Regained." Institute for New Economic Thinking, July 2012.

Mandel, Michael. "There are Only 2 Ways to Save the Economy: Innovation or Inflation." *The Atlantic* online edition, October 29, 2011.

Manyika, James, Michael Chul, Jacques Bughin, Richard Dobbs, Peter Bisson, and Alex Marrs. "Disruptive Technologies: Advances That Will Transform Life, Business and the Global Economy." McKinsey Global Institute, May 2013.

Organisation for Economic Co-operation and Development (OECD). "Ministerial Report on the OECD Innovation Strategy." May 2010.

Parramore, Lynn Stuart. "Big Finance Is Strangling Innovation." Salon.com, July 27, 2013.

PricewaterhouseCoopers. "Government's Many Roles in Fostering Innovation." January 2010.

Acknowledgments

Economorphics started out as a presentation (sometimes with a different name) that I have given to many business groups who are doing strategic planning sessions. So my first thanks go to all those who invited me to share my thoughts, and to the National Speakers Bureau, which continues to match me with groups who want to know how demographic and economic trends will impact their organizations.

Some of the ideas and content for this book originated with my *Globe and Mail* Economy Lab blog: accordingly, I have to thank editor Dave Parkinson and former editor Rob Gilroy for giving me the opportunity to write it. My thinking on the "big" issues has also benefited from my association with the Macdonald-Laurier Institute (I have the awesome title of "Senior Fellow for Economics and Population Change"), so they, and in particular managing director Brian Lee Crowley, have my thanks as well.

With this book I am venturing into the brave new world of "artisanal" publishing for the first time, but with the aid of many people. My thanks first of all go to editor Linda Pruessen: as well as doing everything an editor should, she also asked the questions that a reader would ask, and this book is better for it. Heidy Lawrance of WeMakeBooks.ca guided me through the entire process, answered every question, no matter how trivial, and found me awesome resources for everything I needed. Thanks, too, to Marnie Ferguson, who continues to deal with sales.

Many people have offered support and comments on various stages of the book. My thanks particularly to Lee Anne Davies, who read parts of it, and to Wendy Waters, who helped me formulate my thinking on cities. And a huge and very special thank you goes to Eamon Hoey, who was generous with his time and comments throughout.

Finally, thank you to Lou and Maddie, just for being them.

Index

International Energy Agency, 150, 154
International Federation of Robotics
  (IFR), 268
International Labour Organization
  (ILO), 105, 110, 112
International Monetary Fund, 23,
  71, 98
internships, 132, 242
intra-generational mobility, 134-135
investments, 95-98, 128, 158-159,
  195, 208, 225-226, 259, 266
Investors Group, 218
Ireland, 19, 38, 89, 261
Italy, 85, 89, 106

J

Japan, 23-24, 30-31, 84-85, , 86,
  237, 268

K

Katz, Lawrence F., 45
Kauffman Foundation, 174, 220
Kharas, Homi, 106
Khatiwada, Ishwar, 124
Kohane, Isaac, 180
Korea, 109

L

labor force participation, 20, 26, 49,
  184-185, 218. *See also* gender gap;
  women, and the workforce.
labor market
  and aging populations, 23, 218-219,
    237
  and economic power, 84
  and immigrants, 47-48
labor productivity. *See* productivity.
labor-share of income, 122-124
Lagarde, Christine, 237
Lazonick, William, 265
leisure pursuits, 96-97, 111-112,
  221-229
liquidation, 65-66, 205, 207-208, 209
life expectancies, 17-18, 28, 30
Lin, Carl, 41

luxuries, 129, 144, 149. *See also* leisure
  pursuits.

M

Malaysia, 36, 38-39, 261
Malthus, Thomas, 15, 151, 255
Manhattan, residents of, 68
marketing model, 129
Mayer, Marissa, 178, 240
MBO Partners, 170
McKinsey Global Institute, 22, 63, 68,
  97, 98, 109, 144-145, 148, 156,
  194-195, 269
McWilliams, Douglas, 82-83
meaning, search for, 224-225
meat consumption, 149-150
megacities, 61, 63-64, 69
Meissner, Christopher M., 128
MetLife Mature Market Institute,
  217-218
Mexico, 39-40, 45, 86, 87
Mexico City Pact of 2010, 72
middle class
  decline in, 119-120, 131-132
  defined, 104-106
  and global economy, 107-109
  growth of, 5, 9, 44, 91, 92,
    103-114, 208
  measurement of, 104-107
Middle East, 20-21, 107, 158
middle-market brands, 129
middle-old (MO) ratio, 204-209
middleweight cities, 63, 68, 69
middle-young (MY) ratio, 201-204, 208
migration, 35-55
Milton (ON), 66
minimum wage, 133, 136
mobility, of population, 4. *See also*
  immigration; migration.
monetary policy, 158, 185. *See also*
  central banks.
Mongolia, 236
Moretti, Enrico, 53
mortgages, 25, 52, 127, 130-131, 207,
  210, 217

religious activities, 224

research and development (R&D), 153, 159, 179, 261, 262, 263, 266

Reses, Jackie, 178-179

resources, 70, 112, 154-155, 259. *See also* commodity prices.

retirement, 23, 27, 31 , 49, 52, 65-66, 130-131, 174, 200
and baby boomers, 214-221

robotics, 268

Rosin, Hanna, 238-239

rurban areas. *See* exurbanization.

Russia, 28, 38, 84, 85, 93, 113, 194

S

Salvo, Alberto, 110-111

S&P 500, 201, 205, 206

San Francisco, 64

sanitation, 17, 71

savings, 24-25, 194, 195, 201, 224. *See also* family finances.

Schumpeter, Joseph, 260

Schwartz Center for Economic Policy Analysis, 219-220

second careers, 216, 218-219, 220, 225

Securian Financial Group, 217

securities, 193-194

self-employed workers, 169-170, 173-174

service sector, 53, 71, 96, 239, 240, 242

single-earner households, 125

skill levels. *See also* H-1B program; volunteering.
and immigrants, 44, 45, 47
and income, 8, 123, 133, 135, 136, 186, 242
and migration, 30, 37, 43-44, 50-51, 53, 175

Slate, 241

slums, 72

smart farming, 152

social change, 5, 54, 92

social services, 46-47, 89, 92, 113, 240

social unrest, 91, 92, 113, 133, 144

Solow, Robert, 256

South Africa, 37, 261

South Korea, 94, 268

Soviet Union, 84

Spain, 26, 38, 89

split market, 5

stages of demographic transition, 16-18

standard of living, 8, 156-157, 220, 253. *See also* poverty.

Stanford University, 177

start-ups, 170, 174

Statistics Canada, 44, 120, 176

Stevenson, T.H.C., 105

stock market, 23, 25, 192, 198-199, 218, 259, 266. *See also* bear markets; bull markets; financial markets.

strategic plans, 73-74, 274. *See also* SWOT analysis.

structural changes, in the economy, 276

Sub-Saharan Africa, 17, 20-21

Sullivan, John, 179-180

Sum, Andrew, 124

sunrise countries, 82-83, 84, 94

sunset countries, 82-83, 84

SWOT analysis, 276-281

T

taxation
and aging population, 21-22, 24
and immigrants, 46-47
and income, 126, 135-136
and productivity, 83, 133, 153, 154

TD Economics, 52

technology, 7-9, 40-41, 62, 84, 124, 166
and productivity, 151-153, 255-258

telecommuting, 67, 166, 176-187

Telus, 178

Thompson, Warren, 16

3M, 179

time-crunch economy, 221-223. *See also* leisure time.

top 10 economies, 84-87